THIS BOOK IS
NOT A TOY!

THIS BOOK
IS NOT A TOY!

Friendly Advice on How to Avoid Death
and Other Inconveniences

Chuck Goldstone

ST. MARTIN'S PRESS   NEW YORK

www.stmartins.com

ISBN 0-312-30376-9
EAN 978-0312-30376-1

First Edition: April 2005

10   9   8   7   6   5   4   3   2   1

For my parents,
Bob and Shirle

Table of Contents

viii   CONTENTS

In Lieu of Acknowledgments

I do not know a single person who has ever read the acknowledgment section of a book. Certainly I have not, and it's likely that after I finish writing this one, I won't bother to read it again myself, even to check the spelling and grammar. So if you see some errors, please understand why.

The acknowledgment is part of some quaint, arcane, multi-century-old literary custom. Some authors use it to inflate the importance of a book or share thoughts they feel are important, just not important enough to be included in the book proper. Most often, however, the acknowledgment is what the writer believes to be a highly visible platform to publicly thank those who have lent their help and emotional support, forgetting that no one except the people mentioned in the acknowledgment will ever read it. Personally, I prefer just taking the people I want to thank out to dinner or buying them tasteful gifts.

While mandated by convention, this vestigial section is overwhelmingly ignored by the general public. I can think of absolutely no way it will add to your enjoyment. It is a page-turn inconvenience, an obstacle you have to clamber over as you try to get from the Table of Contents to Chapter One.

As a consumer, you have no choice but to accept this extraneous introductory appendage, since you cannot buy only the parts of a book you really want a la carte. The maddening fact is, these pages add—and I am estimating here—about $1.10 to the retail price. I do not think it's ever worth the expense, and I suggest the money could be better spent on illustrations, or perhaps in the case of a novel, to pay the author to write in another character.

Reading the front piece may be worthwhile if you believe you are going to be mentioned, but realistically, unless I know you personally, the chance of you seeing your name here is slim. Further, the people I *do* mention will mean nothing to you, and even if you track down a few of them because they seem so generous, they are not likely to be nearly so nice to you, a total stranger, as they were to me, a guy they have known and liked for many years.

In truth, acknowledgments are more harmful than helpful to even a well-meaning writer. While someone I recognize will be excited for a few minutes seeing his or her name in type, anyone I neglect will remember my forgetfulness for a very long time. Just wait until I need a favor then.

So, I have decided to thank very few people in these pages—not that I am ungrateful—but I want to (1) avoid offending anyone who can hurt me financially or emotionally and, (2) cut down the length of the acknowledgment section, which will ultimately decrease the cost of printing, with savings I have asked my publisher to pass on to you.

Sadly, I will suffer the financial downside for this brevity. Factored into complex book sale projection algorithms are purchases of books by everyone I cite, so the fewer people I mention, the fewer guaranteed royalties I can count on.

But that led me to an interesting marketing idea. What if I just start listing names, page upon page of people I have met casually though the years, friends of friends, strangers from my voting precinct, celebrities I have never met, names I make up that may coincidentally belong to someone somewhere, or maybe a list of people randomly selected from phone directories in the U.S., Canada, and the principal possessions of Puerto Rico, Guam, and Navassa Island? If I list, say, 150,000 people, and only half buy the book, I am still well on my way to becoming a very wealthy man. I apologize in advance for having you cart around a book that comes with two extra volumes.

In my modest show of appreciation, I would like to start by thanking those from my childhood who humiliated me on the athletic field, enough for me to retreat into seclusion and discover the lonely sport of writing, an activity where neither coordination nor agility are required, and where its well-known practitioners are seldom nicknamed "Dropsy" or "Spaz."

Likewise, I thank Tommy Kalso, a bullying fellow sixth-grader, who, after school on May 17, 1962, did not actually kill me as he had threatened.

I offer a nod of appreciation to my teachers, whose passing statements would shape my self-image, especially to a high school speech club coach who, just prior to my graduation, told the class, "Goldstone will never amount to a hill of beans." She died some years ago, but if she were alive today I could show how, in spite of her discouragement, I am recognized in many circles as a hill of beans.

I also want to use this book to publicly thank all the women who have slept with me through the years. Whether the gesture was offered out of love, boredom, or charity, I extend an equal measure of gratitude.

I offer my heartfelt gratitude to members of my species who have given me so many subjects to squib. I am grateful to anyone whose actions have made them targets of my mockery or who have held up a mirror to my own unwitting foolishness. I thank all the people who actually exist, and even those I have convinced myself exist, but do not.

On the professional front, I extend thanks to my dear friends, past and present, at *Marketplace*: Liza Tucker, Martha Little, David Brown, David Brancaccio, J. J. Yore, Celeste Weston, Jim Russell, and so many others, unmentioned here but appreciated nonetheless. Thanks to Chris Turpin, now at NPR's *All Things Considered*, who produced my earlier work on *Monitor Radio*. I am grateful to the entirety of public radio, which has offered a national loudspeaker through which I have been permitted to yell. Please support your local stations. At their next fundraising, don't waver, don't complain, just make a generous pledge. It's not like they are asking you for a kidney.

I extend thanks to Ron Suskind, my only Pulitzer Prize—winning friend, who, sixteen years ago, encouraged me to do a little more writing. I've always been a bit competitive, so I am anxious to win a Pulitzer myself, or if the quality of my work is going to be a factor, I would be content to buy one.

To Willee Lewis, author and president of the PEN/Faulkner

Foundation, for her farsighted decision to include my work in an anthology alongside the writing of George Plimpton, Tom Wolfe, Jim Lehrer, Emily Dickinson, Sir Arthur Conan Doyle, and Rudyard Kipling.

Thanks to Janice Owens, yet another stranger to the majority of you, who introduced me to my agent, Kit Ward. And to Kit for convincing the venerable publisher St. Martin's Press that the boodles of money they will earn from my book will help pay for some sprucing up of their stately New York headquarters.

I thank my friends at St. Martin's who made me feel like I was a welcome member of their author family—and I assume they are being sincere and not just acting nice because it's part of their job and they do not want to get fired.

To my wordsmithian friends who have lent an eye and ear through the years, including Seth Bauer and John Kronenberger, who I relied on to supply constructive literary recommendations, such as "Maybe you should use conventional periods instead of these little smiley face icons," or "The pieces might read better if you used some verbs."

My thanks to my friends and family.

I have chosen not to acknowledge the woman I am currently seeing, not knowing what the state of our relationship will be when the book hits the shelves. This can be like those who, after a few beers, impulsively tattoo the name of a girlfriend on some body part, forgetting it is easy to end a relationship with a woman, but not with a body part. To erase the reminder of their bad judgment and an epoch of their lives they no longer wish to remember, some undergo painful laser tattoo removal, a process almost as painful as rabies treatment, while others get the tattoo artist to add a few letters, changing, say, "ANNA" to "BAN NAPALM," or if the name cannot be modified, having the words "I no longer like" inscribed above it. In my case, I would need to recall all the books, or worse, phone everyone who purchased a copy to explain that the woman and I are no longer together.

On the institutional level, special thanks to the Peet's Coffee and Tea in Brookline, Massachusetts, which, on many Sunday mornings, supplied a flat table for my laptop and aromatic, fresh-brewed coffee, which, unlike my own, can be described without referring to its "viscosity." At home, I am able to exploit any excuse to interrupt my writing, distracting myself by doing a load of laundry, cleaning the refrigerator, replacing tile grout, or rebuilding stairs. At Peet's I stay focused, never tempted to help them defrost, scour, or grout, no matter how blocked I am. I regret that I have spent most of my advance on lattes.

For this glowing mention, I secretly hope Peet's corporate office will send me a special card entitling me to free coffee for life. If this ploy works, I would add to subsequent printings the names of Marriott and Weston Hotels, American Airlines, Southwest and Jet Blue, Home Depot, Steinway Piano, Apple Computer, and Lexus, hoping these organizations will show their gratitude by sending me room vouchers, tickets, building supplies, a piano, a snazzy laptop, and a luxury sedan. Endorsement slots for a rental car company, a medical insurance provider, and a clothing line are still open.

In advance, I thank those who have purchased this work. I know others of you will be reading parts of it in a book store or may choose to borrow a copy from a friend. In fairness, I rely on your personal honor and ask that you still send me the $3.60 I would have received as royalty if you bought the book yourself. In addition, to anyone who purchased this outright and thought it worth reading again, I do not expect you to buy a second copy, but I do ask that you send the royalty along each time you reread it.

While I am on the topic of money, I salute our wonderful neighbors in Canada, who are willing to pay $33.95 for the exact same book, though we have made no special effort to reprint a special Canadian edition with more familiar spellings of "harbour," "behaviour," "tumour," "tonne," "paycheque," and "manoeuvre," or with measurements converted into the more provincial metric system. Books, I have learned, are important to Canadians, helping them get through their long, fatally-cold, August-to-June winters, where they spend the endlessly sun-deprived days indoors reading by whale oil—incidentally, one of their few pastimes that is not hockey.

Finally, while we are discussing international monetary exchange rates, I suggest that my fellow Americans take advantage of the inviting value of the mighty U.S. dollar in Australia, where you can buy this book for somewhere around US $4.50. My advice to my fellow countrymen visiting Sydney, Melbourne, or Perth is to buy up every copy you can, bring them back here to the states, and be prepared to make a very handsome profit.

Chuck Goldstone
Sometime in 2004. It is evening.

www.chuckgoldstone.com
chuck@chuckgoldstone.com

THIS BOOK IS
NOT A TOY!

The Spirit of Adventure

BACK IN MY SOPHOMORE YEAR OF COLLEGE I LIVED DOWN the hall from a guy named Jeff, who so desperately craved attention that he would put on a nightly pyrotechnic display by igniting his own highly combustible intestinal gases. The public spectacle always drew a large crowd eager for any distraction from studying, even if the diversion did involve somebody's ass. At eleven at night, when all hopes were dashed that macroeconomic theory could all of a sudden start getting interesting, walking down the hall to watch an upperclassman make his flatulence glow even briefly seemed a reasonable enough excuse to get out from behind the books.

As a crowd assembled in Jeff's dorm room, he sat on the edge of his bed, trousers artfully lowered to his ankles and legs lifted upward. Through the weave of his now-visible white cotton underpants, he released a burst of flammable colonic gas, using his highly trained sphincter to regulate the precise volume necessary for combustion. Holding a lit match underneath, Jeff expelled a jet of human exhaust over the flame, which ignited instantly and produced a flash of pale blue light that blasted outward three or four inches like a tiny solar flare, then just as quickly extinguished. The effect was even more dramatic when the lights in the room were dimmed.

In no other situation would a group of heterosexual college freshmen voluntarily train their eyes on a four-square-inch region on the crotch of a fellow dorm mate's undershorts, but the overall effect of making bowel vapors momentarily visible was spellbinding, and we stared in awe, if for no other reason than prior to college, none of us had ever seen flames shooting out of someone's butt before. We watched, eyes wide-open and mouth agape, astonished that any human orifice could be deployed for such a visually enthralling, albeit impractical, purpose and even more amazed that anyone, especially a seemingly intelligent person who scored well over 1450 on his SATs, would attempt anything so monumentally dangerous and stupid. Better Jeff than us was the consensus. For him, the glory was apparently worth the obvious risk. For us, the performance was a welcome break from Statistics and Poli Sci, though none of us really considered it the opportunity to "get out for a little air."

Jeff, whose last name is being withheld because he is now a successful corporate lawyer and prefers not to be known as "the arbitrage attorney who used to light his farts," did not fully appreciate the underlying danger in releasing volatile methane in the vicinity of an open flame. A fluke misfire could send flames racing back in his direction and conceivably detonate his unprotected gastrointestinal tract, producing a tragedy akin to a refinery explosion, simultaneously sending textbooks and the contents of his lower torso spewing across the room. We all stood back six to eight feet and behind his desk just in case, confident we would be shielded from any flying debris produced during the formation of the crater that was once Jeff's bed.

The danger for Jeff was further heightened because his pair of cotton briefs, soon to be saturated with explosive vapors, could themselves burst into flames, causing him unimaginable agony and simultaneously contributing to events that would be awkward to explain in an emergency room. You have to assume that even the most professional and highly trained triage doctors will find it hard *not to* burst into uncontrollable, spit-spewing laughter while taking the medical history of an adult who foolishly ignited his lower abdomen.

Jeff performed his act wearing underpants anyway, not necessarily to heighten the danger, but because he knew there was a limit to what we were willing to watch.

At the end of each performance, Jeff would stand, bow, and against a backdrop of applause and cheering, remind the more impressionable present that he was a professional and that flatus in the hands of someone less experienced could likely result in tragedy. He made all freshmen promise not to attempt a stunt like this on their own and certainly not without a chemical foam extinguisher present. When the crowd dispersed, Jeff would gently dust baby powder on his recently singed hindquarters and get back to his Calculus.

While most of us saw rectal ignition as senseless, Jeff saw it as a platform to win new friends and dormwide acclaim, though throughout his four undergraduate years, he remained unsuccessful at finding a way to exploit this skill in order to meet women.

More important, however, Jeff used this feat to help him bravely face his own fears. He likened his risk taking to that of circus aerialist Karl Wallenda, often speaking of the internationally renowned high-wire artist as his hero, a bigger-than-life role model, and a man he said he hoped to meet someday—that is until someone reminded Jeff that Mr. Wallenda's career was tragically cut short when he plunged twelve or so stories to his unsolicited death onto the pavement in front of a large horrified crowd who, entertainment value notwithstanding, would have preferred that he not splatter in front of them and their children. The lesson lost on Jeff was as follows: You can light flatulence without incident for your entire life, but just one careless move on an off day, and you and your colon are postscript and in that singular moment you will have redefined the concept of "your entire life."

What a tragedy to cut short, by even a moment, any of the limited conscious time we are granted as tenants in this mortal coil. Only when we are frail and elderly on our deathbed, organs failing from eight decades of nonstop use, muscles atrophied, face wrinkled and concave, mouth lolling open because closing it is too exhausting, can we die fully satisfied that we have not cheated ourselves out of even a minute of precious life. Only when we lie in semi-consciousness in a wasting state, organically dysfunctional and incontinent, where it is indiscernible whether we are just still barely alive or if it is OK for someone to pronounce us dead, can we be confident that we have lived as long as our now drained physical housing permitted.

Maybe the best way we can show our appreciation for the brief stay we were granted is to suck every moment out of life before we stall and descend into a spiraling, unrecoverable death spin. Only then can we be confident that we have led a complete existence and have used up all the available loops on the previously mentioned mortal coil.

Tragically, a large number of us perish unintentionally at our own hands, victims of lives cut short in the confluence of ineptitude, poor judgment, and unfortunate timing. It is sad to think that your last earthly thought, that end-of-life insight you will carry with you through eternity, could turn out to be, "I am such an asshole."

My Mother's Warning

MY MOTHER TAUGHT ME TO BE CAUTIOUS FROM THE MO-
ment I could understand flashing lights.

"Be careful," she would say, wagging her index finger, the Official
Finger of Warning, whenever my brother and I left the safety of our
home for any one of the infinite number of dangerous loci outside
her immediate field of vision.

I believe my mother was like so many others, oozing with the innate maternal instinct to protect her prized offspring from all peril,
spirited by a million-year-old tradition she shared with her hominid
predecessors and animal counterparts. Inextricably rooted within her
loving viscera was the drive to keep her babies insulated from harm
and to teach them to stay clear of all that could be physically hurtful.
She would pass on to my brother and me a legacy of common sense,
vigilance, and shamelessly selfish survival, just as her mother had conferred onto her.

"Better to be cautious," she advised. We learned to avoid unnecessary physical pain, puncture, and laceration. Her teachings were
conveyed repeatedly via tersely phrased edicts, through the even
more powerful vocabulary of nonverbal gesture, and sometimes just
by gasping. We discerned right from wrong by watching her face for
its involuntary transmission of the elemental expressions of shock,
horror, revulsion, or paralyzing fear.

That's what mothers do. They are the eyes and ears of sucklings
who have yet to learn that nothing around us can be fully trusted.

By looking at any seemingly innocent action, my mother could mystically forecast the potential for tragedy contained therein. When they do their jobs right, our moms teach us by instilling panic, getting us to obsess about dangers that might have otherwise never occurred to us.

She would routinely chide, "Don't do that!" or warn, "Put that filthy thing down!" when she wanted to remind us how important it was to know the chain of custody prior to us handling any item, especially those destined for our mouths. Nearly any activity could warrant a "Stop! You'll hurt yourself!" My mother knew that unless an object was made of fluffy cotton, it could be easily misused by my brother or me to poke one of our eyes out.

Through her life lessons, we learned that there is danger everywhere—at home, in the car, at school, and even at stores that sell only doilies. In some cases, the peril is obvious, especially when cavorting with something having serrated teeth or with any object equipped with spinning blades, mounted high above the ground, or found near a busy street. Other hazards live parasitically inside an item's core, sometimes concealed, but poised and ready to ambush. Even trustworthy items, including toys and religious artifacts, could be a source of injury. My mother's warning that death and disease coated everything resonated through my childhood and still quietly echoes today.

Perhaps she was a little overprotective. Yet thanks to her, I have not lost an arm to an oncoming bus by sticking my hand out of a moving car window. When my bread lodges in the toaster and spews a pungent thread of burning wheat-smoke, I do not impulsively reach for the closest highly conductive cutlery in frustration to release the jammed slice, remembering that my angry poking and prodding could bring me in contact with the glowing metal coils, redirecting the life-stopping current toward my heart through my conductive jelly-covered hands.

"No toast, regardless how golden brown," my mother taught us, "is ever worth your life."

I have learned about threats that await on the ground, in the sea, and in the air. I reached adulthood knowing that it is reckless to ascend a ladder beyond the third rung. My gutters may be thickly laden with leaves and squirrel droppings, but I remain, thanks to her, safe from a clumsy fall resulting in skeletal fracture or impalement on a picket fence. Furthermore, I am able to swim cramplessly and can recognize in advance when a wild or domestic animal is eyeing me for attack.

I have no interest in the rodeo.

To this day, I heed her periodic caution never to run with anything pointy in my hand, though this sadly ruled out a career for me as an Olympic competitor in javelin, since the sport involves not only holding a pointy stick, but running with it as well. I always knew deep down that you could lose an eye if you threw the javelin.

Such maternal warnings are part of evolution's master plan to keep enough of the species alive to propagate.

Thanks to this upbringing, neither my brother nor I have ever been victims of mudslide, poisoned by rancid candy, and until this point, been kidnapped, or bitten by ponies. I am convinced that if my mother had gone into public safety, the world would be a less risky place, albeit a lot of it would be covered in felt padding and many of its sharp edges would be rounded.

Sadly, there isn't enough of my mother to go around, so society has had to rely on other sirens to guarantee that we don't wipe ourselves out one by one. And offing ourselves prematurely, we do.

Each year, we lose hundreds of thousands of our kind to acts of naïveté, physical oafishness—and let's not worry about being polite here—unrestrained stupidity. Most of these people blindly undertake tasks without thinking about the consequences, often underestimating the risk or overestimating their competence. They ignore common sense, conventional wisdom, and all the obvious warnings that scream out "Don't!"

We increase the odds for our personal survival if we remember the lessons passed on by our parents and teachers. We can also learn from our own mistakes, so long as they were not fatal. But most wisely, we can learn the hard lessons vicariously, standing safely off to the side and watching others take the risks and make the tragic miscalculations.

If I have learned anything from my progenitors that is worth passing along, it is the following trio of life-affirming insights.

Insight 1. The world is a dangerous place.

We live on arguably one of the most hazardous places in the cosmos. Not that the conditions are more extreme here on Earth than elsewhere, but our home planet offers so many more ways to perish than the majority of other venues within the solar system. On rocky and lifeless Mercury, for example, where it is either 900-plus degrees Fahrenheit in the daytime or minus 300 degrees at night, broiling or freezing pretty much account for the only two possible means of perishing. Unlikely you will be killed in a fall, by getting some kind of infection, as a victim of a prank gone wrong, and certainly not by an attack of some predatory life-form, because during the brief moments you are on Mercury, before you turn to charred carbon or harden into a frozen solid, you will be its only life-form. Farther in space, you would have to go quite a bit out of your way to fall clumsily into a black hole. If you stood close to a collapsing star, you might still have to wait a few hundred billion years before it exploded and vaporized you. In such a case, most cosmologists would say you had only yourself to blame if you did not move out of the way of a supernova.

Our own complex planet Earth offers up a buffet of peril, dispensing countless catalysts for our undoing, be they through animal, vegetable, mineral, or mechanical intervention. Wherever we turn, there is a hazard promising to crush, pinch, puncture, split, or in some way jeopardize the intact integrity of our soft vulnerable bodies or to threaten our fragile fleshiness with crippling injury, lifelong pain, and unhappily, death.

Nature, the same mystifying beauty that brings us a pleasant breeze accompanying a gentle rainfall, hypnotic ocean waves endlessly prostrating onto sandy beaches, or a sunrise on a majestic mountain range is the same force that can terminate us with a cyclonic gust of wind, a lightning strike, searing sunshine, a drowning wave, a 7.2 earthquake, or an avalanche of molten lava. Nature is dispassionate and unforgiving. That is why ninety-some percent of animals that ever frequented this planet have gone extinct. If Nature is willing to wipe out entire species after species, what chance do you, a single expendable member of a group with billions of others like you, have for any mercy if you run into trouble?

On the whole, Earth is a good place to live. But you just have to be careful.

Insight 2. We should know better.

We are the dominant life-form on the planet, our million-year ascension courtesy of our intellect, an attribute of humans woefully lacking in lesser animals. The frequent mention of the human being as "One of the Best Animals Ever!" is directly attributable to our brains, which scientists, philosophers, and poets consider the most remarkable and versatile organ in our corporal arsenal. Our cerebral cortex, exquisitely engineered in the first place, has continuously improved through millennia of evolutionary tinkering until finally fashioned into an unparalleled thinking machine.

At face value, the human brain is a visually unimpressive organ—in fact, a rather homely mound of viscera, a mushy gray half-dome of wrinkled pallid cells, characterized by its misshapen lobes and a disturbing landscape of furrows and fissures. Though more powerful than the most advanced supercomputer, the brain has no mechanical parts, no big cavities for storage, and makes no noise when it operates. It is happy to lie deceptively inert, a glob of spongy tissue, offering no visible indication that it is teeming with intelligence and processing billions of instructions per second. While the heart conspicuously pulsates and even the more blue-collar stomach churns proudly to show how hard it is working, the brain quietly goes about its duties behind a facade of stationary squishiness.

For all its responsibility, the brain is fragile, with no internal armature for structural integrity, no bone running through to keep it from collapsing on itself. Poke it too hard, and it breaks into shards like a cake of halvah. Jostle it in cupped hands and does it not quiver? Scratch it accidentally with a fingernail and you are likely to scrape away all memory from 1989 through 1993. Don't hope for its continued reliability if you drop anything heavy on it.

Yet this flaccid and unattractive organ turns out to be the most influential innard in the body, the organ that all other organs turn to for guidance. It serves as puppeteer for all our muscles and as an information processor, calculator, photo album, encyclopedia of memories, and database of sights and smells, often able to perform these roles simultaneously. Our cortex stores a million or so years of collective mammalian knowledge plus whatever else we can cram into it during our lifetime.

Where we have surpassed other animals is in the development of a brain with massive cerebral lifting power. It is our organ's cognitive prowess that allows us to learn, remember, see causal relationships, and draw conclusions. The brain is the organ of judgment and the seat of human free will, lessening our reliance on brute strength and replacing it with the uniquely human characteristics of language, deductive reasoning, insight, morality, guile, sleuth, persuasion, sarcasm, and ridicule.

Although burdened by its own frailty, our brain is vested with the most important of all responsibilities: keeping us alive as long as it can. We rely on our intellect to recognize risks, consider the consequences, and construct a well-thought-out survival plan. Unlike other animals, we are able to override instinct and make conscious decisions.

You would think we would use this enormous cranial firepower wisely.

But this same brain is often the organ of our undoing. Why? Because we are victims of our own free will. Fueled by vanity, a small rogue part of our brain sometimes convinces the rest of the cortex that we are capable of performing tasks we are ill equipped to undertake. Our brain ignores the warning Klaxons, shrouding danger and common sense with cranium-based flattery, duping us into thinking we are much smarter, cooler, and more coordinated than everybody else knows us to be. It convinces us that accidents happen only to others. It is as if deep inside us lives an inner moron, vested with the power to embarrass us or get us in trouble.

This is the part of me that gets the rest of me into mischief. I have to admit that every so often, I do something so astonishingly foolish, so monumentally stupid, that I roll my eyes and shake my head in stunned disbelief. Embarassed, I look at myself from a third-person perspective, no longer seeing me as "me," but instead as "that guy." I am detached, as if I were hovering above myself looking down, much the same way as people who have had a near-death experience do. This out-of-body holiday reflects my wish to get as far away from me as I can because I don't want to be seen with the nitwit below.

Sometimes my embedded moronity causes me to misread directions that are so clear, a fetus could understand them. I walk into a room for something, forgetting eight steps later why I am there. When I become disoriented, I can hide it from no one . . . my face turns pale and my eyes glaze over, which together stir concern in others who believe I may be having a stroke. Sometimes I find I have performed an act that in retrospect clearly violated known laws of physics and eventually resulted in predictable injury. I have left the house wearing two different shoes.

I am convinced that survival compels us to get in touch with our influential inner moron, then to confuse or disable him. We must recognize that no matter who we are, we house an imbecilic lobe capable of all manner of mortifying behavior. We should not hesitate to celebrate our talents, but must be willing to admit where we are apt to falter pathetically and where taking a risk is just plain reckless. As my mother pointed out, "A can-do attitude is a plus when you can do, but a definite disadvantage when you cannot."

Personally, I believe it is the prudent man or woman who understands where peril lurks. It is the enlightened individual who can deftly sidestep it.

Don't get me wrong: I do not consider myself a witless bungler. On the contrary, I do not seek, nor should you even think about offering, your help for most activities. I am quite confident about the many things I do well, and in many cases, I will not be timid in telling you, reveling in my own conceit and quite proud to rub your nose in something I do much better than you ever will. This self-assurance in my cerebral, artistic, and physical attributes is enough for me to live with bouts of transient ineptitude.

Insight 3. There are not enough warnings out there.

Some say there are too many rules. They complain that warning labels that spout the obvious are an insult to our hundred thousand years of human development.

To the contrary, I am convinced that we may actually need more warnings. Sadly, they may be the only tool to help us protect ourselves from ourselves. I do not need to belabor the point. In your heart, you may already know I am right, and if you do not, please just take my word for it.

Many of us drop before we need to. So in the pages ahead, my friends, I will warn you of the many veiled dangers of the temporal world.

That is why this book may be the single most important purchase in your life, and if you do not buy it for yourself, buy it for your children and the multiple generations of their children's children's children, none of whom will be spawned if you ignore the wisdom contained herein and get yourself prematurely extinguished.

I will underscore my points convincingly, citing fact, parable, historical example, scientific study, personal anecdote, undocumented sources, and when necessary, rumor.

Heed the message contained here and I can promise to extend each of your lives by a minimum of fifteen to twenty percent, and I am certain that in years to come, many of you will write thanking me for saving your life over and over again.

For those of you still in the bookstore and on the fence about taking this book up to the register, think about how you'll be kicking yourself later on when you suffer some idiotic injury that I could have helped you avoid—that is, if the accident hasn't paralyzed your good kicking leg.

Don't say you were never warned.

The Home Depot Chain Saw Massacre

I DROVE TO THE HOME DEPOT TO BUY A NO-KILL TRAP TO RID my house of a squirrel that had holed up in my pantry, though in my heart I really wanted to kill the filthy rodent outright—and believe me, I would have if I could have stomached the gory aftermath produced by smacking it with an omelet pan.

As my orange-aproned Lawn and Garden salesman was climbing the shelving to fetch me a humane snare—which, incidentally, costs eight times more than a straightforward trap that works by merely murdering the worthless animal—I noticed another associate talking with a customer who in some strange way reminded me of me. My fellow homeowner stood similarly bent and humbled in the presence of so much domestic technology. He wanted desperately to look and act just like any other competent homeowner, but his eyes, like mine, could not conceal truth to the contrary.

Under his arm was a plastic bag jingling with loose parts.

"My wife and I worked on this thing all evening," the man began apologetically, meekly extending the bag with an outstretched arm toward the flora care salesman, "but we couldn't get past step four. The woman at the customer service desk said maybe you could help me assemble it."

The sales associate nodded, took the bag, and holding one hand on the bottom, tipped the lip downward and gently spilled the contents onto an unoccupied parcel of shelf.

Two dozen pieces tumbled into a shallow pile, and though the parts were contorted in a disorganized heap, I could make out a couple of plastic cowlings, some kind of handle, a little canister with a screw-on cap I recognized as a tiny gas tank, a few dozens nuts and bolts, and a corps of unidentifiable mechanical pieces that were not currently moving but, if assembled correctly and connected to the gas tank, probably would.

The debris mound gave no clue to a novice like me what the assembled product aspired to be.

"This should only take a minute," the salesman assured him confidently, which must have been comforting to the customer who would leave the store presently with a tool he did not have to assemble on his own—yet had to be humiliating, as well, because a recent high school graduate on the job maybe a week could complete the assembly in four minutes while two adults with master's degrees and an impressive investment portfolio could not get beyond the step that said, "Remove bushings from the plastic bag."

The Lawn and Garden guy, knowing the identity of the tool before the last piece clinked out of the bag, reached down for the biggest part. Every object has its nuclear piece, a core component around which all other pieces congregate. In the case of this yet unconsummated tool, its personality was to be defined by an appendageless torso, containing a fist-sized gasoline-driven power plant and some metal flanges onto which its other organs would hang. Holding it in one hand, the sales associate reached down without hesitating for a piece to dock onto it, choosing among all the randomly strewn parts the correct "next one," all of it done without benefit of an instruction manual.

He knew how each adjacent piece would connect by looking for some unique outcropping, working like an expert at jigsaw puzzles who can spot the single correct puzzle piece needed next from a heap of two thousand, just by subtle nuance of shape and color. My Aunt Estelle was like this. After Uncle Sid died, she devoted the rest of her life to the only two enterprises that mattered to her: doing puzzles and making Hungarian dessert pastries. The dining room table was always cluttered with a large pile of puzzle parts, a completely assembled rectangular perimeter with a picture filling from the outside inward. Next to it were piles sorted by color, alongside a large platter of nut-filled baked goods. She could effortlessly find the right piece by eye, as if God himself were a puzzle doer and led her hand by providence to it. She could tell by looking at a little bulge or bulbous growth on a piece in some distant pile that it would lock into the proprietary receptor on the one she had in her hand. She would know from a small dab of color between rounded nodules whether the piece would complete the tinder car of a locomotive or be some part of a puppy. We were never allowed to touch the puzzle, but we were always welcome to have a piece of strudel.

I do not have the patience to do jigsaw puzzles. If I do not have fourteen hours to work in reclusion, but am dying to know what the puzzle will look like when completed, I can look at the picture on the box. Call me unfeeling, but I do not get giddy when I find two piece that miraculously mate. While some people find doing puzzles relaxing, trying to find a one-of-a-kind piece in two thousand from a random pile of cardboard chunks has the opposite effect on me. I get tense, frustrated, finally pushing a sorted pile of pieces in anger back into a big heap. If I were to sit down with a puzzle, it would certainly not be one with more than twenty-five or thirty pieces, and I would probably be most comfortable with one whose pieces were big enough to pick up while wearing mittens. I also have no objection to a jigsaw whose parts are numbered sequentially, or one of a map of the United States, with each of the fifty pieces in the precise shape of the state it represents.

With the same determination I saw in my Aunt Estelle, the Home Depot associate deftly assembled the mysterious tool one piece at a time, never once trying to savagely ram together two components that were not meant to conjoin.

I still had no idea what the tool was, which led me think this would be a good premise for a game show, where contestants would try to identify electromechanical objects whose parts were poured out of a bag onto a workbench and assembled one piece at a time. The player who successfully guessed the item's name first would win a preassembled version of it, a vacation to the place where it was made, a dinette set, cash, or something from the Spiegel Catalogue.

The show, as I envision it, would be most interesting if the items to be assembled were mechanical in nature, such as hedge clippers, a Rollerblade, a CD player, patio furniture, or any item made out of metal, plastic, or laminated wood, but would be less appealing with an object composed of protein-based organic matter, such as an ocean-dwelling mammal.

Transfixed, I watched the sales guy attach each new component. Screws were hand-tightened to keep the tool from rattling apart when turned on. An ergonomically comfy handle extended outward from the tool's hindquarters. As development moved into the final trimester, I stared frustrated, absent any inkling of the object's identity, unable to see what both these gentlemen already could, feeling personally helpless, something like the way I feel when I cannot get an optical illusion to perform dependably for me as it does for others.

"Don't you see the old woman in this picture?" someone will ask, pointing for example to the classic black-and-white line illusion containing either an attractive young woman or a hideously ugly old hag, depending on what your brain wants to show you at that moment.

I have no trouble seeing the nubile twenty-year-old, with her long beautiful eyelashes, soft cheeks, and pearly skin, but I surprise and perplex my friends when I am unable to see anything but her in a picture they claim also seethes "old woman" so unambiguously.

"Come on. What is wrong with you?" my appalled friends ask.

Struggling as hard as I can, and in spite of the jeering, all I can see is the first image, and frankly, she is attractive enough that I see no reason to go off searching for some hideously offensive wart-covered old crone. Yet, I turn the image upside down because I am a little curious. I can make out something that vaguely looks like a child's wagon, but maybe it is a cremation urn. I am told I am wrong in both cases and at this moment, I am thought to be the only living primate who cannot see both images. I stare at only a small part of the page, stuffing the rest of the picture into my blind spot. I push the image a variety of distances from my retina. I put my hand over one eye, as if I am being tested for new glasses. I blink, trying to get my brain to do a manual reset, thinking that as my eyelids rise, a new scene will appear. I strain until my corneas throb. No matter what I do, I am unsuccessful in getting the geriatric woman to emerge from the background. My friends insist I must have a brain tumor.

But then, when I am beginning to believe I am the victim of a cruel ocular hoax and there is no old woman, her image abruptly appears, not in a gentle transformation but in a sudden violent eruption of ugliness. Once visible, she commandeers the page, seizing my visual field, obliterating the illustration of the beautiful girl by overwriting it with her bulbous nose, her hairline, her babushka, and her evil scowl, leaving no trace that loveliness ever existed here. From that point onward, the haggard woman is seared permanently into the optical illusion storage part of my brain, and henceforth she will be all that I will ever see on that page. I will no longer be able to summon back the attractive woman again, no matter how hard I beg. Squint all I want, I cannot even get the child's wagon or cremation urn to reappear.

A more modern version of difficult-to-see optical illusions are colorful computer-generated 3-D stereograms, which appear as flat two-dimensional printed images of random patterns, but will magically transform into three-dimensional structures if you look at them in the right way. Sometimes the printed plate contains a nature scene with a spawning salmon protruding from an undersea field of other fish or a deer bulging out from a page of mountain lions. Maybe it is a landscape, or perhaps in the most bizarre example, a visual fantasy imagined by an artist who believes he was once been abducted by aliens and summarily deposited on a planet that looked like this.

Some people see these three-dimensional scenes as soon as they turn a page, and for them, the images rise upward like skyscrapers. Others will strain for excruciatingly long periods, crossing and uncrossing their eyes, leaning into the book with the more dominant eye, or staring with the book touching their nose and slowly drawing it back. But then, in a moment of eureka, in a visual epiphany, a fully 3-D object pops out of the page like a jack-in-the-box. The image appears to have depth and perspective, belying everything you ever thought possible about a flat piece of paper. The magical picture stays in view for a little while, but eventually retreats into two-dimensional seclusion again.

Some people will never see the image, no matter how hard they struggle, but reluctant to admit visual impotence, will pretend to see it, grumbling, "Sure, sure—it's a bunch of fish," as they indignantly hand back the book.

I avoid staring at these pictures, straining to coax out the 3-D picture, fearful that I will pull a muscle in my eye or that my face will freeze permanently in a cross-eyed stance just as my mother warned. On the plus side, if my eyes did lock, looking at any two-dimensional images from then on, for instance paintings at a museum, labels on breakfast cereal, book jackets, or Rand McNally road maps, I will have the much envied gift of seeing all manner of three-dimensional topography that others can not. I suspect this skill in making a printed image appear realistic enough for someone to want to reach out and touch it could be quite interesting with a page of pornographic photos.

Given a choice, I personally prefer the low-tech mechanical pop-up books for children, exquisitely engineered and activated by turning the page, triggering a set of complicated cardboard gears, levers, and pulleys that unsheathe intricate cardboard scenery previously hidden, revealing such tableaux as the Louvré, the skyline of Budapest, or a panorama of our digestive track. I have no difficulty making out any 3-D image if it actually extends upward eight or nine inches toward my face.

I still had no idea what the Home Depot guy was assembling, and it was almost compete. The salesman picked up a piece shaped like a little beaver tail and attached it the body of the tool, and then added the last part, a four-foot loop of metal that looked like a bicycle chain. He wrapped the necklace of steel around the perimeter of the beaver tail. Sharp metal cups protruded from the links. Just like the old woman leaping out from the printed page, the tool revealed itself all at once, emerging in a cognitive explosion, henceforth preventing me from ever seeing it as individual parts again. The assembled tool was, I am horrified to say, a chain saw. A chain saw, for those who cannot figure out the level of peril from its name, is arguably the most dangerous tool ever devised by mammals, perhaps the tool responsible for more unintended bloodshed than any other implement yet created.

Its crocodilian snout extended outward from the body. The once placid and neutered parts now transformed into an object of pure evil and reckless destruction. As the last piece was screwed into place, I thought about the movie *Frankenstein*, and could hear the voice of the mad doctor screaming, "It's alive!" a disturbing outburst that proclaimed his panic, arousal, excitement, and fear after installing the final parts inside his creature, and watching his previously inert monster successfully kick-started by a jolt of electricity. Neither the deranged Dr. Frankenstein nor the customer could fully appreciate the evil they were about to unleash.

I stood there, aghast that a man who was as helpless and confused as I am intended to leave the store with a fully functioning chain saw. I looked at the chain saw and looked back at the customer, knowing I was a witness to the first of a series of events that once set in motion could not possibly turn out well.

The chain saw is an indiscriminately revving blade whose sole purpose is to chew up everything in its path. It forgives nothing or no one. It is capable of gnawing through a 150-year oak as if it were runny Brie. It is a device that does not know the meaning of "hard," supremely confident that everything bows to its ferocity. The blade is an endless ring of butchery. Simply touch a tree with this powerful instrument, and robust trunks explode into flying shards of woodpulp and sawdust. Neither neatness nor precision are on the tool's list of attributes.

This is the reason the chain saw is the voracious no-nonsense tool-of-choice of professionals who need to get a lot done fast and don't need to be pampered by such inconveniences as the Department of Labor's occupational safety regulations. Armed with a chain saw, a lone logger can topple a forest in an afternoon. Their operators are hardy enough to live in the wilderness, scale trees, and jump from log to bone-crushing log to break up a floating jam on a rapidly flowing waterway. These rugged outdoorsmen are likewise able to brush off the kind of injury a chain saw can inflict. Severing an appendage or aorta, undaunted lumberjacks wrap their wounds in some flannel and tend to the bleeding after the rest of the forest has been clear-cut.

Ice sculptors, who prefer working no more time in a walk-in freezer than absolutely necessary, use chain saws to hew the rough shapes of swans and other ice subjects quickly, rather than by the more tedious Michelangelo-an techniques requiring chisel and file. Packers who work in slaughterhouses find the tool has merit in reducing an unwieldy side-of-cow hanging on a meat rack into smaller, meal-size chunks with unprecedented swiftness.

Life expectancy of these workers is directly proportional to the size of the saw they choose. It is also a generally accepted maxim that if you use a chain saw enough times, your body will eventually be disfigured with scars and you will someday only be able to indicate a maximum of eight items by holding up your fingers.

Other breeds of saw have some kind of admonishing blade guard to prevent injury if you brush up against them or inadvertently reach up with one to wipe a little sweat off your brow. Not so with the chain saw. Nor are there safety features to stave off the most common accident, called kickback, caused by the saw binding on a wood knot or a nail, whipping backward, and rebounding upward toward your face. More than one owner of the implement has been divided vertically over the years. In all of tool-dom none has ever been as effective in executing a person whose innocent intent was to get a handful of kindling.

If you learn nothing else so far, let it be this: It is hard to have a tiny accident with a chain saw.

Power-tool injuries in general are not particularly funny, though if I had to pick one, I suppose I would giggle most over pneumatic-nail-gun accidents, mishaps where especially inept carpenters, using high-pressure fastening tools that blast nails into timber in a single stroke, staple their own hands to a kitchen cabinet or feet to a roof or patio deck. Believing pain preferable to the unmerciful taunting of coworkers, nail-gun victims will often wait for hours until their fellow workmen go home before they call for help. Others, working alone and just out of reach of their cell phones, are forced to consider desperate acts, like those of the snare-trapped beaver in the wild that must bravely gnaw off its own foot.

I cannot envision any circumstance in which I would voluntary fire up a chain saw. What has always stopped me is the sobering vision of trying to hold on to a dangerous machine that is flying about irrepressibly by its own torque. I see myself clutching the saw tightly with both hands, desperately holding on like a rodeo cowboy. I am haunted by the image of the tool whirring out of control at the end of my involuntarily outstretched arms, spinning me centrifugally about my own axis. Trees limbs are indiscriminately dissected as the working end whips wildly on its own, self-propelled and as if purposeful in its mission to destroy everything within view. The blade, buzzing like a swarm of bees, plows deep furrows of ruin, dragging me helplessly behind it. I careen about my yard, colliding with solid objects that shatter as the nozzle of the saw glances off them. I refuse to let go, fearing the saw will ricochet off something, bounce back in the direction of my retreat, and sever whatever body part is closest to it.

Sure, the chain saw is hazardous, but if you are especially careless, so are other tools, even those with alleged guards. Lathes, radial arm saws, table saws, scroll saws, and band saws cause horrible injury and, in rare cases, fatality. Even a power drill if mishandled can induce circular trauma, though the puncture is generally a neat little hole that can be patched. Palm-sized electric sanders are perhaps the only safe power tool, considered trustworthy enough to be used by children, since the most serious complication to accidentally brushing up against one is that you will just end up a little smoother.

It is possible to get hurt with the simplest hand tool, as well. Whack your hand with the blunt end of a sixteen-ounce claw hammer, and your normal-sized thumb will inflate and your thumbnail will turn the color of cheap Beaujolais. Even the most careful tradesman has skewered his palm with a screwdriver or pinched his finger in the hungry jaws of pliers, leaving the telltale parallel furrows of crushed flesh that will take a few hours to level out. Though something like a hand saw can exact injury, unlike a power tool, you can prevent it from doing further cutting damage if you simply stop moving it. A power tool is different. Once you give it permission to proceed by turning it on, it will keep running whether you are in the way or not, performing its work unabated until you purposely turn it off or until it jams as it embeds itself in you.

I have concluded that our attitude about power-tool accidents perhaps defines our philosophical worldview. When it comes to serious injuries, I am more of a pessimist than my traditionally more positive and uplifting brother. Whereas I would see an injured appendage as half-severed, he optimistically views it as still half-attached.

I watch the Home Depot associate quietly slide the assembled chain saw back into the bag and bid the customer a productive day in his yard. It surely does not take too vivid an imagination to imagine the soon-to-be muffled screams coming from the do-it-yourselfer's property and the gruesome discovery made by his children of his lifeless body—and not far away, a gas fueled chain saw, still whirring and spinning in circles by itself like Curly of the Three Stooges, until it eventually runs out of gas and stops on its own. If the man is lucky, he will survive, though I envision him henceforth solely dependent on his spouse to feed and toilet him.

It is just as likely that sometime in the future, the man's wife will approach a doctor in her local hospital's emergency room.

"Excuse me. My husband recently bought a chain saw," she might interrupt, holding a plastic bag under her arm. "Someone at the front counter said you might be able to help me reassemble him."

You've Been Warned

WONDER JUST HOW MANY LIFE-SNUFFING INJURIES ARE
caused each year by home improvement stores callously putting instruments of personal destruction in the hands of the inept.

Some say retailers should be held criminally liable for blithely
ringing up a $149 sale with its forty percent margin, knowing that
the power tool they sell may be used thrice before its inexperienced
owner is maimed in a totally preventable mishap. A store should
know it has no right to sell someone like me a dangerous device such
as a chain saw or 240 amp arc welder.

But then I wonder what responsibility we must assume for our
own well-being, and simply, whether we should make it someone
else's job to prevent us from being schmucks.

Some people will insist that you only have yourself to blame for
not understanding that some objects are obviously dangerous if used
improperly. You should already know not to take an electric Crock-
Pot into the tub, no matter how pleasant a bubble bath along with a
bowl of chili sounds.

Likewise, it shouldn't take a Fulbright Fellow to watch the muzzle
end of a formidable tool gnaw through a chunk of rebar or crosscut
a 4×4 pressure-treated timber without figuring out that it can do
great personal damage to one of your appendages if things go terribly awry. For God's sake, a porpoise, a tree shrew, a flounder, or just
about any animal with more than a rudimentary brain stem would

jump back in horror if it fired up a wood chipper or pneumatic impact hammer.

Indeed, we ought to know that certain implements can be a hazard
to us, but we should also know that *we* can be just as much a hazard to
us. You would hope that inexperienced or known-to-be-awkward
people, many who have also scored 1450 on their SATs, would be
smart enough to realize that they may personally lack the aptitude,
coordination, good sense, and overall luck-in-life to do home roofing
or install new power-mower blades without incurring tragic consequences.

I am beginning to believe that we, as bipedal, linguistically advanced mammals, may still not have evolved sufficiently to be entrusted with our own safety. In the case of, say, the chain saw, there is
convincing evidence to suggest that some of us need a bold faced,
fiery, crimson-printed warning on the box to remind us that we are
buying—and forgive me for being redundant—a chain saw, and that
such an uncontrollably rowdy piece of machinery, with its history of
unsolicited carnage, is not for everyone. Maybe text translated into
multiple languages ought to begin by saying, "The manufacturer
cannot more emphatically warn that if you cannot assemble this
chain saw on your own, it is really not in your best interest to use it."

Next to the words, taking up its own entire panel, would be a big red
international NO circle and diagonal slash overlaying a graphic illustration of a person standing upright, holding a saw in one hand, while off
to the side, a detached other-arm lies on the ground, motionless.

Certainly, no one will argue that an item shouldn't include a clear
warning if it contains hidden explosive bolts, an easily triggered
squirting acid bladder, or dangerously sharp, removable pieces which
are small enough for a toddler to choke on, and, coincidentally taste
a little like a Snickers bar. Likewise, you should not expect that operating a coffeemaker known to cause house fires, or blow up and blast
shards of carafe into its users, their cabinets, and children is simply
"part of the price you pay for brewing a mug of decaf." Any company that knowingly makes a faulty product should be whacked un-
mercifully with the heavy metal scale carried by blindfolded Lady
Justice.

But today, we look for any excuse to blame someone else for a mishap, even when it is clearly our own fault. It is bad enough that we foolishly throw ourselves in the path of peril, but worse, we often try to make others morally and legally responsible for our own unparalleled foolishness

That's why dockets are choking with lawsuits. Many people whose lack of common sense ought to make them the butt of our jokes are instead walking away the beneficiaries of giant judgments, proving that being profoundly dim-witted may not necessarily prevent someone from getting ahead.

More and more manufacturers, lacking confidence in us—their customers—and fearful of lawsuits, are proactively slathering their packaging with detailed warnings, for their own protection as much as ours. While the cautions may appear to be overly simple, obvious, and condescending, I think they may actually be a pretty good idea.

Take the message printed on plastic bags that protect new clothing or recently retrieved dry cleaning. Garments often come packaged inside ultra-thin, see-through, polyethylene-film wraps—ethereal, jellyfish-like, gossamer windows—designed to keep their contents shielded from dirt, greasy smudges, fingerprints, and tiny tears, while still offering customers an unobstructed view of the garb inside.

This lightweight polyethylene sheathing is cheap, wispy, easily torn, and too frail to support even the most delicate sandwich; it is barely scrappy enough to undertake the duty it is asked to perform. Still, people misuse the otherwise fragile plastic bag, and through their own acts of stupidity or carelessness, have turned it into an instrument of death, capable of wiping out the families they are lovingly trying to clothe.

So garment makers and cleaners have been forced to stamp a message on the plastic as a stern notice, in case it is not already obvious, that THIS BAG IS NOT A TOY! The unrestrained text reminds adults and literate children that if one of the principal criteria for a good plaything is that it "will not lead to suffocation," this plastic wrap falls disappointingly short. Dry cleaners and apparel makers are afraid, and rightly so, that some children will discard their Play-

Stations, Barbie Victorian Dream Condos, and expensive Hasbro Weeble-based products, and will reach for lightweight industrial packaging materials instead. They fear that imaginative youngsters will pretend these bags are make-believe space helmets and place them over their little heads. Only after it is too late will the tykes find, to their chagrin, that the bags do not provide sufficient oxygen to keep them alive during their pretend intergalactic trip. Asphyxiation will cut short the children's fanciful excursions to Mars in precisely the same way it would for a real astronaut whose air supply ran out in deep space.

Personally, I cannot imagine how a normal child could consider the shirt-bag as a toy-of-choice. Nor can I see how a bag of any kind could provide any amusement whatsoever, except perhaps to carry around other toys. From my own experience, I do not recall any childhood buddy ever coming to the door and asking, "Mrs. Goldstone, can Chucky come out and play? And can he bring his toy bag?"

But apparently, death-by-bag is so widespread that society must now make sure each one is boldly emblazoned with the caveat, targeted especially to those who may have forgotten about it since last handling a similar bag a few hours earlier. This warning may be the only hope civilization has of keeping our clothing free of schmutz, while preventing the loss of a few hundred-thousand children annually.

Soon, we may also want to consider an even more important alert on new clothes, this one indicating the precise number of straight pins holding a new garment in its neatly folded origami rectangle. I will probably never suffocate myself while trying on a new Polo shirt, because I am smart enough to remove the packaging before I pull it over my head. However, I may more readily pierce an important artery with an undiscovered straight pin that sometime later plunges into my throat. By letting me know that there are, for example, twelve pins, I can be certain I have removed them all, and therefore can confidently go about my business without fear of leaning forward a few hours later and puncturing my abdomen on one I missed. I would gratefully welcome a printed warning that says, "This is an eight pin shirt. Do not attempt to wear it before all pins have been successfully harvested."

Perhaps the most ubiquitous warning found in America today is on our coffee cups. With newly discovered dangers lurking within our lattes, our baristas are working behind the scenes to help keep us scald-free. The carefully worded text on the container reminds us in tiny, tiny type that hot coffee is, by definition, hot, and further implies that using your crotch as a cup holder while driving is ill-advised.

I have to admit that this is one instance where such a recommendation might "go without saying." Written warning or not, I can think of very few situations where I would voluntarily place a container of boiling liquid, an electric stapler, a chain saw, or anything with potentially hurtful parts anywhere near my prized genitalia. If I sustained some injury there, some might smugly suggest that I rightly deserved it, considering my mishap to be one of those important-yet-costly life-lessons that I will not soon forget or repeat.

It follows that we may be just tiny steps away from more detailed, paragraph-long instructions regarding the handling of paper beverage-containers, including an advisory explaining that we live on a planet with gravity so, "It is prudent to carry this container with the big round opening facing up," and perhaps even proposing that if you are planning to use this cup as a toy, wait until it is empty.

In the future, don't be surprised if you buy an espresso and Starbuck's makes you sign for it.

What coffee shops and fast-food restaurants have not yet realized is that by trying to protect patrons and themselves with these warnings, they may actually be increasing the likelihood of injury, caused when customers bring the cup to eye-level, inadvertently tip it as they try to read the extraordinarily tiny print, and dump the scalding contents onto their laps.

In a society rife with disclaimers, scarcely an item purchased today does not have a "Read Me First" insert or a list of provisos. Caustic drain openers not only have to inform us explicitly that they are "Not for Internal Use," but need to further explain that "Internal Use" refers to inside you and not the drain. Medications, even sleeping pills, caution that they will make us drowsy. Machinery discourages operation if you are woozy on medication or intoxicated, warnings which will not be clearly understood or will be ignored if you are woozy on medication or already intoxicated. Dumpsters warn children not to "play in or around" them, assuming that garbage, rotting food, discarded syringes, and medical waste are tempting playthings for children, and scaling a five foot metal wall will be no obstacle to gaining access to this debris funhouse.

For the most serious hazards, we attach the stern warning of the nation's biggest gun, the Surgeon General, whose primary duty is to investigate all things that are the least bit dangerous and then to caution us about them, using the full force and authority of the United States government to get our attention. We learn about products that will cause cancer, about jobs that are perilous, and activities that will cause disease or injury to us or our unborn offspring.

For decades, the Surgeon General's most reoccurring theme has been that smoking causes cancer. The only people who do not know this by now are newborns, those who have been in coma since 1963, or are French. It could also be argued that the only people who smoke today are the diehard addicted who have been inhaling since childhood, and for them, a warning is no longer necessary because by this time, they already have cancer. We have also learned that second-hand smoke, expelled from the malignant lungs of smokers into the public ether, is a problem for the rest of us too, not only because the discarded and besmirched air we will breathe in is rich with recycled carcinogens, but because it has taken on an unpleasant stench, having recently commingled with the exhaled air of people whose breath is already offensive because, frankly, they have been smoking.

Perhaps our most colorful Surgeon General was C. Everett Koop who served in the Reagan Administration. With his Maine fisherman chin strap beard and his iconic bow tie, the avuncular Koop, who appeared to be part Walter Cronkite and part Captain Kangaroo, was America's family doctor: serious, authoritative, yet looking friendly enough to approach. He could lecture without it seeming like he was yelling at us.

Dr. Koop warned us of the dangers of fatty foods and additives. He forecast an increase in morbid obesity throughout a population hungry for burgers and fries. In the name of yummy, we consume nutritionally shallow food, resulting in portly children, jeopardizing our individual health, cutting short our productive years, increasing the costs of health care for everyone, not to mention putting added strain on our already deteriorating highway bridges and overpasses.

The Surgeon General additionally admonished that if you are a pregnant woman, alcohol may be harmful to your unborn child. Should you be irresponsible, ignoring your body's role as a cocoon for your offspring, and you get yourself selfishly shit-faced drunk, your baby will get a slight buzz as well, and while you can throw up in a back alley, your fetus is in a place where throwing up is inconvenient, if not impossible. The irony is that so many women were made pregnant only because they got themselves shit-faced drunk in the first place.

When C. Everett Koop warned you about something, you stayed warned.

The Consumer's Union offers warnings in more detailed white papers, acting on our behalf and trying to use items in the same stupid and irresponsible way we do, testing them vigorously under strict laboratory conditions, trying to anticipate every bone-ass or irresponsible move we could make, and finally publishing their recommendations in their monthly *Consumer Reports*. Their testing process is so studied and comprehensive that the model in question is generally discontinued by the time the report is in print. Although this does you no good, you can take some comfort in the fact that there was once a product safe enough for you and your children to use had you only purchased it six months earlier.

Similarly, many electrical products carry the Underwriters Laboratory Seal, acknowledging that anything connected through your home or office directly into the North American power grid is potentially hazardous, but you can sidestep fatal injury if you use these products properly. Should you have a chance to visit the UL headquarters, you will see a wall of memorials honoring the unselfish laboratory scientists who have given their lives so we can enjoy better toasted bagels or dry our hair more safely.

In the years to come, as government and industry begin to fully recognize the supervision we need, we are apt see more and more warnings. We are not too far upstream from finding warnings adhered to the barrels of guns informing users that "firearms shoot a very small pellet of metal very fast from the nose end, so be careful not to point one at anything that is moving unless you want the moving to stop." In the future, you can count on seeing large print on the side of children's inflatable swimming pool horsey rings or swan-shaped water wings to remind waders that these will not be effective in Class V whitewater. In addition, you will be advised not to fill them with propane. In this particular case, you may actually see a warning printed on the side that says, "This IS a toy!"

Warnings will no doubt save the lives of many who are absent minded, careless, overly confident, or foolhardy. But critics claim that we also need to be warned about the downside of warnings.

In America especially, we are becoming so dependent on others to keep us from committing folly, so numb to potential danger, we are losing our ability to respond to danger on our own. The less we rely on sound personal judgment, the more it will atrophy, and eventually we will not be able to trust ourselves for anything. After so many years of natural selection and sharply honed survival skills, we are rapidly losing the good sense it took 100,000 years to accumulate. Incidentally, this is just another reason why the Europeans are laughing at us behind our backs.

Others claim that bold printed warnings alone will not make the products themselves any safer. In the end, blades will remain sharp, weed killer . . . poisonous, and electricity . . . provocative.

Warnings may actually contribute to more people losing an eye or dispatching a neighbor's child in the future. We are becoming so inundated with messages of caution, detractors tell us, that the frivolous ones are crowding out those that are really important. At some point, we might just ignore them all.

Neither will they stop lawsuits. In fact, they are helping the litigious generate new strategies about whom to sue for what. Personally, if I did something intergalactically stupid, I would not want to go public with a civil proceeding and risk the details of my ineptitude becoming part of case law. Instead, I would choose to simply hobble about with my injury claiming I fell when skiing or got scorched while saving a member of a clergy from either a burning church, synagogue, or mosque, selecting the house of worship depending on the person to whom I was speaking. I, for one, would prefer not to be remembered as the guy who sued the Girl Scouts of America because I pulled down a crate of Samoa cookies onto me. If I carelessly dumped steaming hot peril onto my crotch, I would be content to live the rest of my life secretly in long trousers, my face and inner thighs a little redder for the experience.

Finally, there are some who see our hardship as a form of entertainment, and relish hearing about the occasional incident of accidental brain damage or dismemberment.

Let's get used to it. Warnings are here for the long haul, and maybe a reminder every so often describing the perils around us isn't such a bad idea. While some will consider the wording insulting, the rest of us may be quietly content that we have been so forewarned, thankful that a few well-placed phrases may be enough to keep us ambulatory and fully sighted. Perhaps we would even be better off with a few more.

While we are on the subject, I would like to remind you that my publisher, a venerable institution with an unblemished reputation for almost one hundred years, is not made of money and could not sustain a class action lawsuit resulting from injury caused by this particular work, so they have insisted that I inform you that THE EDGES OF THESE BOOK PAGES ARE VERY SHARP AND IF YOU ARE CARELESS, YOU COULD SUSTAIN A PAINFUL PAPER CUT. REMEMBER, THIS BOOK IS NOT A TOY!

Bully for Fear

IF YOU HAD TO POINT TO THE SINGLE CHARACTERISTIC MOST responsible for survival of life on this planet, you would be wrong to assume it to be the development of mighty defensive paws, a ferocious threatening roar, serrated razor-sharp teeth, or venom sacs spilling over with paralyzing sputum. It would not be speed, agility, or unfaltering bravery. Nor would it be courage. Likewise, cross off keen senses, insight, compassion, and spirituality.

Many of us believe that the attribute that has most mightily contributed to the long-term endurance of any species is fear: trembling, humiliating, wet-your-trousers terror, that scaredy-pants response to dangers, both real and imagined. Chickenhearted panic—shrinking, weak-kneed, yellow-bellied timidity—has arguably done more for animal preservation than anything else nature has yet to devise.

Fear, though unsettling, provides the biological mechanism for an entity to (1) recognize that life-threatening danger is imminent, (2) put a responsive survival plan into action without much dilly-dallying or unnecessary fumbling, and (3) prepare physically, emotionally, and spiritually for a very disquieting next few moments.

The brain is always at work, suctioning in images, sounds, and smells and comparing each one quietly to those stored in our personal database of dangers, not interfering with the mundane activities we are performing until there is a match. At such point, the brain arouses what the non-medical person might call the "Yikes! Center," a part of the nervous system empowered to take over when trouble is afoot and to broadcast an alert to drop everything because "what is about to occur is not going to be pleasant."

The fear sequence is automatically triggered by an electrical SOS broadcast from a cashew-shaped portion of the brain called the amygdala, located deep inside the cranium. While other lobes are assigned the functions of speech, problem solving, memory, locomotion, reconciling checking accounts, remembering locker combinations, judging the speed of objects as they are flung toward the face, and the even more esoteric duties of laughter, breathing, and controlling our bowels, the primary purpose of the amygdala is to act as the early warning system of the body—the watchtower, sentry, monitor, dispatcher—from which an appropriate fright response is ultimately deployed.

Within milliseconds, the amygdala trumpets its panic alert to the hypothalamus, a neighboring region of the brain empowered to execute a carefully programmed, corpus-wide emergency plan, rallying the rest of the body, urging it to don battle gear and to suspend all nonessential services until further notice. Dramatic physiological changes occur as organs at various bodily outposts are pressed into service.

Adrenaline, the most invigorating of secretions, acts as the body's charcoal-lighting fluid. With one endocrinal squirt, we ignite an in vivo explosion of heat and energy, firing up a metabolic afterburner, giving us superhuman abilities, if only for a brief moment.

Hormones increase the heart rate. The upper body hammers rhythmically, each low-frequency throb vigorous enough to be heard as well as felt as it punches the inside of the thorax and percussively flushes waves of oxygen-rich blood to our cells in greater-than-normal volume, an advantage in keeping the muscles aerobically fueled, yet in a cruel circulatory irony, a response that contributes to us bleeding to death much faster should we be attacked.

On the respiratory front, the once unobtrusively ventilating lungs now bellow rapidly in shallow staccato cycles. Our nostrils widen, our eyes dilate, and our mouth dries. Suddenly, we are no longer as hungry, an autonomic defense to ensure that we won't slow down during our retreat if we happen to be distracted by some pizza.

The liver treats our tissues to a burst of sugar, encouraging the muscles to work harder by enticing them with some sweets. All our musculi poise in a catlike crouch, temporarily conferred with an uncharacteristic ability to perform in astounding ways, by running faster, jumping clear over obstacles that we would normally plow into, or if necessary, fighting with ferocity that we will consider disturbing in retrospect.

Concurrently, we produce a thin layer of sweat, so if we are caught, we will be very slippery and hard to hold for very long.

We are wound tight as a mainspring, alert, our senses hyperacute. We rely partially on instinct, our archetypal tool for well-being, which contains millennia of hand-me-down survival instructions, hardwired directly into tissue and fiber circuitry. Stated simply, instinct is having the answers to frightening situations in advance, preloaded and accessible. It is a remarkable set of guidelines that prevents a given species from falling for the same trick over and over again.

Now buffed up physiologically, we are braced to react to frightening stimuli. We select one of two opposing yet equally effective survival options, to defend ourselves or to flee, sometimes making the either/or choice through careful cognitive debate or just as often at random as a result of what the literature calls "chickenshit panic."

Psychologists have dubbed this autonomic fork in the road as the "fight or flight" response, where we either (1) puff out our chest, crouch in a defensive pose, and fight or (2) turn and run like mad in whimpering terror, retreating without the least concern for how pathetic we look, just praying we can outrun, outjump, or outswim whatever is thinking about hurting us.

Standing our ground and preparing to fight is the noblest option. In certain situations, we confront danger head-on no matter the cost, putting on a stern game face and doggedly digging in our heels.

Animals in the wild will snarl, raising their lips to show teeth or fang. They hiss, screech, rear up, and posture to make themselves look more ferocious, hoping their adversaries will back down. Sometimes a dance of aggression will be enough, defining a winner and loser without anyone getting bloodied in the process.

Just like most other animals, we humans, too, raise our hackles and fight to protect our territory, or the rest of the pack, if we feel it is being threatened. We also defend ourselves with uncharacteristic viciousness when we are cornered and are certain we are about to be hurt or killed anyway.

Even where we know our resolve will be no match for a bigger adversary and where resistance is futile, we may still bravely duke it out, often with predictably tragic consequences, yet occasionally with astounding courage that surprises both us and our adversary. Once in a while, even the surliest of animals will bow to a smaller one exhibiting unusual balls.

Throughout the animal kingdom, some oppressors enjoy toying with frightened victims, bullying the smaller, younger, frailer creatures, bolstering their own cheeky animal esteem through the fear they produce in others. Being among the physically smaller children in my elementary school, I could identify with the life faced by tiny defenseless animals in the wild, such as the marmoset, the brine shrimp, and others who were easily taunted, hectored, and beaten up by the brawnier animals that shared their habitat.

In McKeesport, Pennsylvania, the small mill town outside of Pittsburgh, where I grew up, many of my classmates were the sons of burly steelworkers. Their fathers were fearless men who spent their working lives in silhouette against the Hadean aura of the blast furnaces, ever covered in grime, adding their own sweat to the recipe for steel, as they turned hot liquefied metal into pipe and girder.

Many steelworkers emigrated from Europe to Western Pennsylvania in order to escape poverty or persecution, coming to the New World with a satchel of clothing, a few coins, and a glossary of even fewer English words. Here, they found work in the hot and dangerous steel mills, where the universal language was fearlessness, and the only English necessary was understanding a coworker saying, "Excuse me, that cauldron of molten pig iron directly above you looks like it's tipping."

The mill towns attracted men strapping and courageous enough to withstand the harsh condition of the mill, willing to ignore the oppressive, flesh-searing heat, poisonous gases, splattering molten alloys, or silently moving railroad cars. Their massive arms, bulging from decades of continuous backbreaking labor, held hooked pikes as they muscled blocks of glowing orange steel along rollers toward presses that would squeeze them into I-beams and rails.

Their offspring, mesomorphs all, and sired from this mighty stock, inherited brawn and daring. With all their pent-up kinetic energy and no ingots to push around as a release, these children of steel-workers used my friend Howie and me as substitutes.

I was no match. The Goldstone DNA, shaped by its own work history, has not provided for the strength and ability to defend ourselves against the kind of threat posed by mill children. As descendants of five generations of haberdashers, members of my family were to grow only as strong as it took to lift shoes, dress shirts, and men's hats.

So it was no surprise that my family, who could not seem to produce a male over five feet eight inches, would pass this defect on to me, condemning me to a lifetime of bullying by anyone even a bit taller, which in the fifth grade included all the boys except Howie. I was fortunately taller than the majority of girls, apart from the hulking Lucy Doherty, who long before there were reports of steroid abuse was assumed to be at least partly boy. To the larger featured and better developed schoolmates, the smaller among us were tiny, anonymous, faceless targets, easily accessible and useful to strike repeatedly with their knuckles if they wanted to build up calluses.

Following one particular day of after-school effrontery, my father found me in my room huddled under a blanket, where I felt momentarily secure that my adversaries would not be looking for me. Dad sat on the edge of the bed, addressing a bell-shaped lump underneath the bedspread, and delivered a character-building lecture about confidence and courage, hoping to mold me, his eldest son, into a citizen who would not be such an embarrassment to him. Bullies, he promised, such as those I feared at school, picked on us only because we empowered them to do so. They bothered only those who they were certain would crumble in the face of their bluster. They sought out the fearful, the insecure, the beleaguered, those they felt would willingly submit—in short, a sure thing, which I appeared to be evidenced by my frequent outbreaks of trembling in the corner of the schoolyard for no apparent reason.

Bullies, he continued, were generally cowards themselves, and the surest way to get one to stop was to stand up to him or, in the case of bulky Lucy Doherty, to her. "If you bravely hold your ground," my dad assured me, "a bully will always back down."

He encouraged me to face Ronny McKasson, an exceptionally aggressive sixth-grader, who saw me as an inanimate object and used me routinely for his physical exercise and personal amusement. Ronny's reputation for brutality was so widespread that most children would walk blocks out of the way to safely circumnavigate his neighborhood. He carried himself in the manner of an oppressor, strutting arrogantly in any direction he surveyed. Crowds dispersed like iron shavings around a repelling magnet. He was able to crush galvanized metal garbage cans in a bear hug, and just to flaunt his coolness, he would spit through a gap between his ill-fitting front teeth, and did not much care if you were standing between his mouth and the ground.

Ronny McKasson was oversized even for an upperclassman, in part because he had the added years of growth that repeating both the second and fourth grade provided. His wrist and forearm were the same diameter. I imagined that as he grew older, any barely observable definition of his massive neck would no longer be visible and would just dissolve in an amorphous shape between his shoulders and head. He got the worst grades in all of Versailles Avenue Elementary School, but academic achievement was unimportant to someone who could get whatever he wanted in life just by making a grapefruit-sized fist.

Each day, Ronny and his friend Tyler waited at the schoolyard gate, leaning symmetrically against opposite fence posts in Gothic gargoylelike poses. They owned the gate and were the toll takers en route to the school yard, extracting a payment of fear and respect from those who passed by, or sometimes, collecting actual cash. Tyler followed Ronny's every order, acting in the role of loyal lieutenant and referred to in schoolyard parlance as the "under-bully." He knew he was only a heartbeat, or school suspension, away from the principal oppressor position.

There was no convenient way to get from the outside of the schoolyard to the inside except through this portal of terror. The only other option was the long walk all the way around the schoolyard fence to the forbidden and dangerous loading dock, used exclusively for the daily truck delivery of 300 half-pint cartons of milk. So we were forced to ceremonially travel in review of Ronny and Tyler if we had any interest in continuing our education.

We never knew if we would pass ignored and unharmed or whether we would be singled out for harassment. Ronny randomly selected each day's prey from a list of about six of us. Even though we could never predict the exact day it would be our turn, we could count on a good three, sometimes four encounters each month, excluding snow days.

The cruelty would usually begin when Ronny got our attention, calling us by some clever name he invented, "Hey, Shrimpy," for me, "Freckleboy" for Howie, and "Gimpo" for Paul Dorini, who, no fault to him, suffered from polio. Once the bullies selected one of us as the *victimium diem,* we could count on them batting us back and forth for a few minutes like a volleyball. I am certain this violent jostling caused long-term damage to our internal organs. Ronny and Tyler often followed shoving with a round of slapping, the theft of our homework, and, if time permitted, some humiliation to our bagged lunch. Those of us even less fortunate to be chosen after school could look forward to a degrading and sometimes painful walk home, which might not end until well after dark, and only after we finally figured the best way to get our pants down from a tree.

The day after my dad's lecture, I decided to confront the miserable bully whose secret life as a pathetic wimp himself would finally be revealed. Ronny outsized me in every dimension: taller, more muscular, and heavier by a good twenty pounds. The logic of me calling his bluff was not easy to understand. Still, I knew my father would not purposely expose me to harm.

I spotted McKasson standing alone across the playground, and in order to throw him off guard, I proactively approached, briskly walking toward him, my eyes narrow and locked on his, treading forward as erectly as my fifty-inch frame would permit. I was pumped up hormonally, my heart beating quickly. I felt both a little scared and exhilarated, prepared to face down the spineless bastard, strike him definitively, and watch him whimper off defeated and humiliated. I was eager to see his expression turn flush and fearful.

"My dad says you are a big coward," I blurted, stopping a bold six inches away from him, though unable to get the phrase out entirely before Ronny lifted his arm casually and slammed his mallet-sized fist downward into my face. All he apparently heard was "My dad says you are a big cow—," which I believe only made him madder.

The lesson excluded from my father's sermon was that sometimes a bully is not a coward at all, and such was the case for Ronny McKasson, who, as it turned out, enjoyed beating up others and was actually quite good at it. If you think you will take a terrible thrashing from a guy who is calm and happy when he is hitting you, you will be astonished to learn that it is far worse when you piss him off.

In retrospect, I would like to amend my father's wisdom to include the following disclaimer: Even if a bully is easily frightened, it does not necessarily mean of you.

I finally saw Ronny McKasson, now going by Ronald, at a high school reunion many years later, and as I predicted, he had aged more quickly than the rest of us. He blimped up morbidly and was now a pitiable character who had apparently peaked physically at age twelve and was now barely contained in an abused, failing body that gave no clue that it once housed a tyrant. He sat friendless at a table with his comparably overweight wife, his face bloated from medications, feebly holding on to an asthma inhaler he brought to his face to periodically jump-start his wheezing lung. Likely, we thought, the guy would not make it to middle age, and it would not surprise any of us if he didn't make it to the end of dessert.

He was unable to wear a tie, his shirt opened wide at the collar to accommodate a neck that had continued to grow unabated since elementary school and was now either the same size or slightly more circumferential than his head. Seated, an obese half-dome of lower abdomen draped out toward his knees like a gelatinous lava flow, pushing downward and wedging his legs out at a forty-five-degree angle, hanging where a traditional lap on the rest of us would be expected. Bending forward, he was barely able to reach around himself for a goblet of water and had to reposition himself on his chair frequently to prevent pressure sores. He battled strenuously to move even a little, like a turtle on its back trying to right itself. I watched him struggle and pant pathetically, thinking this might be the perfect occasion after so many years for Howie and me to beat the crap out of him in the parking garage.

Again, standing up to adversaries, whether in the human or lower animal world, is sometimes surprisingly effective. Souped up with energizing fluids churning, an animal can transform temporarily into a machine of awesome aggression. This display of uncharacteristic ferocity sometimes makes a small creature look like it is packing a tremendous wallop, so disconcerting and unexpected that a predator may turn and leave, perhaps frightened and confused. In rare cases, the sight of a creature snarling or spinning its arms around like a windmill might be so amusing that the predator has to leave because he is about to pee himself laughing.

The advantage to winning such a fight, or at least making a gesture, goes beyond the benefits of mere victory. Should you win, word of your triumph will spread, and the news that you are not a pushover may dissuade others from bothering you in the future. An arms-flailing, maniacal defense will similarly earn you the admiration of the rest of your pack. In the animal world, your den mates would show gratitude by elevating you in the pack hierarchy, allowing you to eat first, or giving you the pick of females with which to mate, though for civilized adult human beings, this does not necessarily translate to getting a restaurant table any faster or facilitating an evening of casual sex.

If you choose to battle, whether as aggressor or defender, it is wise to engage only when you know you can win for sure. Obviously, you can better your chance of victory by fighting with something crippled, infirmed, or very, very old. Once you taste blood, and assuming it is not your own, you could someday even gain the confidence to become a bully yourself, and when you are bored, you might enjoy the simple primal pleasure of harassing creatures smaller and frailer than yourself, until one of them can take it no longer and stands up to you.

In any event, fighting may not guarantee that you won't be beaten to a bloody pulp, but by displaying courage as your last living act, you leave this temporal plane with dignity, and in the worst scenario, you will make killing you as inconvenient for your adversary as you possibly can.

Weaker animals rightly fear confrontation, and when all options are equally accessible, the alternative of fleeing is the preferred choice. Running in disorganized terror has proven time and again to be a much more reliable mechanism for self-preservation. Statistically, the life expectancy of the craven far exceeds that of the foolishly brave.

Two safety tips regarding flight: First, heed thousands of years of maternal wisdom, and make sure you do not run while holding anything sharp, whether scissors or spear, and second, make certain that you are not retreating from one predator and into the waiting arms of one of its friends nearby. In either case, you are best served by making a decision promptly, not wasting valuable running-away-time by vacillating.

Most of the scientific literature stops at the conventionally accepted binary option of either highly charged escape or fisticuffs, often failing to acknowledge the third, infrequently discussed but equally valid response of curling up in a tight little hedgehog-like fetal ball, tucking in anything tuckable, covering our heads with our hands, and making our crotches as inaccessible as possible, hoping that what ever has chosen to attack will not hurt us too badly and, more important, will go away presently.

Wildlife Television

EVERY SATURDAY MORNING, MY BROTHER AND I WOKE UP early to watch *Bwana Al's Safari Adventure,* hosted by a man we believed was a real bwana, the Swahili word for "jungle boss." We figured he had previously been an African explorer, but with fewer and fewer good jungle boss opportunities available abroad, he decided to move back to Pittsburgh. In reality, Bwana Al was Alvin Markowitz, a booth announcer during the week and the only station employee who happened to fit inside the size 42 regular safari jacket the station owned. Donning his jaunty pith helmet and smartly pressed khaki shorts, snake protective black knee socks, and a bandanna tied nattily around his neck, he stood against a jungle background of thatched huts and a tribal drum, surrounded by a weave of hanging vines.

The ambient chirping of tropical insects and distant call of the bonobo looped endlessly under his on-camera narration. Every week between 8:00 and 10:00 a.m., Bwana Al introduced a badly spliced jungle movie pulled from the station's scant movie library. Since the show drew an audience of children between age eight and twelve, programmers did not spend a lot of time choosing the film featured each Saturday and the only scheduling criterion was that the movie had not been shown the week earlier. All the jungle films on *Bwana Al's Safari Adventure* were in black-and-white, and the majority had been produced on a Hollywood back lot sometime between 1941 and 1945, at a time when maps still referred to Rhodesia and the Belgian Congo. Since this was also the period when we were at war in

Europe and the Pacific, most able-bodied males had been drafted or enlisted, so the cast of these films was comprised primarily of militarily deferred men, many who wheezed asthmatically or limped as a result of childhood bouts with polio. Likewise, the African warriors hired were generally older black gentlemen whose median age was sixty-three, retired from their jobs as porters on the New York Central Railroad.

Jungles, especially those of the African subcontinent, were portrayed as dark, mysterious, moist, and foreboding, overgrown with ripe jungle weeds and pocketed with suctioning pools of quicksand. Back in the 1930s and '40s, jungles were thought to have no ecological purpose except to house danger, being not yet appreciated for the botanical treasures they held and having not yet been renamed with the more environmentally inviting term "rain forest."

Each week, the film would feature a small group of amiable explorers trekking through the jungle proper, nobly intending to discover new cultures, to find a cure for disease in an obscure plant growing near a cannibal enclave, or to save jungle animals from the dangers of the wild, where their survival was always at risk from animals superior to them on the food chain. The explorer's altruistic goal would be to transport as many animals as possible away from the jungle's indwelling hazards and to relocate them to a much safer home inside zoos across America.

In jungle movies, the wild was regularly breached by a safari. Safari-ing as an occupation was not easy. Danger lurked everywhere, often from animals that patrolled the jungle, from African warriors who seemed to be overly territorial, or from groups of evil explorers or soldiers of fortune intent on stealing jungle gold or defiling some tribal voodoo shrine. At least one or two safari members would die some miserable death before the movie ended, which you would think would be a deterrent to subsequent groups who were considering a visit to the jungle the following week.

Through much of the footage, a group of explorers slashed its way with machetes through an overgrowth of vegetation, traversing a dense jungle floor that was more cluttered than lush, balancing on crumbling ledges suspended above raging waterfalls, and wading through swamps with rifles held dry above their heads. A concerto of generic animal sounds supplied an eerie backdrop. Vines hung from trees, able to camouflage hungry yet patient cougars or aggressive bushmasters.

Each week, we could count on a scene where a snake dropped down from a tree onto an unsuspecting safari member, and after a few unsuccessful moments of trying to uncoil it from around his neck, the victim would gasp, and as the lone woman on the safari "eeked" in terror, the unlucky victim would die a violent choking death. These scenes permanently imprinted in our young minds that (1) all snakes were dangerous, and (2) most trees contained them.

In Bwana Al's movies, you could also rely on all visiting adventurers to be white. They were fashionably dressed in khaki safari garb and sported safari helmets, which provided some protection from the equatorial sun and torrential rains but apparently not from the cascade of reptiles that regularly fell from overhead branches.

Jungle parties would also come in contact with the indigenous tribespeople, who were by nature malevolent, primitive, and minimally dressed, hiding in wait with curare-tipped spears, eager to puncture trespassers. In other horrific scenes, disoriented jungle explorers who were captured by Pygmy tribesmen would undergo terrifying ceremonies of torture, either as a test for bravery or just for Pygmy amusement.

In a test that I vividly remember, the jungle chief forced his prisoners to undergo the Ritual of Poisonous Snakes. Toeing a line, each captive was forced to hold a lethally potent serpent, carefully grasping it with quivering fingertips just behind the head and at the tail, barely squeezing it at the length of outstretched arms. Then, the captives were ordered to raise the linear and horizontal viper above their heads repeatedly, a move that was terrifying for the safari members, but no less comforting for the snake.

When being tortured, it is important to remember not to panic, especially with a lethal and ill-humored animal in hand. As long as the snake was securely gripped around its collar and at its terminus, it posed no danger. It was only if an end got free that the angry snake's flailing could produce misfortune.

Usually one captive, a dispensable member of the safari, would lose his resolve, letting go of the poisonous front end of the snake—incidentally, the less favorable end to drop. This oversight was apparently terrifying for the snake, as well, and in its innocent attempt to break its fall, it would instinctively try to grab something, and since a snake can realistically clutch an object quickly only with its mouth, it regrettably did so by biting onto the miserable explorer's face.

All of us find that certain memories fade as we get older. Sweet memories of long-dead relatives are now a bit harder to recall. To my detriment, I have forgotten anniversaries, birthdays, and library-book due dates. Yet, the disturbing image of this snake ritual, seen only once when I was seven, is permanently etched into my memory and cannot be erased from the cerebral tablet no matter how hard I try.

Most of Bwana Al's movies were Tarzan adventures. The most famous of all Tarzans was Johnny Weissmuller, an ex-Olympic swimmer who secured a career in Hollywood in 1932 after apparently finding no steady work as a "professional swimmer." Tarzan, as author Edgar Rice Burroughs describes in his series of books about the Ape Man, was the only child of a British nobleman named Lord Greystoke and his wife, the fetching Mrs. Greystoke. The couple were passengers on a steamer but were abandoned on the African coast by a mutineering crew who found it difficult to run a successful mutiny and provide decent cabin service to passengers at the same time. Dumped on shore and forced to live in a handmade hut, the Greystokes survived by their wits, foraging through the jungle for food and taking on chores that they had previously relied on butlers and nannies to perform. The couple conceived a son, who would not be born to a life of privilege as would have been his destiny, but instead, to this primitive and hostile world. Shortly thereafter, the Greystoke parents were killed at the hands of a moody she-ape. The abandoned baby boy named Tarzan was adopted by some of the local animals, who chose to raise him and show him the ways of the jungle rather than eat him outright.

Tarzan's strength and courage reflected the patient training of his ape stepparents. But Tarzan would bring to the jungle the unprecedented gift of human intelligence, which would separate him from the rest of his simian pals. Harnessing his brain and the jungle savvy he learned on-site, he was eventually able to rise above the rest of the animals, getting himself elected Lord of the Jungle, using his advanced human intellect to convince the other animals to vote for him and not for his opponent, the ocelot.

Tarzan learned to speak a form of "broken English" surprisingly well for a child tutored exclusively by gibbons, and even with his halting command of the language, he was still able to make himself understood. However, having no human role models, Tarzan was unable to effectively master grammar and the proper use of pronouns, always referring to himself by his first name.

"Me Tarzan," he would say, continually forgetting that "me" is used exclusively as a direct or indirect object. Confident in his knowledge of the jungle and his animal-like prowess, he was equally gracious in accepting his grammatical shortcomings. "Tarzan regret not good with syntax," he would say self-effacingly, admitting to both animals and people of his ongoing struggle with English structure.

Each week, Tarzan would prevent jungle evil through his direct intervention or, when necessary, in league with his ferocious animal friends, summoning them with shrill jungle calls and somewhat embarrassing animal impersonations. In response, a herd or two would reluctantly come over to see what Tarzan wanted, and as a favor to him, would end up pouncing on the people who had pissed Tarzan off. To function in this primitive environment, Tarzan learned to communicate with wild creatures, speaking the primordial language of the jungle. Not being his native language, he never learned to speak jungle talk fluently, though he did speak "broken animal" well enough to be understood.

To give the movies more human appeal, and to assure viewers that Tarzan was not having sex with animals, the films introduced a love interest, Jane, a woman attracted to his jungle passion and willing to give up a life of privilege to live atop trees. Tarzan and Jane stayed together for many years until the Ape Man got a little restless and broke off the relationship, one day saying, "Tarzan need space. Think good idea to see other people."

Some years later, our local television station responded to complaints that Tarzan jungle movies unfairly portrayed all indigenous African people as cannibals, savage and barbaric primitives. Not to be accused of insensitivity and racial stereotyping, the station eventually took *Bwana Al's Safari Adventure* off the air and replaced it with *Charlie Chan Theater.*

My earliest images of animals and the concept that they are inseparably linked to uninvited injury and death came from Bwana Al and his ilk. Television is a powerful medium to share ideas and shape phobias.

Through the years, nature documentaries have offered me a way to learn about my fellow living things vicariously, permitting me to visit especially dangerous plants and animals while sitting in the safety of a comfy chair in my living room. It is here in front of a TV screen that I got to see the coyote, the hammerhead shark, and the aggressive wombat, confident none of them could see me.

Baby boomers like me learned about creatures of the wild by tuning in on a Sunday afternoon program called *Wild Kingdom,* sponsored by the Mutual of Omaha Insurance Company and hosted by a rather chipper older gentleman named Marlin Perkins. We welcomed him into our homes each week so he could introduce fauna heretofore unfamiliar to us. Both vicious animals and kindly petable types were treated with equal respect by Perkins.

An unlikely-looking outdoorsman, Perkins was a man in his sixties, gray haired and dashing, with a smartly trimmed white mustache. He condensed everything we could ever wish to know about wildlife into a half-hour visit, bringing us into the animal's natural habitat, whether we were welcome there or not.

Perkins, who was a zoo curator when he wasn't tromping around jungles, was accompanied by his easily gulled and compliant young sidekick, a man who could be talked into approaching all manner of confused and vicious wild creatures. These encounters were captured on film, giving viewers a hitherto unseen week-to-week comparison of how different animals go about mauling an adult human. But it also provided fans with a reasonable explanation why it made sense for the show to be sponsored by an insurance company.

Without *Wild Kingdom*, many of us would know nothing about the wallaby, bandicoot, badger, the coatimundi, the macaque, the Andean condor, and the loggerhead turtle. We learned about animals on the brink of extinction, many of which have finally gone extinct since the programs were first telecast in 1963. By learning just how rare and treasured some species of animal were, Perkins and his associate no doubt motivated many of my contemporaries to pursue careers in veterinary medicine, biology, and nature studies, while at the same time influencing some of our African counterparts to explore lucrative careers in wildlife poaching.

But most important for me, *Wild Kingdom* provided the only means for my brother and me to have an animal in the house, albeit inside the TV screen.

Today, educational TV, science channels, and cable networks airing programs about animals exclusively offer round-the-clock exposure to life-forms other than our own. The daily schedule includes compelling wildlife documentaries, stories of animal murder and mayhem, shows where huge menacing animals beat the stuffing out of darling little ones, and even game shows where trained animals compete for title or money. Based on the popularity of funny-home-video shows, most of which feature clips of people being accidentally whacked in the testicles with one kind of object or another, there are even funny-nature-video programs featuring clips of animals being whacked in the testicles. There are animal courtroom shows where one animal, wronged by another, can sue for damages, as well as the authorized biographies of such nonhuman celebrities as Seabiscuit, Flipper, Fury, Shamu, and the first six generations of the collies who played Lassie, a heroic dog loved by a young farm boy named Timmy. I learned that the producers of the *Lassie* TV series always chose male dogs to portray the bright and selfless she-dog Lassie, but you must remember this was the male dominated 1950s, when it was hard for female dogs to get work. The collies did all their own stunts, explaining why they would ultimately need six of them. Legendary Hollywood dog handler Rudd Weatherwax raised and trained all the various Lassies used through the program's decade-and-a-half run, and I hear he raised and trained all the different young Timmies, as well.

Today's most popular animal shows feature wild and dangerous beasts, animals with fangs, land and water creatures with poison barbs or venom sacs, and animals able to crush or gut other animals.

The program hosts, following the Perkins model, are usually zoologists, naturalists, or individuals whose family businesses dealt in the vicious animal trade—people who are happy to pick up anything that (1) is disgustingly slimy; (2) urinates when lifted; (3) pinches, bites, injects poison, or breaks bones; or (4) kills with no warning. They seem to be willing to cavort with snakes, crocodiles, scorpions, poisonous insects, and just as willing to have their untimely deaths recorded on film if they are one day so unlucky.

A few of the more outrageous of these shows are emceed by animal experts from Australia. The country-continent, as it turns out, is home to some of the most deadly reptiles, spiders, and plants that evolution has ever to conjure up.

The venom-fertile Australian land mass, pushed to a remote South Pacific location by tectonic movement, has been long untethered from the other continents and has therefore given poisons thousands of years to marinate in isolation within various members of the animal pool. So once the continent got more widely settled, the animals were just itching to try out their venom on someone.

Australia is a fascinating country, founded by prisoners, rogues, varlets, scoundrels, and rapscallions who were dumped there by the English in the early 1800s. Australia was the Empire's Devil's Island, which means that the majority of its citizens today are descended from Britain's misbehaved. Over the years, the settler's progeny built a great nation, tamed an unruly land, and created a booming civilization out of a continent that was geologically challenging and inconveniently located. Its modern cities are examples of what the discarded dregs of British society and their offspring can do when you just leave them alone.

Australians are supposed to be the friendliest, most charming people south of the equator. They will interrupt their day to help you tow your car out of a sinkhole or saltwater marsh using the winches they all have connected to the front of their vehicles. The locals will come up to you if you look lost and ask if you want to come to meet their families and join them for a barbecue. If you were ever in desperate need of a kidney, you would find most Australian strangers happy to give you one of theirs. Down to a person, they go on long walkabouts deep into the outback on a regular basis. Pub-drinking, shark-infested-water-swimming, coral-reef-protecting Australians are a people who love their country and the outdoors, no matter how perilous they may be.

And peril there is. In both the outback and cities, you will find legendarily assertive organisms. Here you are likely to stumble upon the deadliest of plants and animals, with more venomous treachery per square kilometer than anywhere else on Earth and a fertile medium just brimming with creatures that will slaughter you as soon as look at you.

Make a list of the most poisonous snakes, and you will find most of them here. Likewise, Australia boasts the majority of the planet's deadly spiders, virtually all of them living within a short bus ride from Melbourne. Great white sharks, in greater quantity here than almost anywhere else, continually patrol the coastline waiting for chubby little surfers to float by on bodyboards.

Travel any more than a few kilometers inland, and you might come face-to-face with the saltwater crocodile, the larger and more dangerous kin to the American alligator. In the less reptile-accommodating United States, alligators claim only an occasional careless onlooker and are not instinctively combative, getting defensive only if we taunt them by dangling small dogs in their faces or when they think we are eyeing them for wallets. Reports of attack are infrequent, making the U.S. a much safer place to retire than Australia, the reason I convinced my parents to relocate from Pittsburgh to sunny West Palm Beach and not even consider Perth.

Production costs for dangerous animal shows are low in Australia because you don't have to walk more than a few steps to stumble upon something that would be happy to kill you.

The program hosts, thick with down-under accents and buoyant in their excitement about the accessibility of so many horrific animals, are quick to reveal the beauty hidden within even the most sinister creatures. They share their love for these animals, dispel misconceptions, and try to teach us to see the aesthetic magnificence of them in the same way they do. Where others just see death, they see beautiful death.

Walking through areas known to be the last address to the fer-de-lance or green mambo, a host will creep silently, relaxed in the deep obscuring brush, wearing skimpy warm-weather clothes, usually khaki short pants and ankle socks, rather than the more conservative protective outdoor wear made of Kevlar or some kind of aluminum alloy as you or I might demand. He walks without hesitation, even with his easily reachable ankles accessible and a target of exposed and unprotected bare shins teasing predators from a few inches away. Hunkered low, the host trains his eyes on the forest floor, looking for signs of life cloaked by the luxuriant brush or in tiny pools of brackish water. Suddenly he stops. Pointing at something he has found hiding nearby, he puts his finger to his mouth to shush us—by the way, unnecessary because we are thousands of miles away in our living rooms watching video footage shot in 1998. He throws himself to the ground, turning to the camera to tell us that he has come across a nest of very lethal boomslangs. Reaching in a burrow up to his elbow with the intent to grab one, and while still looking straight toward us, the host tells us just how poisonous these critters are, and if any one bites him, he will die a horrible convulsing death, and while he hopes this will not happen, he assures us that it would be entertaining to watch.

Spotting a particularly big specimen, he snags it with his bare hand and scoops it up by its hindquarters. The snake dangles and thrashes. The host explains that this is a snake's way of expressing its preference for staying on the ground.

Like a mongoose, the host is agile and successfully dodges a few targeted strikes, chuckling as he tells us, "Cripey, she almost got me that time." Like other wild animal experts who are still living or not on respirators, he parries its attack.

Once the snake is in hand, the host continues to speak to the camera, completely ignoring the snake as it whips and writhes. "She's so beautiful," he coos, seeing something in the snake that we are either unable or unwilling to acknowledge, and though intoxicated by its markings, he is still a realist, "but if she bites me, mate, I will surely be a goner." He calmly describes the lethal qualities of the aggressive snake, how there is no known antivenom, and why it is a good idea to put it down right now.

To get a close-up view of the most ornery animals, he is willing to wedge himself under a rocky overhang, crawl headlong into a narrowing cave, hold his breath and slip under the surface of a briny lagoon, or squeeze into a dark burrow, where a new wild animal mom is protecting the remaining newborn she has chosen not to eat. The host slides belly down, narrating his progress and reminding us how risky this maneuver is, always whispering so the animals do not know he is talking about them. "If I come face-to-face with the contentious mama Gaboon viper that lives at the end of this tunnel, she will probably latch herself on to my unprotected face. And if I have to back out quickly to get medical attention as the father Gaboon is returning, I will really be screwed."

As long as he does not frighten the snake, it will possibly ignore the intrusion. Wrangling demands years of experience, knowledge, patience, resolute focus, and a respect for the animal's potential for harm. Unremitting vigilance keeps the host healthy. In many ways, the work is no different from people in other dangerous professions, a good example of which might be those who manufacture fireworks or handle high explosives. They can work a lifetime around gunpowder-based pyrotechnics without incident and retire after forty years of accident-free service with a gold wristwatch, which is obviously a thoughtful memento only to those safety-conscious employees who have been meticulous enough not to blow their arms off. Inexplicably, the host survives and is back the following week to scamper with another deadly animal.

Animal shows are big business. To boost ratings, a few are becoming even more graphic and realistic, now depicting the wild at its goriest. Some go out of their way to excite the viewer with jungle violence, happily displaying the gratuitous brutal murder of frail and lovable animals by bullying big ones. Television production companies shoot depraved nature snuff films to titillate and shock, drawing in an audience of debauched carnage voyeurs by promoting series with alluring titles such as *Little Animals and the Big Animals Who Eat Them* or *Creature Evisceration Funhouse*.

As much as wildlife photographers tell you about their deep love for animals, you can't help but conclude that many of them are actually sadistic, horrible people with no regard for the sanctity of animal life.

Cinematographers perch themselves behind a jungle blind, camera trained on a prairie clearing, watching a family of huggable otters politely foraging for food. Clumsily walking behind the mama otter is an adorable baby, followed by his waddling little brothers and sisters, who are discovering new sights and smells as they learn the ways of the forest. The caring mother otter picks up little morsels, making sure that all her fuzzy little babies are fed. Taking tiny otter steps, they stroll down to a stream, leaning over, sipping water through their little pursed otter lips. Not far away is papa otter, grateful to have such a loving otter wife and beaming with pride as he watches his brood frolicking. The entire sequence is tenderly captured on film.

Known to the photographer but not to the carefree otter family, a leopard is lurking nearby, eagerly eyeing the family of moist and luscious mammals who are unaware of the danger. The opportunistic photographer shoots this, as well. It does not take a member of the Nature Conservancy to figure out that what is about to happen is not going to be good for the slow-to-retreat chubby otters with whom we have just spent the last ten minutes bonding.

The cinematographer continues to shoot both the leopard and otters, knowing that the predator is crouching and poised to strike. If the filmmaker really cared about animals, he could easily prevent the upcoming massacre and save the life of the entire otter family with just a little warning, perhaps whispering, "Psst. Behind you," or a more discreetly cryptic pig latin caution, "Eopard-lay! Eopard-lay. Un-ray for your ife-lay!" At the very least, he could shoo the otters to safety by gently nudging them with the fluffy windscreen end of his microphone pole.

But instead, he callously keeps the camera rolling and thus becomes a willing accessory to murder, panning and tilting to record the butchery as the jungle cat springs out of the bush in a surprise parabolic leap, pounces squarely on a couple of the slower moving family members, and consumes them directly. The documentary cameraman happily captures the bloody slaughter, offering no assistance to the unsuspecting victims. Then even more heartlessly, he moves in for close-ups, filming the grieving of the surviving otters. I would think if the tables were turned, and a ravenous leopard were stalking the cinematographer from a clump of bushes, the cinematographer would appreciate the courtesy of a little heads-up.

We Are No Match

IF I HAVE LEARNED ANYTHING ABOUT NATURE, IT IS THAT WE humans arrogantly perch ourselves above other animalia, self-proclaimed as the global ruling life-form, boasting that we are the coolest thing evolution has come up with to date.

We have usurped decision making, committing the planet to choices that affect not only our own kind, but every other plant and animal, as well. We have dragooned our way to the top, commandeering the role of spokes-species for all organisms. We have unapologetically exploited the environment, appropriating its precious resources for our selfish gain. We don't seem to care if we inconvenience other animals or if a breed or two go extinct in the process.

As a species, we are self-absorbed, pushy, and domineering, rudely cutting to the front of the phylogenic line, rubbing our highly developed brains in the faces of all other living things, and acting as if every one of them owes us a favor.

We are advanced cerebrally, sure, but need to understand that we are no match for most other animals physically, and should they ever decide to turn on us, we are in deep trouble.

While we have been wasting evolutionary time refining our brains, ignoring our muscles, and not making any effort to develop stingers, talons or venom sacs, other animals have used the clock more wisely to work on physical attributes that make them better prepared for both offense and defense in a cruel and dangerous world.

Compared with so many other animals, we humans are soft, frail, and very easily damaged.

We proudly walk upright, forgetting that our bipedal configuration exposes our soft defenseless underbelly to attack. We are structurally flimsy, with fragile flesh as easily torn as parchment and insufficient protection for all the delicate organs inside. We bruise easily. We are, in fact, quite easy to dispatch under the right circumstances.

We are nowhere near the largest creature. Nor are we the strongest. All varieties of bear defend themselves better. Even the muscular raccoon or chimpanzee can tear a human limb from limb. Pythons and constrictors, their entire torso no thicker than our puny, weakling wrists can crush all the wind out of us in less than a minute. The tiny black widow spider, injecting a barely visible droplet of paralyzing toxin, can stop a 250 pound man—intent on squishing it with a shoe—in his tracks.

We do not have the speed of a jungle cat, and we cannot escape like lesser animals by scaling trees, trapezing from branch to branch, tunneling through underground filth, or flying away.

We are unlike the porcupine, that defends itself by erecting a barrier of pointy quills, and we lack the protective exoskeleton of the invertebrate lobster, which is difficult to crush, even if the lobster has been boiled and even with the use of special crustacean pliers.

We even lack the self-defensive mechanism of the lowly, fist-sized spiny hedgehog, safeguarded by its cowardice and programmed to retreat by compressing itself into a prickly warm-blooded sphere.

We humans have no sharp claws, no packets of poison, and no pointed fangs. We cannot easily maul an invader nor can we swipe a predator off its feet by the swish of a muscular tail. We are pathetically vincible even when compared with a small, feisty claws-extended house cat, a muscular and rabid opossum, or an irritable monkfish.

Most animals can beat us up very easily, and won't hesitate to do so, especially when they feel we are encroaching on their space, if we are annoying their babies, when they are hungry, or if they just want to mess with us. It is impossible to reason with any animal once it has made up its mind to harm you.

If I have learned anything, it is that animals are, by and large, out to get us.

While my mother would suggest avoiding all of them just to be safe, I believe it makes more sense to identify those flora and fauna expressly gunning for us and to learn what to do to avoid them. A working knowledge of the food chain is also helpful.

Size gives some of these creatures license to do whatever they want and ingest just about anything they would even remotely imagine to be tasty. To a ravenous meat-eater, you and I are nothing special and from a culinary standpoint no different from a tree shrew or ibex. A carnivore driven by primal instinct would dispassionately devour a member of our species without a moment's pause, never taking into account that we are the same food group that produced William Shakespeare, George Gershwin, and Albert Schweitzer. Predatory beasts do not value education or achievement and would gladly sup upon a dignitary just as readily as they would a non-prolific and unpublished gazelle. Such a wild animal would not hesitate to guzzle down Mother Teresa, though given her diminutive size, a hungry animal, if given a choice, would probably prefer one of the larger and much more filling Nobel laureates or visionaries instead, perhaps Thomas Alva Edison, widely considered one of the more succulent inventors of the early twentieth century.

Much of our wild fauna, impressed by their own ferocity, will tear you to shreds for no other reason than they are bored and believe eviscerating you with their claws would be momentarily entertaining. Take the rapacious polar bear, for instance, which lives comfortably in the hypothermic waters and sea ice of the North Polar Basin. Its nastiness makes it a threat to both Inuit and non-Inuit alike.

Covered with a layer of snowy fur, the polar bear is the largest member of the Ursine family, weighing in at up to 1,750 pounds and equipped with powerful short limbs, broad shoulders, and catcher's-mitt-size spiked paws. As it walks plantigrade on land with its thick layer of insulating fat and coat of fluffed white-hued fur, the graceful creature undulates with each heavy step like a feral Jell-O mold. It swims effortlessly in the clear and frigid waters of the north, submarining like an obese, hairy, yet delicately poised ballet dancer, one who is also uncharacteristically accorded the brutish endurance of a long-distance swimmer, able to venture out fifty miles or more and return tirelessly to land hours later.

Those who are lucky enough to observe them in their native surroundings are awestruck by their hulking arctic charisma. Many people would describe polar bears as majestic and resourceful land-water creatures. In return, polar bears would likely describe people as "sufficiently tasty." A stealthy hunter, the white colossus blends invisibly against the alabaster backdrop of its gelid habitat, so even though it is the biggest of all bears, neither you nor any other prey may see it until it is way, way too late.

At nearly a ton and always hungry, it is a dangerously aggressive carnivore that will feast on just about anything edible that crosses its path. But who can blame this impulsive and nondiscriminating behavior on an animal assigned to the near lifeless arctic north, where the available meat-per-square-foot ratio is about the lowest on the planet?

Nature has compensated polar bears with an uncanny sense of smell, allowing them to sniff out food sources from great distances. They are masters of their frozen and inhospitable surroundings, efficiently navigating the stark white landscape in search of a meal and eking out a relatively successful lifestyle in spite of the obstacles. If you find yourself alone on a desolate ice floe in the Arctic with a starving polar bear anywhere nearby, the survival advantage will accrue to the bear, who will advance fleet and sure-footed on the sheer ice as you helplessly scamper in adrenaline-surging retreat, slipping and sliding like Lou Costello, looking for any kind of protective shelter, which you will sadly not find because you are of course alone on a desolate ice floe. Polar bears in captivity—any inbred crankiness not at all moderated by the intolerable heat they are forced to endure when relocated to non-Kodiak places as the Atlanta Zoo—will routinely reach out beyond their enclosures and snatch a curious toddler who has leaned in just a little too far trying to pet "Teddy."

Campers are warned about the polar bear's southern brother, the grizzly, one thousand pounds of hair and muscle that can rear up on hind legs and tower ten to twelve feet above frightened campers, arms arched menacingly above its head and looking like a huge ocean wave about to crash. Omnivorous, munching on nuts and berries as a light snack but preferring a good piece of meat when it's available, these forest monarchs are able to pummel prey, humans included, into edible submission. They can run fast, climb trees, and swim, a triathlon of forest skills that makes escape futile. Living in the timberland full-time, they also know all the woodland shortcuts, so as you round the last bend in the trail on your breathless sprint to the safety of your SUV, you will find the bear already there casually leaning up against it. If a formidable grizzly approaches you, experts suggest, play dead. This may not save your life, but will give you a general idea what it will feel like in a few moments to actually be dead.

With the popularity of amateur camping and the spread of suburbia to the brink of the wildwood, humans are pushing civilization into the bear's once-unencroached forest habitat. At one time, these nervous, shy, and easily frightened creatures would avoid all human contact, but of late, they have learned we bring coolers filled with food and beverage, and knowing that we carelessly leave our campsites littered with our leftovers, bears have become—and permit me to borrow a phrase from wildlife behaviorists—much ballsier, approaching humans fearlessly with a brazen disregard for property rights. Drawn to campgrounds by the smell of discarded taco chips and shriveled hot dogs, they boldly bound into our clearings unannounced, intent to rob us by any means necessary. Attempts to shoo them away will neither be effective nor well advised, and the phrase "bad bear," though initially thought to be a promising deterrent, has time and again brought on tragic consequences.

Campers are thus advised to keep the tent site clean and make sure that all food is out of a bear's reach. Guidebooks will tell you to store your rations in leakproof, airtight plastic bags, tying them securely, and dangling them from an overhanging tree limb.

Yet, experienced campers know that grizzlies will get frustrated trying to jump for the high-hanging food and will become equally irritated and impatient as they fiddle unsuccessfully to undo small plastic baggies using their massive, clumsy bear paws. They will eventually abandon the project when they realize that you and your family, asleep inside a tent a mere ten feet away, are now a more easily accessible food source and do not require unraveling some granny knot to get at. Your untouched food, still fresh and suspended from the overhead branches, will make a welcome repast for the coroner after his long hike up the mountain to identify your remains as human.

The deceptively docile, always smiling giant panda looks cuter than any other living bear, fuzzy little brown bear cubs included. With their black and white yin and yang pelts, their stocky black arms and legs stick out of a squatty white torso, giving the appearance of a black bear in a sleeveless alpaca vest. Two black circles of fur around their eyes and inky-dark ears stand out sharply against the pure white of their enormous heads. They sit quietly, stubby legs extended like fat little children as they pluck at their bouquets of bamboo, the only food these pickiest of eaters consume, spending the better part of the day fixated on the task of pinching off leaves and chewing on shoots. The appear chronically happy and peaceful, though hiding under this adorable sweetness is an animal that would maul you to shreds without hesitation if it believed you had even the slightest interest in its limited bamboo inventory.

Sadly, the panda is rapidly disappearing from the animal roster. Today, fewer than one thousand are known to exist in their only natural habitat, the highland bamboo forests of south-central China. A few others are working as emissaries of the People's Republic, living comfortable but sexless lives in "animal assisted living" quarters inside a handful of American zoos.

With so few examples of the species, animal parks are doing all they can to breed the panda in captivity. Hoping for panda offspring, a zoo will go to extraordinary lengths to fix up its male with a female from another zoo or from the wild, assuming the couple will hit it off immediately and make what we Americans might call "Panda Whoopee" and what the Chinese describe with a phrase that translates literally to "Happy Panda Make Humpity."

Animal behaviorists, puzzled by the male panda's lack of interest, have not considered the simple explanation that the majority of the female pandas that are set up on these animal blind dates are just not attractive, and are available for arranged zoo marriages only because they cannot get laid on their own in the wild. An otherwise horny captive panda will often decline the coupling, refusing to go out with her, "even if she were the last panda on earth," which sadly might actually be the case. Other zoologists believe that many pandas are gay, but would consider adopting.

A circus elephant is another animal whose size makes it ominous. Normally passive, a bull elephant can just as easily stomp you to death on a whim. Sometimes experiencing an emotional breakdown akin to cabin fever, these intelligent, usually rational beasts will go a little berserk under the stress, and in a psychotic episode of obviously gigantic proportion—which they are reluctant to remember later on, cliché notwithstanding—will lose it, and with their extending prehensile trunk, which is essentially a very flexible nose powerful enough to uproot trees, they can pluck you from the bleachers and bash you repeatedly against a tent post.

Less accessible but equally dangerous are jungle predators. The irascible armor-plated rhinoceros will predictably attack the moment it senses your presence, pointing its sharp nasal horn in your direction and charging at you at full tilt in order to skewer you, by the way an unnecessarily excessive use of force since the inertia of two thousand pounds of fast-moving rhino alone will kill you on impact.

Jungle felines—the lions, tigers, and cougars of the Serengeti—stalk their prey as do all cats from Bengals to tabbies. Those interested in you will crouch slowly in wait before they pounce, then leap out and pin you to the ground, toying with you at first as if you were a big ball of aluminum foil, until their playful mood decidedly turns more somber and they remember amid all this merriment that they are still hungry. Running is useless, since it is folly to assume that you can outdistance an animal with twice as many legs as you. All you will do is expend energy you might better use screaming for help. Even if others are nearby, your call for assistance will likely be answered by any weaponless onlookers with an inquiry such as "And what specifically would you like us to do?"

The meat-eating cheetah, a feline rocket and one of the fastest mammals alive, has been clocked at sixty miles an hour. It is widely held that the only way to get away from one in the open savannah is if you happen to be in a Porsche.

Indonesia is the home of the largest, most aggressive lizard alive, the Komodo dragon, the only reptile brassy enough to hunt down and kill an adult human being. Growing to ten feet in length, these monsters are hair-trigger sprinters, and will be upon you and gnawing on one of your body parts before you have a chance to take your first step in retreat. Inside the dragon's mouth incubates a form of bacteria so deadly that a bite brings agony and certain death to its recipient, humans included. Ecology be damned, we should consider ourselves lucky that the Komodo dragon is on the brink of extinction.

Swim in the warm ocean currents of the South Pacific, and you risk an encounter with the Portuguese man-of-war, a rather delicate, gelatinous bag, translucent and wispy as it peacefully floats just under the surface, trailing nearly invisible tassels of jelly behind it, so harmless looking and frail, you wonder why it doesn't just break apart in the ocean current. Its undersea cousin, the box jellyfish, shimmers in see-through pastel hues as it drifts aimlessly through the ocean like a beautiful laced parachute, with its fringed hem of gossamer-thin tentacles dangling underneath it.

But brush up against either of these flimsy invertebrates, and you will trigger thousands of explosive, poison-secreting barbs called nematocysts, which will inject you with a dose of venom nearly as potent as a cobra's. An assault from these nasty coelenterates will cause such paralyzing pain that you will likely die of convulsive drowning long before the toxins do you in. Even dead and washed up onto a beach, these creatures threaten us, able to continue to let loose a barrage of stings from beyond the grave, interrupting the peaceful sound of crashing ocean surf with the periodic screams of curious barefooted beachgoers just moments after they were heard to ask, "I wonder who dropped this plastic baggy here?"

The inoffensive-looking stonefish—blending half-buried in the sandy sea bottom, stationary and perfectly disguised as a faux rock, igneous textured and motionless—surreptitiously lies in wait for prey to swim innocently nearby. Then bursting upward, it gulps down the unsuspecting and careless passerby. But it is the stonefish's ancient disguise that obscures its true danger to humans. Lying hidden just under its granite exterior are rows of poisonous dorsal spines, spring loaded and equipped with the most deadly of all fish venoms, potent enough to kill any pitiable human unlucky enough to misstep on its camouflaged torso. Hypodermically injected, the toxins instantly produce indescribably searing pain. If treatment is not administered promptly, the sting is fatal, not a comfort when you know that a stonefish's home can be in the deep regions of the ocean and you are likely to be many miles and many hours from the closest medical care. So unless you happen upon the serendipitous, one-in-a-million chance that a Red Cross Hospital ship is steaming above you at the exact moment you are stung, you may have to concede that you are going to die slowly and painfully. If you are lucky, your bleeding may summon the interest of sharks who will take mercy by eating you.

And speaking of sharks, many species, for instance the nurse shark, hammerhead, and of course the great white, will dispassionately attack and devour any prey they feel they can overpower, tracking down a meal using their olfactory radar to beam in on the tiniest morsel of blood. The shark's mouth is equipped with large, functional hinges that allow it to open like the front of cargo plane. Inside is a set of sharp and pointed triangular teeth, never housed long enough to become dull, but instead designed as disposable dentures, used for a short while, then replaced by a recently generated row of brand-new teeth pushing in from behind. You might think that you, a fully skeletoned vertebrate, could outmaneuver a boneless animal with an internal armature made entirely of cartilage and one based on a nearly unchanged four- or five-million-year-old design at that. But no, a shark is a streamlined swimming and eating machine. Perpetually moving and in search of food, the shark will guzzle down a human swimmer in a few bites, not because we humans are its first food choice, but because our silhouette often mimics that of a moist and tender sea lion. In the wild, it is usually "eat first and ask questions later." That you know you may not be particularly tasty to a shark, and in fact may be stringy and bitter compared to a plump little seal baby will ultimately be of little consolation to you.

Though horrific and violent, shark attacks on humans are rare. The ecological record proves that sharks are in greater jeopardy than we are. For every one human casualty from shark attack, upwards of ten million of them are killed annually. What this means is clear—if we are willing to merely sacrifice another one hundred people, we can finally be rid of these pesky animals forever.

Fall in the Amazon in the wrong place, and a school of hungry red-lipped piranhas could polish you off in a churning feeding frenzy. Should you go fishing for dinner along the beaches of the Caribbean or off the coast of Japan and cook up the corpulent little marine-dweller known as globefish, blowfish, or puffer, be prepared to convulse to death in waves of suffocating anaphylactic shock even before dessert is served, as the fish's nerve toxins race through your body, shutting down your respiratory passages in neurotoxin retribution.

Crocodiles like those living in Australia are aggressive and extremely dangerous. Crocs are savvy hunters, giant and uncompassionate, cannibalistic when expedient, willing to chase down and gobble up anything fleshy. At four hundred or more pounds, they can still move faster than we can on both land and in water. Always prowling for any animal unlucky enough to be working or playing nearby, they are armed with weapons at both ends, a muscular tail on the back that can knock an adult Aussie thirty plus yards and an even more dangerous mouth generously provisioned with sixty to ninety interlocking teeth, more than is really necessary and sharp as X-Acto knives. Members of the crocodilian family have immensely powerful jaws that can flatten an animal as they slam shut with a bone-crushing force of thousands of pounds per square inch. Paradoxically, the muscles they use to open these same jaws are very weak, so the upper and lower lips can be held together with one hand. If you are cornered by a crocodile and are somehow lucky enough to get a hand on both jaws and can hold them shut, you will be safe from a severe bite so long as you never—and let me stress *never*—let go.

Most victims of attack are unaware that one of these monsters is nearby. Crocodiles float silently just under the waterline, their nostrils and periscoping eyes skimming the surface like water bugs. Stealthy creatures, they are able to sneak up behind their prey, their pineapple-reminiscent dermis hidden below the ripple-free lagoon. In the wake of the croc's a surprise leap, a giant wall of water explodes like a depth charge; then with its massive jaws revealed, it grabs the unsuspecting mark.

Death does not come instantly from the bite of a crocodile's powerful viselike jaws or the blunt trauma from a thwack of a brawny tail. Most quarry die by drowning, as the croc pulls the wary victim under, initiating a frightful maneuver called a death spin. The crocodile, with a firm hold on its prey, rotates rapidly about its long axis, whirling like a top in the thrashing, reptile-induced white water until its captive tires and eventually drowns. Then the croc quietly consumes a meal that is no longer inconveniently flailing about for its life. It also goes without saying that if a crocodile pulls you in within a half hour of your last meal, your cramping will make the animal's work even easier. In the unlikely event that you do escape the crocodile's ancient death spin, you will emerge from the lake dizzy and possibly quite nauseated.

Many Australian families that lose a loved one to a crocodile attack accept the loss as the cost of doing business with Australian nature. In interviews following a horrific attack, a mother and father will be sitting on a log at the edge of a marsh, rescue boats still crisscrossing the waterway behind them, dragging trawling hooks, as the parents calmly relate the episode that tragically ended with a twenty-foot female crocodile lunging out of the water, snatching their children, and pulling them under in a splashing, churning cauldron of swamp water.

"We do not blame the crocodile for eating the twins," the parents stoically respond, understanding the dilemma for the crocodile. "The boys were encroaching on *its* territory."

"This will probably be a good lesson to our other children," the mother continues, "Now when we say, 'Don't play near the swamp,' their surviving brothers and sisters will know just how serious we are."

The tiniest of creatures, too, can pose a great threat to our survival. Poisonous spiders such as the brown recluse cause crippling pain and occasional death, a regretful surprise to scores of the hapless each year who blindly put a socked foot into a shoe they were convinced did not contain a brown recluse spider. Deer ticks carry Lyme disease. Mosquitoes are the vehicle for the sometimes fatal West Nile virus and dengue hemorrhagic fever. Field mice and otherwise harmless looking vermin have been linked to the deadly hantavirus and bubonic plague. The bite of an otherwise healthy Old World monkey can be the infectious trigger for Ebola.

Cattle, even those not prone to stumbling and breaking their bovine hips as the result of mad cow disease, can be placidly grazing on the prairie in our nation's midsection one minute and stomping over you in disorganized stampede the next. Farm animals have been known to turn evil, and more people are injured each year by fluke barnyard incidents where ducks and piglets run amok than are mutilated in thresher-harvester-combine accidents.

City dwellers are no less at risk. The bite of an urban raccoon or skunk infected with rabies is fatal 100 percent of the time if left untreated. Visit a petting zoo, and don't be so smug to think you and your kids are immune from an unprovoked attack by an enraged llama.

Even plants pose unforeseen dangers and can cut short the lives of unfortunates who ingest them or just wander into a thicket where they live. Raging flora carrying life-limiting ingredients grow in jungles, in swamps, along the roadside, in rolling meadows, and even in our gardens. For humans, a vicious plant attack can shut down digestive tracts, barricade respiration, and cause lagoons of internal bleeding.

Leafy and photosynthetic, plants supply a thankless service to our planet. They are happy to inhale carbon dioxide from our breath without complaint, no matter what we have recently eaten, and convert it back into fresh pure oxygen. Yet many of these same plants are just as willing to melt your internal organs and force your central nervous system to go flooey if you consume them. Some will cause total muscular paralysis, which is a plant's ultimate revenge, as if it is saying to you, "If I am staked here in the ground and cannot move about freely, henceforth neither shall you."

Sweet-sounding plant names—the kalmia, oleander, and wisteria—belie the illness and death lurking in their leaves, stalks and roots. Some of their names give you fair warning: poison sumac, poison ivy, poison hemlock. Others do not: daphne, the youthful cocklebur, and the kiss-motivating mistletoe. There are quaint names that deceptively summon up the image of a mighty fine pie, for instance, baneberry or wild cherry, though a wedge of either would prove fatal. Other botanical specimens have parts that do make a decent pie, such as the rhubarb, but contain poisons such as oxalic acid in their leaves, which can quickly turn their consumers' otherwise squishy and healthy livers into an inoperable solid. Some plants just look tasty and similar to berries and leafy vegetables we find prepackaged in produce departments. Do not trust them.

Forest floors are clustered with varieties of mushroom, both the delicious and the wicked. Edible woody fungi, which mushrooms happen to be, have been used safely for centuries to enhance salads, sauces, and sautés. Common gastrointestinally-friendly varieties include the readily available commercially grown button-style generic white mushrooms, the honeycombed morels, the chanterelle, portobello, oyster mushroom, wood ear, porcini, straw, and shiitake.

The heavily scented truffle, which is extremely rare and the most expensive, highly prized of gilled fungal species, is found underneath parts of Europe. Specially trained truffle sniffing pigs snout out the fungi, which are so pungent, they can be detected even interred many meters below. Once truffle seekers lead their working pigs into the woods, the animals point their noses downward and go about divining for the treasures. Because truffles are one of the trendy mushrooms, their aficionados ignore the inhospitable odor, which has been compared in putridity to the "feet of the homeless."

The edible mushroom's poisonous fungal brethren, sometimes invitingly similar in appearance, contain chemicals that cause serious illness, vomiting, homicidal diarrhea, jaundice, coma, and death. More than two hundred mushroom varieties are known to be aggressive, some carrying names such as the jack-o'-lantern and the fly amanita, which conceal their mercilessness. The death cup and death angel, as their cautionary monikers suggest, are among the more lethal you can pick.

Because of the huge number of dangerous mushrooms and the difficulty differentiating the good from the bad, gathering them is not recommended to anyone unschooled in the subtleties of fungal physiognomy. For the amateur mushroomer, there are no hard and fast rules for distinguishing poisonous specimens, and there is no such thing as just a tiny mistake. As such, we are still better off trusting the safety and efficacy of freshly harvested mushrooms to a lowly fungus sniffing hog than perhaps to your cousin Mark, the accountant, who brought a basketfull back after one of his infrequent strolls through the woods.

You do not have to ingest a plant to suffer its wrath. Merely touching some plants such as poison oak can trigger an allergic attack. Oily, lacquer-like resins on the leaves and stalks provoke a painful, skin-reddening reaction, which spreads over the body in itchy, flaming welts.

Without the application of a soothing topical cream, clawing to relieve the unquenchable itch follows, and as an outcome of this self-mutilation, the victim's arms and legs will quickly look like a cat's scratching post. Dermatitis caused by the toxins that coat the leaves of these plants can spread like a brushfire over any area that is subsequently touched. This is one reason why men in the landscaping business—unlike restaurant workers who are required to wash their hands after using the bathroom—are advised to wash vigorously beforehand.

Behind the leaves, roots, and stems of hundreds of varieties of other beautiful wild fauna and houseplants, verdant death lurks, so avoid putting anything in your mouth you do not get from a greengrocer. Shun plants with such names as the star-of-Bethlehem, nightshade, dumb cane, jimson weed, and the oozy milkweed. Castor beans in the chili if you have run out of red kidney are not a good substitute. I have recently seen a bit of an anti-vegetarian backlash, and personally, I now refrain from eating anything that is not pure protein and does not have a birth canal.

There is only small risk of being done in by life-threatening botany if you do not consume it or roll around naked in it. Plants do not attack on their own. There is little chance of waking up to find yourself covered by a cantankerous fern. Be secure in the knowledge that it is easy to outrun a plant, and even those that do move, as their names imply, can only "creep." A tragic plant-related accident is more likely in your attempt to avoid contact with hostile vegetation, should you try to sidestep some dermatological peril on your hiking path and fall backwards into a hedge of nettles.

I guarantee that you, armed with this knowledge, will remain safe from plant and animal hostility, and even more so if you also avoid hikes, flower shows, and most pet stores.

Some people will try to tell you that plants and animals pose very little danger to us. They will quote some study, telling you for example that you are ten times more likely to be mugged in a large city than to be mauled by a wild animal. Even if this is true, it will be no comfort to know that at the precise moment you are being gutted by a cougar, nine other people are getting robbed at gunpoint somewhere in Manhattan.

To Be Safe, Always Carry a Mongoose

I POLLED FRIENDS AND COLLEAGUES HERE AND ABROAD TO determine which animals people feared most, and found that snakes incite the highest levels of anxiety per running foot of any living creature. As a group, these are animals capable of producing both physical and emotional anguish.

It might be said that we can conveniently lump people in the civilized world into a few categories based on their snake tolerance.

In the first category, you will find those who neither love or hate snakes, and as a result of their neutrality, have adopted what they call the "Swiss Approach to Reptiles." They are not repulsed and will not fly into a screaming frenzy when a snake is present. On the other hand, if someone offered them one, their response would be a polite, "Thank you. No."

Another group of people loves snakes. Some of its members dedicate their lives to herpetology and zookeeping, while others may not want to make a career out of them but believe snakes are fun to have around. These are people who delight in the intense color, disturbing designs, tiny flicking tongues, and the squirming—just the things that the rest of us do not. We are happy to let these people go off and amuse themselves with snakes, because it means shorter lines when we are looking for a fluffy puppy. More extreme devotees in this group include followers of snake-handling religions who worship while fiddling with poisonous breeds. Surprisingly few congregants die from handling vipers or are bitten by one that, on a particular Sunday, may not be feeling particularly spiritual.

The majority of us fall into the third category. We are vocal about our disdain for snakes. We make no excuse for it. We love other animals, but for reasons we believe are no one else's business, we rebuff anything that slithers.

Some of us are a little queasy around snakes. Others are paralyzed in fear. I know women who shriek and men who rear back in horror. I also know cases where the reverse is true. Some people cannot look at a snake without shivers shimmying up their spines.

The startling presence of a snake may trigger a physiological response marked by trembling fear and nausea. As the heart thumps furiously, the skin turns a cadaver-like gray, all moisture in the digestive tract from the neck up evaporates, and the once-sure ankles, the bulwark of upright hominids, go rubbery and melt into ineffectiveness like warm taffy.

Sometimes a snake in a still photograph, painting, or harmless book illustration printed on 100 percent venom-free paper is enough to cause people to flee a library in terror.

As a child in the fifth grade, I remember the immediate body-jarring shock if I happened to flip open a page of a book containing a photograph of a snake. I jerked back, my face was sucked of color, and my blood chilled as I confronted an animal that had been coiled, ready for ambush, waiting patiently there on page 186 since the day the book had been printed. My body trembled uncontrollably, reacting the same way it would've had a real snake turned up unexpectedly in my underwear drawer.

The page now forever taboo, I slammed the befouled book shut, touching the outside edges of its hard cover as briefly as possible. I hoped the snake was equally frightened of me and would retreat to some part of the book I had already read. But in my heart I knew I would probably have to go through the entire fifth grade never knowing what else was on page 186.

Even today, show me a picture of snake, and I still reflexively shiver a little, my head involuntarily twitching back. A sudden icy shudder ripples up from an epicenter in the mid-region of my spine and exits through the hairs on the back of my neck. The temperature of the room plummets fifty or sixty degrees, but just for a fraction of a second and apparently just for me.

I must immediately obscure the picture with something—a piece of paper, a handheld calculator, anything at least the size of the picture insert—just not with my hand directly. I squint in order to dim the offending image on its path to my retina until the picture is safely shrouded. If I still need the information contained in the book, I will look for it somewhere else.

For most people, all it takes is watching a lone snake slither to trigger a psychotic episode. Snakes are squirmy and move with slippery choreography, advancing without legs, wheels, or any other apparent means of locomotion, menacing forward, hypnotically compelling yet simultaneously repellent, formfitting themselves around poles and branches and quickly scooting into a hole in the ground or wall as if they were being slurped up by a vacuum. Snakes are pseudo-amorphous, constantly changing their profile, a solid acting much more like a liquid and one of the few animals that can be placed in a box or jar and will comfortably conform to the shape of its container.

Perhaps we are revolted by the most disturbing natural behavior of a snake, the periodic shedding of its skin, a trait that is a hallmark of snake maturity. A snake's rind does not grow, although the underlying snake will. So, a few times a year, the reptile must slough off the old, dulling, ill-fitting skin, replacing it with a better-tailored dermis. It does so by bursting through its scaly seams and slithering out from within itself, a concept of a snake-within-a-snake that appears to be the reptilian version of Russian stacking dolls.

When two or more reptiles gather, queasiness and revulsion increase exponentially. A nest of snakes collectively squirming in a wriggling pile is anxiety's nuclear strike, an image so repugnant, a weapon so viscerally disturbing, that even the least squeamish among us join in a communal gasp of horror, as we slam our eyelids shut to protect the brain from this, one of the most unsettling of all images in nature. Snakes crowded together create an ever-changing, wriggling mosaic, a writhing nest of clashing colors and shapes as they move sibilantly, more content to keep slithering than stay put. They sideswipe each other, creeping in their aimless rambling, in a continuously changing collide-o-scope of color. Knots of serpentry twist and creep effortlessly, frictionless, as if they had been lubricated with a thin glossy film of petroleum jelly. They slide, moving in a way that no life-form should be permitted to move, squeezing into the tiny voids left between associates. After such a vision of terror, a single snake is a welcome sight.

Freudians will tell us that the obvious explanation for our crippling fear is the phallic connection and a deep-rooted flaw in our ids, a theory repudiated vigorously by non-Freudians, based on the observation that most of us are not thrust into hysterical paralysis at the sight of a belt or garden hose. It cannot be the scaly skin either, because once a snake is bereft of life and manufactured into a change purse or pair of stylish Western boots, it can be handled quite comfortably by most of us and will no longer trigger a panic attack. Snake hide, penetratingly repulsive while still on the snake, is quite fetching as a fashion accessory. Most people have no further hesitation holding on to it, looping it in belt form around the circumference of their pants, or even more confidently filling it with credit cards and stuffing it into a back pocket near their own vulnerable buttocks.

While debate will continues as to the cause of snake phobia, the majority of the phobic will remain content just knowing they are terrified, not feeling obligated to explain why to anyone.

So I tend to avoid circus sideshows that feature a pit of snakes. I camp in snake-free forests whenever possible. I love Cajun food, but do not plan to visit the swampy, viper-resplendent Louisiana bayou anytime soon. At a zoo, I will happily spend extra time viewing the fecal-juggling gorillas just so I do not have to visit the serpent lounge. Personally, the thought of these animals anywhere but in remote parts of faraway continents makes *my* skin, which I cannot easily shed, crawl.

Statistically you have a better chance of dying by lightning strike or getting sucked into a jet engine than you do by the chomp of a snake. Still, a snake-related death, like a plane crash or sex with an attractive twenty-one-year-old, seems so much more dramatic when we think it could happen to us.

Not that fear of snakes isn't justified. Many are long tubes of poison, able to kill you faster than most other animals or a gunshot wound.

If a snake is to kill you directly—and by "directly" I mean by its own action and not as a result of an aneurysm you sustain when you startle upon one—it will do so in one of two ways: either by envenomization or by constriction, or more simply stated, either by biting you until you are dead, or squeezing you until you are dead. Either way will produce a terrible and agonizing last few moments of life. If you are truly unfortunate, you might encounter a snake that will squeeze you until you are almost dead, and just when it relaxes a bit and you think there may be some hope for your survival, one of its associates will come by and bite you.

Biters outnumber squeezers by a long shot. Some manufacture highly concentrated toxin in their salivary glands, storing it for later use in puffy little sacs adjacent to their cheeks.

Paranoid as you might be about snakes hiding in the woods just waiting for your bare ankle to hike by, snake venom is not always "about you." The purpose of the poison is to give the snake a fighting chance to capture food or protect itself. Obviously absent arms and legs, a snake cannot maul or batter another animal into unconsciousness. So to live long enough to produce a subsequent generation of snake offspring, some have learned to mix up a toxic protein cocktail internally. Snakes administer it with lightning-fast strikes, injecting victims with stunning poisons in order to immobilize them by convulsions, paralysis, or catastrophic respiratory failure. Even if you are not seen as food, you may still trigger an attack from a snake if you inadvertently step on its neck.

Snake venom is among the most concentrated poisons on the planet, but in some cases, a good example of unnecessary overkill. The inland Taipan, for instance, carts around a poison so robust that a single drop could kill a quarter million mice—that is, if the snake had the time. I do not have the mouse-to-human conversion formula accessible, but it is safe to say that a snake like this one could single-handedly take you out along with a congregation of one hundred or so of your friends.

Venomous snakes are found in abundance on every continent except Antarctica. In North America, the copperhead, cottonmouth, various rattlesnakes, and the coral snake are a routine cause of outdoor vacations cut short. North Carolina currently holds the title as the "State Where You Are Most Likely to Be Bitten by a Poisonous Reptile." If you are planning to drive from New England to Florida, AAA maps suggest taking a right off Interstate 95 into Virginia, then driving south through some back roads in Tennessee, making a right and joining 95 again in Georgia, avoiding the Carolinas altogether. This rerouting, however, will be unnecessary if you promise not to get out of your car anywhere between Roanoke and Atlanta.

Outside the United States, you will find an abundance of serpents, as well. In Europe, if you step on a venom-rich snake, odds are it will be a common adder or Pallas' viper. Africa is home not only to the asp and the cobra, but also the boomslang, puff adder, krait, saw-scaled viper, and the mamba. The Amazon offers about two and a half million square miles of hiding place for the bushmaster and the fer-de-lance. Remote islands, even those that have been cut off from the larger land masses for millions of years, are populated by such demons as the yellow-bellied sea snake and the death adder, whose name is probably self-explanatory.

When traveling, you may want to avoid countries that are home to the Okinawa habu, watu, jumping viper, jacaraca, the Wagler's pit viper and any waters containing the beaked sea snake. Avoid the diabolically dangerous Gaboon viper, whose bite feels no worse than an insect's and is often ignored, until you turn to your travel companion and ask, "Does it always get this dark and foggy at one in the afternoon here?" just as you begin to drift into the hazy pitch-blackness of an irreversible coma.

King cobras, the serpent mascot of India, can grow to eighteen feet and carry offensive saliva that can immobilize a multi-ton elephant in just a little more than an hour. The green mamba of the sub-Sahara is believed to be among the most toxic serpents of them all. Even the most optimistic among us will admit that it is a waste of remaining breath to cry for help.

It must be hazardous for any venomous snake to carry a mouthful of poison around all the time, especially with its own pointy, hollow injector fangs protruding outward like giant buckteeth, sharp and just itching to pierce something fleshy. It is a wonder that we do not hear about snakes inadvertently poisoning themselves more often. I bite my lip accidentally all the time, and thank my lucky stars that I do not carry around teeth filled with venom.

But it isn't just poison that can bring death from a reptile. Non-poisonous snakes in the boid or constrictor family compress the life out of their prey, artfully wrapping around victims and squeezing more air from their ever-compacting lungs with each lap, tightening a little more every time the victim exhales. Death does not come from crushing, as most people think, but through suffocation, as if this distinction really matters.

Snakes such as the boa and the reticulated python are measured in linear feet, somewhat like lumber, and once stretched out, can reach ten feet, although it is not uncommon for the really lanky ones to hit twenty feet end-to-end.

Once a constrictor gets an inappropriately called foothold on you, it will cleverly coil around and around, tightening as it moves, dodging and weaving with its bobbing head to elude you as you try to snatch it, outmaneuvering you by darting in a new direction at the last second, and sliding itself securely under an unprotected arm or leg. You twist and contort, trying to remember the moves you have seen magicians do when they try to escape from a straitjacket, but with each circumnavigation around your body, the snake becomes all the more difficult to extricate. Compare escape with trying to unravel a fifty foot extension cord, but one that is constantly moving and retangling around you on its own. Once this reptilian wrench gets its powerful musculature around your torso, there is little chance for any meaningful loosening. This death squish is a reptile-human pas de deux, a ballet move that would be graceful and beautiful if didn't always turn out badly.

Supersized snakes, the anaconda of South America, for instance, can grow to the circumference of natural gas pipelines, reach thirty feet or more in length and can weigh upwards of 550 pounds. This is a snake that can swallow a deer whole. Depending on the size of its prey, a constrictor may take several weeks or longer to digest its food, and consequently may not need to eat again for half a year. So, even though the remaining deer will be overcome with grief over the loss of one of their own, they will all sleep a little easier in the months to come.

I am like many other people, being so uncomfortable around snakes that I would be willing to take my chances rollicking in the company of more dangerous animals instead. Given the choice of using a sidewalk occupied by a friendly bug-eating green snake restfully sunning itself or crossing a busy thoroughfare to use a walkway crowded with a promenade of bone-splintering and carnivorous wild animals, I would gladly join the parade across the avenue, feeling a bit less stressed marching unprotected between a battalion of wolves and the puma.

This seems as good a time as any to discuss how you, perhaps having spent a lot more time indoors on your liberal arts education and less on becoming forest-wise, can remain safe, using lifesaving poetry and erudite literary devices to remind you of the dangers.

Such cautionary balladry has a precedent. What nautical Westerner has not heard

> Red sky in morning,
> Sailor take warning.
> Red sky at night
> Sailor's delight.

Simple rhymes and onomatopoeic devices have likewise warned visitors to the forest and jungles of the dangers coiled under rocks and in gullies.

The lethal Arizona coral snake, for example, flaunts vibrant red and yellow bands that predators learn to associate with a toxic bite. Interestingly, some nonvenomous breeds, such as the Sinaloan milk snake, glom off the disorderly reputation of coral snakes by counterfeiting the coloration, mimicking the venomous snake's rings to trick other animals to leave it alone, switching the order just enough so it does not violate nature's copyright. To remind hikers of the difference, a well-known outdoor poem warns:

> Red near black
> Venom lack,
> Red near yellow
> Kills a fellow.

For those traipsing outside during the summer, may I suggest some additional cautionary wildlife poetry passed on to me from my maternal grandparents. Simple. Direct. Life extending. Feel free to memorize them and tell them to your own grandchildren, if you live long enough to have any.

On vigilance in the forest

> There's danger lurking in the woods
> Found under rock
> Or tufts of clover.
> Though careful steps will save your life
> It's best to stay
> In the Land Rover.
> —*Courtesy of the Goldstone Family Trust*

For generations, this jump rope rhyme has reminded youngsters in the snake-infested Southwestern corner of the United States of the neurological consequences of a venomous snakebite.

> You lapse into coma
> From bite of a viper.
> You'll feed through a tube and
> You'll poop in a diaper.
> —*Courtesy of the Goldstone Family Trust*

The poem confirms that, beautiful weather notwithstanding, it will be better for Arizonan and New Mexican children to grow up entirely indoors.

In many Japanese prefectures, all literate men, women, and children are required to commit this life-saving limerick to memory:

> The habu found in Okinawa
> Has venom with life-stopping pow-a
> You'll eat no more sushi
> From bites on your tooshy
> 'Cause you will be dead in an hou-a.
> —*Translated from the original katakana text, courtesy of the Goldstone Family Trust*

You can thank me for these poems later.

That's Entertainment!

I HAVE KNOWN STEVE SINCE COLLEGE. HE HAS NEVER BEEN A stranger to adventure, celebrating a zest for life and bountiful curiosity that the rest of us secretly considered unhealthy.

Steve looked every bit the part: brawny and self-assured, sporting the kind of outsized frame you would imagine peril merely glanced off. Steve was unafraid of most things because he was bigger than most of them.

Barely contained in this barrel of a man was massive confidence and an eagerness to face any challenge without flinching.

If someone wondered if it were possible to vault over a Dumpster, Steve happily volunteered. If there was some question of whether a graying piece of meat, leftover moo shi shrimp, or some crusty potato salad unearthed in a remote region of a refrigerator had gone bad, Steve was the guy willing to taste it. He disappeared for days on road trips, sometimes coming back a bit tattered, but always enriched by his wanderlust. He loved visiting places and plunging headlong into adventures no one else would undertake, for no other reason than—no one else would.

Now, decades later, Steve is still the jovial explorer, and not too timid to stray off life's more conventional and paved thoroughfares.

In Thailand on business, he ended up with some free time. He had already eaten his fill of pad thai and had visited a number of temples and live sex shows. So by now, Steve was eager to explore something a bit more unusual. His hotel concierge suggested a visit to a poisonous snake farm, a popular Bangkok attraction, where Steve could learn about the lovely homicidal snakes of the region—Siamese cobra, Russell's viper, banded krait, Malayan pit viper, green pit viper, and Pope's pit viper. If he were lucky, he could catch venom-milking, the hand-extraction of poison used to produce antivenom which, ironically, might be used to save the lives of the people who were bitten while milking the same snake the very next day.

Steve has never liked snakes, but thought there was no better way to confront his uneasiness than through total immersion. Thailand offered a controlled, risk-free laboratory environment where Steve could put his personal grit to the test and see just how close to his emotional boundaries he could get without dire autonomic consequences. Even if he freaked, making a spectacle of himself as he ran screaming for help, he wouldn't feel too embarrassed about it since no one here in Thailand knew him.

A local and reputable snake farm, not far away and part of what was once the Pasteur Institute, was listed in the tour book, but the concierge further volunteered, "Very busy and has many tourists." He suggested Steve hire a boatman for the day instead and travel upstream to one of the more remote mom-and-pop snake ranches.

I was not surprised to learn that non–risk averse Steve consented to visit one such farm where locals raise and handle snakes by the tubful. Personally, such a junket would be much lower on my own Bangkok tourism to-do list, probably somewhere between eating dog and watching a ritual suicide, but Steve, braver than me in college and likewise as a middle-aged man, told the concierge that he was ready to go.

Steve cabbed to the pier, where he met his river master, a Thai version of Humphrey Bogart and owner of the little charter outboard that would transport him upstream. The boat was shaped like a Venetian gondola, pointy end in the front, swelling out toward its middle just wide enough to seat a slightly-larger-than average adult, then narrowing to a flattened stern with a paint-chipped wooden seat for the helmsman. It bobbed merrily on the surface of the river, affirming that it was seaworthy, although its shape did put into question the boat's non-tipworthiness.

Steve stepped off the stable pier and lowered himself into the marginally buoyant vessel, causing it to seesaw in response. He carefully made his way to the plank located halfway down the boat's torso, which would be his seat during the hour-plus cruise. As Steve settled in, the gondola readjusted itself in the water. The boatman nodded hello, started the outboard motor, and lowered its blades into the river. The boat dug its stern assertively into the sludge and the bow nosed up. A thick churning spray of dirt-clogged water shot upward as the boat left its footprint, a V-shaped wake, behind them. In Bangkok proper, they passed cargo ships, large tankers, fishing boats, and floating houses. Soon they headed up one of the less traveled tributaries, where the spaces between boats grew larger and modern buildings gave way to primitive shacks and dirt roads. A half hour farther upstream, dense trees canopied the river. Animals murmured in the distance. The boat passed decaying objects floating on the surface of the waterway. Steve was both unable and reluctant to identify any of it. The river was calm now except for the trail of rippling water that chased after the boat.

After all contact with civilization had terminated, the boat puttered through a few miles of jungle. If the tiny dinghy capsized in these waters and the pair became nutrient for carnivorous fish and reptiles, no one in the western hemisphere would even think of looking here. Months later, tourists might see other unidentifiable objects floating downstream, loath to guess what they were. The bigger pieces would probably be Steve.

An hour and fifteen minutes into the trip, the boatman throttled down the vessel, the engine's pitch dropped an octave, and the boat turned toward an outcrop of trees and a rotting pier jutting out into the river. The boatman jockeyed the little gondola into port, bumped it a few times against the dock, and tied off. Steve climbed out and in response, the boat happily postured higher in the water. Steve headed down a tree-lined dirt path, logically the only direction he could travel.

The snake farm was surrounded by lush jungle. Trees and vines overhung the trail giving the sunlight only a narrow slit to squeeze through. There was nothing close by, and this included medical assistance. The same species of poisonous snakes that awaited Steve inside were probably wandering around free here on the outside, since the owners of the snake farm obviously put it close to the place where they could get the snakes in the first place. Knowing that the venom of many deadly breeds is fatal only if left untreated for more than an hour was no comfort to Steve, remembering the trip upstream took over seventy minutes.

The footpath wound through the dense thicket of trees and brush, finally spilling into a small clearing and the entrance to the snake farm proper. An archway with some Thai lettering and a badly painted portrait of a snake arched over the gate. A flimsy fence defined the outside perimeter of the snake farm, but you could only see a few feet of it before it disappeared in the overgrowth on each side. The frail barrier could not actually stop anything from entering or leaving, but it served more as a visual reminder where the snake farm ended and where the rest of the identical jungle carried on.

Steve paid a woman at the gate in the way he paid most people in countries where he had no clue how the monetary system worked, by holding a little pile of money in his cupped hands, encouraging her to take whatever number of baht she thought fair.

Inside the farm grounds, displays containing live snakes rimmed the meandering dirtway. Some specimens were crated in splintery wooden cages, faced with a chicken-wire mesh to contain the resident while protecting the viewer as best that splinters and chicken wire could.

"One-way chicken wire!" volunteered the boatman, who had surprised Steve by walking up behind him.

"One-way chicken wire?" Steve asked.

"Yes," answered the boatman, apparently misinformed by someone in the past but willing to pass along the inaccurate data enthusiastically anyway. "We see snake. Snake no see us."

Steve politely smiled, now with a little less confidence in the man he was relying on to get him back to civilization alive.

Inside the makeshift wooden crates, the snakes lived in an environment meant to replicate their natural habitat, furnished with whatever the keepers could scoop up from the ground next to the crate after they put it down: some twigs and branches, piles of leaves, a few rocks, candy wrappers, and pieces of broken Styrofoam cup. The snake-in-tenancy generally sat curled in a corner under the debris, sometimes making it difficult to determine whether a snake was really in there, or if it had escaped. Camouflaged by its marvelous coloration, a shy green reptile could disappear against a backdrop of foliage, and an evasive beige one could blend in invisibly against sand. It is this kind of natural subterfuge that permits the legless animals in the wild to capture prey and to keep themselves safe from other predators. Yet this same talent also makes them undetectable to campers who have perhaps chosen an unfortunate place to sit for a moment, with untoward consequences for both the snake and the hiker's ass.

Steve visited about a dozen of these cycloramas. Along the path were shallow pits containing bigger snakes. Some occupants sat motionless like solar-array panels sopping up sunlight. Others were busy moving from place to place, as if with purpose, pretending to be busy and self-important. Around the upper lip of the pits were spindly wooden railings, halfheartedly nailed, and apt to collapse under the weight of anyone leaning on them who is considered anything more than "petite."

A half hour into Steve's visit, a loudspeaker squealed, followed by a woman's voice broadcasting a short message in the local dialect. The boatman rushed over and grabbed Steve by the arm, informing him that the reptile show was about to begin, and all those visiting the farm, which at that moment included only Steve, a Japanese man, and their respective boat drivers, should move into the tent in an orderly fashion.

Steve ducked under an opening and entered a dimly lit canvas amphitheatre. A big metal fan in the back panned back and forth and provided the only incentive for the warm air inside the tent to move. Chipping metal folding chairs arranged in haphazard rows on the dirt floor ringed a six-foot-by-six-foot platform covered with some remnant of heavily stained indoor-outdoor carpeting. Elevated two feet above the dirt and having all chairs facing it suggested that this riser was the stage and would be the focus of the entertainment about to unfold for this small matinee crowd.

The usher escorted Steve to his seat, a good one, Steve thought, about a foot from the stage. The Japanese man and the boat drivers were seated a few rows behind.

The house lights dimmed, in this case by the usher unscrewing a bulb, signaling to the audience and the snakes that outnumbered the audience about 2 to 1, that the performance was about to start. The show would not begin at a predetermined time as on Broadway when lobby lights flash to indicate that you have only a few moments to get to your seats and the show is going on with or without you. In the snake theater, the performers and crew would just wait patiently until Steve, representing a significant percentage of the audience in number and more than forty percent of it in mass, was comfortably seated.

Two remaining columns of spotlight converged in the middle of the stage as a small middle-aged Thai man wearing short pants and sandals emerged on stage holding a burlap sack, which looked like it had originally contained tree bark mulch. The top of the bag was tied securely and the entire weight of its contents concentrated on the bottom thrashed about wildly, confirming to anyone in eyeshot that the bag did not contain the traditionally more passive mulch, but in fact probably contained one of the professional snakes.

Steve spoke no Thai nor did the handler speak much English, so the show would have to be self-explanatory or at least include an element of pantomime. Through a series of gestures, the man signaled that the snake he had was very, very big (spreading his arms as far apart as he could), and if it bit him anywhere from the waist up (pointing to his own pelvis), he would drift into unconsciousness, rapidly succumbing to death (throwing his head back suddenly, lolling his tongue off to the side, and slamming his eyes shut). Steve assumed that this is what the sign language meant and not an alternative interpretation indicating that the handler's genitals (pointing to his pelvis), are very large (spreading his arms as far apart as he could) and if you see them you will faint at their enormous size (throwing his head back suddenly, lolling his tongue off to the side, and slamming his eyes shut).

Alone on the stage, the handler loosened the rope closure on the top of the bag and poured out a nine-foot squirming snake onto the carpet. Now freed, but having been dumped discourteously onto its head, the snake was unsure whether it should be happy to be released or justifiably angry. Thrust into bright lights from the pitch darkness of the bag, the snake found the glare disorienting, but having no eyelids, it was unable to squint as its pupils struggled to adjust to the brightness. It quickly collected itself and settled in a more comfortable semicoiled pose.

Thus, the performance began. The handler crouched down, eight inches in front of the spiraling snake, staring directly into its face. Their eyes locked, and both moved in tandem. As the man sashayed, the skeptical creature followed, its head hovering a foot and a half above the ground and always the same distance from the trainer. It was a gliding human-serpent dance in 2/4 time, with the passion of tango, but replacing a posh Argentine dancehall and the radiant face of a beautiful partner with a mosquito-harboring rotting-canvas gazebo and a consort sporting deadly neurotoxins.

Just as it seemed this was going to be a long and not very interesting floor show, the handler reached over and slapped the snake on the top of its head, startling both Steve and the snake. The snake drew back, and the handler reached out and swatted it again, then again, repeatedly taunting it, making mocking noises, and doing whatever he could to agitate the animal. The slaps did not hurt the snake, but did rather humiliate it. It was clear that the handler wanted to get the snake livid enough to kill him. Having no arms is decidedly a disadvantage for an animal trying to block an uppercut.

When the snake finally had enough, it lunged forward, fangs engaged, trying to hook on to this guy and to inject him with a good mouthful of stashed-up poison. The handler artfully dodged, and the snake glanced off to the side, missing the man by inches. As the viper reloaded, the handler smacked it again under the chin, followed by a few left jabs, and a kidney punch. The snake was always one move behind. When it looked to the right at the direction of the last blow, one came from the left. Each time the handler approached, the enraged snake attempted another strike, and as its indignation grew, so did its inaccuracy.

Then, as the snake sprung airborne toward him, the quick-reflexed handler reached out and caught it midair just inches behind the head, bringing it to a sudden jerking stop. To assure the audience that the performance did not include trick snakes or optical illusions the handler slammed the captive's little reptilian face into the carpeting. The snake flailed and hissed in protest, angrily driving its fully-armed poisonous overbite into the rug and squirting a dose out to show that this was not some rehearsed act.

The handler released the snake. Trying to regain its dignity, it raised its upper third off the ground by sitting up on its snake haunches, assuming a more defensive posture, only to be thwacked again and again by a Thai man bobbing and weaving around the stage like an Asian Muhammad Ali. The handler laughed devilishly, taking a certain bullying delight in embarrassing the snake in front of an audience. The snake struck sloppily, and no matter what the harassed animal did, the nimble Thai man parried.

As the snake made one last pitiful lunge, the handler reached out, grabbed the attacking viper by its nape, and plunged it downward toward the carpeting again. Anticipating the impact, the snake tried unsuccessfully to close its eyes just before its face was smashed flat onto the rug like a pug's, sadly reminded that this would be yet another one of those occasions when eyelids would be so very useful.

The snake hissed, fanging the nappy pile, which was soggy with venom. Holding the still openmouthed and hissing snake by its throat, the showman smiled at the audience and bowed. Steve, the Japanese man, and their respective boatmen politely applauded.

The handler laid the snake down on the tarmac and exited momentarily, leaving it alone on the stage with nothing else to stare at but Steve. As a good judge of distance, Steve calculated that the snake was about four feet closer to him than the handler was to the snake, so if the snake decided to attack, it could get in quite a few successful licks before it was restrained by any nearby employees. Steve could die there on the snake farm just as anonymously as he could have on Bangkok's backwater rivers.

It was unclear to Steve whether, as an amateur, he should stare into the eyes of an aggressive animal. On one hand, he might intimidate it and cause it to back off. Yet making direct eye contact may be an animal call to arms, an insult, like thwacking it in the face with a glove to initiate a duel. So Steve pointed one eye toward the snake to watch for any sudden forward moves and the other on the slit in the curtain where the handler had disappeared. What seemed like many minutes later, the serpent wrangler reemerged, carrying an even bigger burlap sack, which by this time Steve was praying actually contained mulch. The guy dumped the contents onto the carpet, revealing a longer, squirmier, and much less accommodating serpent. It writhed on the floor in confusion and agony, flopping and twitching as if its back itched and it could do nothing to reach it.

The handler mimed his introduction of the second snake, using similar arm-spreading and groin-pointing, which told Steve that either this was a much more prodigious and deadly snake, or to remind him that he would be really awed by the handler's truly enormous organs.

One snake was to the Thai man's left and the other to the right, exposing two reptilian fronts to defend. The trainer reached over and smacked one snake and then quickly leaned back to smack the second, now alternating his pummels and dividing the whacks fairly evenly. In reply to attack, each snake jolted forward individually. Now the handler was sparring with two snakes, slapping one and dodging its strike, then slapping the other, which had strategically repositioned itself but was still unable to get a clear shot of its assailant. Whether the snakes struck one at a time or simultaneously, the guy was able to jump agilely out of the way.

The snakes followed him around the stage, and at one point, they lunged in unison. In a move that Steve concedes was very impressive, the handler caught them both at the same instant, one in each hand, immobilizing them mid-strike. Before the now-stunned pair could make eye contact with each other, the handler slammed them into the carpet, both heads clunking against the stage at the same moment. Twice the dosage of venom spritzed into the carpet.

More applause erupted. The handler put the smaller, less zealous snake back in its burlap sack, though it kicked and knotted as best it could to make relocation as difficult as possible. The second snake remained on the stage alone, watching his rug-burned colleague man-handled, perhaps wondering why he had been left behind.

The handler jumped off the stage and took a seat next to Steve, using clownish flapping-arm movements to draw the remaining snake toward them. Now Steve understood why a giggling usher led him to that particular chair. The snake, still throbbing with tiny welts, swaggered across the stage, confident it could more easily hack a chunk out someone sitting. With the snake now firmly coiled at the edge of the platform and directly in front of Steve, the handler reached out and smacked it broadside, first from the right, then as the snake turned in the direction of the assault, he surprised it with a dis-respectful bitchslap from the left. Assured he had the animal's atten-tion, the trainer leaned over and started to gesture wildly just inches in front of Steve's face, in kinetic language interpreted by a snake as "fightin' words." The easily ired creature now made more furious by these nonverbal slurs, assumed that that these obscene messages were emanating from Steve's head.

"Hey, you most miserable of all animals," the hand signals sug-gested, "go screw yourself," a supreme insult to snakes just because a few breeds of mutant hermaphroditic reptiles actually can. "By the way," the handler's miming continued, "Steve told me to say this."

For the past thirty minutes, the snake had been slapped, smashed into cheap carpeting, and disgraced in front of strangers. By this time, all it wanted to do was kill somebody, and at this moment, it was not particularly choosy about whom.

Despite the knowledge that a ten-foot poisonous reptile that had been provoked to attack was looking him in the face, Steve was con-fident that the handler knew what he was doing and would not be endangering people in the audience if he weren't a professional, in total control, and practiced in his art. "No one would come here if this was really dangerous," Steve thought, forgetting that there were only three other people in a tent that held forty, two were paid boat chauffeurs, and all of them were sitting safely a number of rows back.

The handler was in his late forties. Steve figured the guy made a lifelong career out of goading venomous snakes and dodging their strikes. He convinced himself that the guy had probably been doing shows six times a day, six days a week since he was fourteen years old and was probably good at his job because, look, the guy was still alive. But then, Steve's own skeptical brain countered, (1) this may be the only work out-of-work middle-aged Thai men can get, (2) he was hired after about two hours of training, and (3) the snake farm goes through three or four of these guys a week. Perhaps gravestones across Thailand are carved with the inscription, "In Loving Memory of a My Husband, A Man Who For a Few Days Was Faster Than a Banded Krait." Steve looked out of the corner of his eye, praying the man had the courage and talent to keep all three of them—the handler himself, Steve, and the snake—alive.

For the finale, the handler leaned over and, from a starting point just in front of Steve, punched the snake broadside, not with a gentle slap or even a bullying jab, but a full-body assault with a bony clenched fist. Now spurred by pure rage, the snake hurtled forward, fangs exposed, flying toward Steve, whom it blamed for this afternoon of torment. Again, if I can remind you of Steve's overall girth, the snake didn't need to be accurate and could be off by a foot or so in either direction and still plunge itself successfully into some part of him.

The snake flew off the stage, launching itself horizontally, its mouth open, eyes squinty, and brow furrowed, unambiguously displaying agitation, one of the few distinct facial expressions within a snake's limited gestural repertoire. At the last second, just before the snake plunged into Steve's now more-wan-than-usual facade, the handler reached up and caught it in flight just behind the head, stopping the lethal serpent within an inch or two of Steve's eyes, in a move that recalled Houdini's bullet catch.

The man held the snake just out of striking distance of Steve's face for what seemed longer than necessary, with its forked tongue oscillating and venom-dripping fangs desperately straining to reach out just a little farther. Finally, the performer pulled the reptile a safe distance back, stood up, and bowed, an appeal for applause, which by now could come only from the Japanese man in the back, since the boatmen had recently exited knowing that the show was about to end and their passengers would be anxious to return to the safety of the unpredictable river. Steve was either unwilling to applaud in principle or could not because he was still partially paralyzed with fear. The handler obviously could not applaud himself because his hands were currently encumbered with a dangerous, angry, and irrational snake.

The handler put the show-snake back in the bag, bowed once more, and left. The usher in the back screwed the lightbulb back into the socket, signaling Steve to rise from his folding chair and head back toward the relative calm of an unstable riverboat, though as he left the tent, he could feel that his knees no longer operated in a reliably wobble-free manner.

Steve retreated up the trail, passing through the gate too quickly to nod good-bye to the woman posted there, up the path, under snake-filled trees, toward his waiting boat. He leapt off the pier and would have produced a huge cannonball splash had the boat not been stationed underneath. Two hundred and sixty pounds of North America landed in the flimsy vessel all at once. The gondola reacted defensively to survive a capsizing, finally settling back in the water. The boatman jerked the rope to start the outboard motor and lowered the prop into the water, which sent brown river froth splattering back onto the pier. The boat nosed its pointy-end toward Bangkok, where in his seventy-plus-minute downstream trip, Steve would re-examine his life and try to figure out what faulty part of his brain had permitted him to visit a questionably reputable snake farm miles from civilization. He was thankful to be alive, and on the trip back, he promised God he would be a better person and give more to charity.

Back in his hotel room, Steve stood in the shower for a long time, making sure he rinsed off any contact neurotoxin that might have splashed on him earlier in the day. He was also thankful that he had not visited Ebola Virus Village.

Dating a Woman from Snake Country

HAVE I MENTIONED THAT I DO NOT LIKE SNAKES?

Poisonous or not, a snake has the linear capacity to ruin a life, not from quadriplegia, degenerative neurological decay, respiratory downsizing, or blood-clogging contamination, but rather from emotional scars, self-doubts, unfulfilled dreams, and paths not taken because snakes were sunning on them.

A few years ago, I dated a woman named Michelle, an otherwise perfect woman whose only flaw was that she had recently purchased a house in the country. Her rapidly developing community, twenty miles outside of Boston, was now classified as a suburb, but had been built right on top of what had previously been the country. In the rush to put up new homes, no one informed the local wildlife about rezoning, so many of them could still be seen wandering aimlessly around the changing neighborhood, cautious, confused, and looking desperately for now backfilled ponds or any familiar grove of brush.

Michelle's property butted up to an old stone wall that had for many years been the sanctuary for generations of snakes, and her house, only a short commute for the creatures, offered an appealing place for them to explore. A few times a month, a garter or a few feet of some other kind of harmless snake would shimmy down the walkway and make its way onto the front porch. It was not uncommon to find one had wriggled under an Adirondack chair. On a few occasions, she would discover a pair of corn snakes sauntering all the way into the kitchen. Michelle admitted that prior to moving in, she was snake neutral, not quaking in fear at the sight of them as many people do, but certainly no friend to them either. Spotting field snakes regularly, she soon considered them only a minor nuisance and ignored them altogether, hoping her rudeness would subtly encourage them to leave on their own. She would eventually just step over one in the basement if it was in the path to the washer–dryer. If she knew company was coming, she would shoo a snake aside before anyone arrived or just pick one up and transport it away from the house, carting it far enough away so it would be inconvenient for the thing to return.

Remove snake infestation from the relationship equation, and Michelle was a woman brimming with undeniable love potential. She was intelligent, sharp-witted, attractive, and since she was a physician, I knew she could be extremely valuable to have around during times of pandemic. Most important, Michelle possessed a quality absent in the many other women I had dated recently in that she seemed to like me.

The relationship was doomed from the start. From a purely statistical perspective, it was unlikely that I could avoid a confrontation with a snake for very long, and it would be only a matter of time before some corn snake would barricade her front door, forcing me to drive forty-five minutes back to my house, call her, and pathetically ask if she would please clear a reptile-free path between the street and her porch.

Acknowledging that snake encounters were an integral part of her daily life, I sadly realized that I could not spend my days with a woman who frequently consorted with the animals I so loathed. Because I lose virility in the presence of most reptiles, I knew an egalitarian relationship built on mutual respect could never prosper. I knew that if it were ever necessary for me to save her from a life-threatening snake skirmish, I would falter, selfishly saving only myself. I would live the rest of life not knowing how to express my sympathy to her elderly parents.

In nearly any perilous situation, I will not hesitate to valiantly and selflessly throw myself between a person I love and certain danger.

With extreme prejudice, I will rid my home of any form of mammalian vermin. I have bravely captured bats, feeling no guilt in my dominion over a six-ounce intruder, four hundred times my junior. Admittedly I held an unfair advantage, since I was much more familiar with the domestic terrain and was, unlike the bat, fully able to actually see it. A mouse that enters my kitchen in search of food or warmth will find me an unyielding adversary and can count on me to thwack it senseless with a seldom-used skillet, smashing its little skull into rodent pulp without mercy as the hunter in me takes over and as testosterone explodes through my bloodstream in concentric tsunami-like surges.

Mammalian-crushing bravery aside, I knew I would be powerless in a house regularly invaded by snakes. I knew I could not be comfortable constantly looking over my shoulder and walking through Michelle's yard only if I were wearing hip waders. I knew that I could not live with even a fragment of personal dignity, if I were continually calling out to her for help from my safe-house, perched atop a patio table, where humiliated, I would watch her calmly pick up the bullying garter snake with some wadded-up toilet paper and gently carry it off the deck.

Communing With Exotic Pets

PERSONALLY, I DO NOT UNDERSTAND THE APPEAL OF AN ANimal that is not furry, cuddly, or capable of performing applause-provoking tricks. Given all available pets, I am surprised to find a number of people who opt for any kind of snake, poisonous or not, not because "all the other animals were sold out," but do so willingly, even after conducting an exhaustive feature-by-feature comparison with gerbils, orange tabbies, and ferrets. These owners of nontraditional pets view slithering reptiles no differently. "We just see snakes," committed serpent owners might say, "as slender, legless dogs."

Sure, there are some advantages. Snakes are generally inexpensive, and if you do not choose to buy one, you can head out into the woods and find one under a rock. They eat very little and only every few months, so a single bag of Purina Snake Chow will last for the life of the pet. Kids find them easy to handle because a six-foot-long cylindrical pet is in effect one big handle. From head to tail, they are prehensile, so they can always loop around one of your body parts to maintain a suitable grasp.

Luckily, neither you nor your children will get as emotionally attached to a snake as you would to a puppy, bunny, or kitty. Its loss will certainly be acknowledged, with someone in the family casually mentioning, "I think the snake is dead," though it will be brought up in terms of inconvenience rather than sadness. The family's collective thoughts will generally be focused on how to get rid of its corpse. When a snake dies, it is sometimes possible to discard it by flushing it down the toilet, a decided advantage over time-consuming burial or costly cremation. Communities that do not allow you to burn leaves will probably have even stricter bylaws about incinerating snakes. Pet owners with finicky septic systems can stuff the flaccid remains into a plastic garbage bag along with the coffee grounds and nonrecyclables, leaving the deceased out on the street for the Monday-morning trash pickup. Snake owners smugly boast, "Try *that* with a golden retriever."

Snakes are incapable of supplying the same benefits that accrue to owners of traditional pets. Should you decide to adopt a snake, be prepared to compromise.

How can I say this without offending snake fans? Snakes are, frankly, stupid. I am not being judgmental. Snakes cannot help it. They have tiny heads, some no bigger than a human thumb, and once you subtract the space needed for a skull, eyes, fangs, cheek-mounted poison bags, and the like, there is not much space left for a brain. They are low on the neurological development scale, have dismal memories, no powers of reason, and no recognition of causal relationships. If you ever try to train a snake, you will find yourself explaining the same concept over and over. In short, do not expect much from a snake intellectually.

While they may surprise you by eating the occasional rodent, they cannot be trained specifically for this or any other useful purpose. In theory, a reptile could keep your condominium free of mice, chipmunks, and squirrels, but because they eat only once every few months, you might have to invest in many of them for complete coverage. From my perspective, if a home were overrun by rats, I would consider a half dozen snakes freely roaming from room to room to be just one more inconvenience.

Likewise, you cannot rely on a snake for protection from home invasion as you would with, say, Dobermans. Neither will you find the literature filled with too many stories of snake heroism as you might with, for instance, dogs and cats, which will dodge flames to save the lives of a sleeping family whose home is on fire. Even if a snake had such noble intentions, you would be long dead from smoke inhalation while it was still desperately trying to figure out how to get up the stairs.

Furthermore, their benefit to the physically impaired is questionable. Some canines have selflessly dedicated their lives to assist those who are blind or deaf. Old World monkeys have been trained to perform domestic chores such as turning on lights for people with physical disabilities. Though the snake's most powerful attribute is an amazing sense of smell, we have yet to find a way to successfully exploit its sensitive olfactory receptors to assist individuals who may be, say, smelling impaired.

Unlike more cerebrally versatile pets, snakes cannot be taught even the simplest household tasks, so you will have to get your newspaper and slippers yourself, just making sure the snake isn't already curled up inside. Nor will you find reptiles as entertaining as you would a mammal-based pet. You cannot teach a snake to sit, catch a Frisbee, or speak on command. Based on its simplistic external physiology—essentially a long, thin organic cylinder—"roll over" may be as close as you will get to a trick. The problem is that once snakes get rolling and gather some momentum, it is hard for them to figure out how to stop.

You will sadly realize that even "fetch the ball," where you gently roll one a few feet across the yard will be a painstakingly difficult concept for a snake to comprehend, and you will eventually discard the project when the snake slithers back proudly ten minutes later with a huge round bulge a few inches down its neck.

Finally, and this may ultimately be their single biggest failing, snakes are not warm and furry. Being cold-blooded, your snake will be the same temperature as the room, the tabletop, and your stemware. While reptile lovers have managed to convince us that snakes are not slimy and wet as fear-lore has suggested—and we will gladly just take their word for it rather than actually touching one ourselves to find out—even the most steadfast of herpephiles cannot look us straight in the face and tell us that reptiles are cuddly. To snuggle up next to one would not be too different from curling up with a piece of vinyl.

Snakes are, frankly, not puppies, and nothing that even the most devout herpetic animal lover can say to the contrary will change our minds. While snake owners are absolutely convinced that their snakes love them, empirical data do not support this. In fact, it is best to discourage your snake from showing affection. Owners of huge reticulated pythons learn very quickly that when returning home after a long day to a snake they missed, it is not a good idea to greet it by saying, "How about a big hug?"

There are people who are not content to own reasonably safe, nonthreatening snakes, and instead seek out peculiar, dangerous specimens. For these risk takers or for those who delight in shocking others, a milk snake or a cute little hognose is not quite snake enough, and they are drawn to lengthy and muscular constrictors or even poisonous strains—the bigger and more poisonous, the better.

I live in Massachusetts, a state that spawned freedom, birthed some of the most noteworthy advancements in science and technology, and helped to ignite the information revolution. With only a vision and a few dollars, entrepreneurs here built giant computer firms and sired the biotech, genetic engineering, and pharmaceutical industries. Harvard and MIT are in rock-throwing distance of each other, and the state is home to some of the nation's top publishers, universities, and consulting firms. Physicians conduct lifesaving medical research in the shadows of Boston Common and Beacon Hill. The state's think tanks have influenced government leaders and the captains of industry for many decades. Frankly, we have a lot of really smart people here.

Yet, there appears to be an incontestable law of nature that says for every really smart person, there must be an equally moronic person nearby to serve as a counterbalance. A few years ago I read about a man who had evidentally been assigned to the Boston area to cancel out the genius of someone doing cancer research. He lived a few miles north of the city and decided that it would be really "neat" to raise a deadly Egyptian banded cobra in his suburban home.

Remember, a cobra is a snake that can grow to be eighteen feet long, houses one of the world's most astonishing venoms, does not really want to be a house pet, and cannot be trusted to refrain from striking a loved one because honestly, it loves no one.

While a warning of the cobra's inherent dangers may not be written on the side of the snake, it is information that is readily accessible. No one has ever purchased a cobra "by accident," and a thinking person should know better than to have such a snake within striking distance. Yet this man in suburban Boston apparently went out of his way to acquire one.

It is not legal to own a poisonous snake in Massachusetts. There is a law on the books. Sad that we need legislation to remind our fellow citizens how dangerous it is to keep a fully loaded poisonous reptile in a residential neighborhood, but apparently, sometime in my commonwealth's lawmaking past, the prohibition was made official, if for no other reason than to dissuade those who were "on the fence" about getting one. Our state legislature, whose members had dedicated their lives to public service, took valuable time away from debates about the economy and the pressing needs of our children. They forestalled votes on unemployment, tax reform, the homeless, school textbooks, and meals for the elderly to discuss and pass into law a reminder to our populace that it is a bad idea to own a pet capable of killing family and neighbors. The law was written in the arcane language of legislation, but its meaning was unambiguous: If you are stupid enough to bring a snake filled to the brim with venom into Massachusetts, "we will arrest you and drive you directly to one of our prisons. Then we will put you in one of its cages and kill the snake. Or vice versa."

Bucking the laws of Massachusetts and the very laws of self-preservation that have kept our species alive for the past hundred thousand years, the man went ahead and acquired a huge coil of cobra as a companion. A single specimen comparable to his could produce enough toxin to wipe out the entire Massachusetts legislature in an afternoon and still have enough juice left over to put the judiciary and their appointed staffs in intensive care.

So why would anyone want to chum it up with one of Nature's deadliest breeds? This is not a snake you can play with or wear to parties. It is not an animal whose owners rush out of work early, thinking, "I cannot wait to get home so I can pet him." A cobra is an animal version of an automatic assault rifle: always loaded, cocked, and dangerous to handle. Considering the already dubious benefits of owning any kind of snake, there seems to be no "value added" in having one with a poison feature.

The witlessness of the owner would be story enough, but he saw no reason to keep the snake indoors in its secure snake house, and he routinely took it into his front yard to let it relax and sun itself, within shimmying distance of parks, school grounds, and a nursing home, where the elderly in walkers would have no chance to outrun even the slowest of snakes. Still, no one would have even known he had the cobra had it not wandered off one day and, in doing so, no longer endangered just its owner, but everyone from Portland, Maine, to Cape Cod, as well.

The snake was lounging one afternoon, when the owner apparently left for a moment, walking away and forgetting he was leaving the third-deadliest thing on the planet unchaperoned in his front yard. Having never known such freedom, the cobra saw a hitherto unavailable opportunity to explore the Bay State, and swiftly slithered past the patio door, across the driveway, and over the guy's set of lawn darts, thought to be the fourth-deadliest thing on the planet. It wandered off, maybe because it wanted a between-quarterly-feeding snack or maybe because it was tired of living in captivity and missed Egypt.

I cannot begin to fathom the panic suffered by this guy when he returned to find his unleashed snake gone. It may be like coming back to a parking lot and discovering your car has been stolen. You continue looking at the empty space in denial, looking away, then back again, hoping you had just missed seeing it the first time. Perhaps his first thought was that he had walked over to the wrong part of the yard, and the snake was elsewhere, some feet away, patiently waiting for his return. Maybe he thought the snake was sleepy and had gone back inside on its own to take a nap in its comfy snake quarters.

After running in terror throughout the yard, frantically looking for anything that was (1) up to eighteen feet long and (2) moving, the owner concluded that the cobra was missing and, by now, bellying past children playing in the street, past housewives carrying bags of groceries through kitchen doorways left invitingly open, over bicycles and toys, finally taking temporary refuge in landscape shrubbery.

The snake had bolted, leaving the frightened owner with the incontrovertible conclusion that aside from misplacing an expensive animal investment, he would have to explain to local officials the bad news that (1) he had been cohabitating with an illicit cobra against their best legal advice, (2) he does not quite know where it is at this time, and (3) he might need their help looking for it before it killed someone. He was now painfully aware that putting up a lost-snake poster would not be sufficient and that the pet returning on its own in an hour and scratching on the back door was equally unrealistic.

So in the weeks to follow, terrified families in this north Boston suburb hid their children indoors, cancelled Little League games, sealed their garage doors shut, and moved the patio furniture inside. Dogs, no longer taken on daily walks or even given access to the backyard, were allowed to squat freely in the kitchen and dining room. Homeowners cancelled barbecues. Vegetable gardens went to seed, lawns weeded over, and previously well-coiffed hedges turned haggard and unkempt. Married couples slept in shifts.

Receding into the suburban landscape, the snake that had previously been one man's pet was now everyone's problem. It could be hiding, coiled, ready to strike anywhere. Some people calculated that they were statistically no more likely to be killed by the snake than win the state Big Game Lottery, not frightening until you remember that there is usually at least one lottery winner every week. Neither the police nor reptile experts could comfort a frightened community by confirming the snake's whereabouts. At any given moment, they could only tell the concerned citizenry where the snake wasn't.

Herpetologists speculated that a cobra that had gotten used to a cushy life inside a posh carpeted terrarium—with branches for it to crawl about and its own fluorescent light under which to bask, all to simulate fluorescent life in Northern Africa—could not survive long on its own. News stories hoping to quell widespread hysteria reminded residents that with each passing day the probability of the snake dying of hunger, dehydration, thirst, or just being flattened by an oil delivery truck increased measurably. The fact that a snake cannot cover a lot of ground quickly was also reassuring, especially to homeowners west of Bloomington, Indiana, who were confident that a cobra starting in New England, even a very fit one, could probably make it no farther than Ohio.

Officials continued to assure quaking residents holed up in their split-level homes that the odds of a cobra turning up in a silverware drawer or inside a laundry hamper were remote. Still, I doubt a single townsperson was able to slide a foot into a sneaker or reach into a dishwasher without at least a moment of hesitation. Zoologists tried to prevent further panic, reminding everyone that the snake, even if it were alive, would probably not appear in public because, as they claimed, "It is probably more afraid of us than we are of it." They failed to acknowledge the more important fact that Egyptian banded cobras are poisonous, and we are not.

The escaped cobra story remained newsworthy for about three weeks, and as confidence built that the snake had to be dead, life slowly reverted to normal. Draperies were slowly reopened. Sun-deprived children, pupils constricted and skin pallid, returned cautiously to the streets, able to finally forgo their daily hypodermic injections of vitamin D.

But a few months later, the snake story reemerged, proving once more that truth is much more bizarre than even the most brilliant literary irony. The snake turned up, not dead in some sewage culvert, not flattened and a bit longer and wider on Route 93, but inside a local elementary school, sleeping peacefully curled up on a library shelf. I read the *Boston Globe* article about the discovery and subsequent rescue while I was on a flight out of the area. I sighed in relief, certainly because the deadly preditor was finally apprehended and no one got hurt, but more important, because I was at least forty thousand feet away from it at that moment.

The snake had somehow survived, still healthy, a little hungry, and fully lethal. No one, including the cobra, was injured in the capture. A community with pulse rates finally approaching normal was relieved that the school administration had not stumbled onto a trail leading to the card catalog littered with the convulsing little bodies of children thrashing wildly on the ground, or worse yet, had not discovered a snake sitting content in some dark corner of the gym with the unmistakable bulge a third of the way down its back in the shape of a fourth-grader.

Not to belabor the point about snake intelligence, but the only reason they do not bite or crush us is because we are not threatening or hurting them at that particular moment. With its rudimentary just-barely-more-than-a-brain-stem brain, a snake is a live-for-the moment kind of animal. A snake does not know of loyalty or love. It is not good with faces and does not remember how well you treated it yesterday. A snake does not see you as its caring pet owner, but just another animal who does not happen to be stepping on it. It forges no emotional attachments as you do with it. It might forget all about the kind stroking and the playful intertwining you've provided in the past. Your ongoing safety is entirely the snake's call, and a good day with a dangerous snake is defined as one where it does not actively attempt to take your life

Every so often, you will read about a boa owner who is deflated by his own snake. It is not as if the danger should come as some surprise, since the snake is, after all, called a "boa constrictor" and not some benignly misleading name like "boa snuggly."

Not long ago, a guy from New York was done in by his own crushing constrictor, abruptly ending a man–pet relationship of many years. Apparently the man was making his own dinner, and while cutting up chicken, splattered a little pullet juice on his T-shirt. While waiting for the meal to roast, he decided to play with his snake, forgetting that he was drenched in appetizing chicken fluids. Although the constrictor was not scheduled to eat for many weeks, it was aroused by the aroma and concluded that eating a month ahead of schedule wasn't such a bad idea, perhaps the snake version of an "Early-Bird Special." Momentarily convinced that dinner was at hand, and with the smell of fowl in the air, it decided to wring out a little from its owner's T-shirt.

Imagine how the man struggled with his own pet, as the python grabbed him and wrapped its massive, muscular trunk about the guy's chest, squeezing tighter and cutting off blood and oxygen flow, strangling him like a full-body garrote. Imagine how disappointing it must have been for the pet's owner, knowing that he failed to convince the snake that he was not a chicken but was, in fact, Larry.

In any event, the man was crushed to death, sad for him because he died at the hands of a beloved pet, and sad for the snake, which killed its dutiful owner and still did not get any chicken out of it. Fortunately, the snake could go a little longer without food and was able to hold out until the police were called in a few weeks later, after the neighbors complained of the smell.

So my advice: Do not share your home with an animal that can surround you 360 degrees. If you decide on a large snake against my advice, just don't let it sleep on the bed. You don't want to wake up at about three in the morning, look toward the foot of the mattress, and find that your snake has already swallowed you up to your thighs.

While we are at it, let's not let warnings stop at snakes. Every day, thousands of Americans buy house pets. Among them will still be many people who will not be content with a fish or a cockatoo. If you are one of those people who needs to be warned that it is not prudent to own an animal that (1) has a fully functional poison injection mechanism or (2) can strangle you in your sleep, perhaps you need to be reminded about other pets that you would likewise be ill-advised to bring back from the mall pet store.

First, avoid baby alligators, which you can still buy at one of a number of reptile ranches located on your way out of Florida on Interstate 95, a road thought to be as potentially deadly as the alligators themselves. Gatorettes, as these minis are called, may be adorable in their pigmy size, four or so inches from snout to tail, but remember that they are wild creatures, not destined to be happy if marooned in the frosty Northeast snow belt and deprived of other alligatorial companionship. They will mature and grow muscular tails, and not knowing their own strength, will eventually destroy your dining room furniture and inadvertently knock your aging stroke-infested uncle and his walker across the den, sadly as he is slowly straining to make his way to the bathroom on his own for the first time.

If you are intent on having a pet alligator, treat it with respect from its babyhood forward. If alligators have memories, and many people believe they do, your kindness will pay premiums or at least guarantee that the reptile will not put you into a death spin as it tries to drag you under the surface of the bathwater. Rumors about baby alligators flushed down commodes and growing to dozens of feet in length in the New York sewers are urban legends, but being an aquatic animal, an abandoned baby alligator sluiced down through your waste plumbing would be capable of swimming back upstream, and to avenge itself for your insensitive and loveless neglect could quietly reemerge one evening up through your toilet as you are using it and take a large chunk out of your genitals.

Remember when you see the baby alligator smiling up from the pet store enclosure that it will invariably grow to be eight or ten feet long, and in a ironic twist is one of the few leather objects that would enjoy chewing on a dog.

Some eccentrics think that creepy spiders make handsome pets. Topping their list are oversized hairy ones, including the tarantula, a large hirsute spider generally found in southwestern United States, Central America, South America, and other New World tropical regions. With thick jointed legs, a take-no-prisoners face, and a body the size of a clenched fist, they look to be a genetic hybrid of a conventional spider and a Yorkshire terrier.

Carnivorous as all spiders are, tarantulas will eat insects and small animals, ridding your house forever of nuisance mice and your children's gerbils. Some people claim these creeping invertebrates are no uglier than Shar-peis or hairless cats, and will not wince at reaching in a terrarium to pick one up. I would more likely reach into a moving food processor. While tarantulas do bite and maintain a working set of poison glands, a chomp from one is not fatal, but it will produce a painful reaction and trigger the impulse to smash it with a hardcover book just as you would if it did not enjoy pet status.

Finally, avoid exotic cats. Some less-than-forward-thinking individuals have actually purchased cougars, mountain lions, cheetahs, or Bengal tigers. These felines do not behave like house cats, and at a few hundred pounds, with sharp claws and teeth, they will not be content with one of those springy toy feathers that bob about playfully at the end of a stick. A jungle cat is wild and will remain wild no matter what you do. The operative rule here is this: Be leery of any pet that is higher than you on the food chain. Never buy a pet that looks at its food bowl, then at you, and has to decide.

Remember, if an animal cares so little about members of its family that it devours its young, you will not have much luck reasoning with it if you are cornered. My advice—stick with a puppy. It isn't as exciting as an exotic creature, but if one eats your shoe, it is far less likely you will be in it.

Not An Animal Family

MY BROTHER AND I WERE SHELTERED FROM ANIMALS. OUR parents did not buy produce from farm stands, because of their proximity to the outdoors. We visited Lion Country Safari only once where, if I remember correctly, the rangers asked my family to leave after my father, attempting to retreat from some grazing gazelles, backed over an animal that we later learned (from the invoice) was an ostrich. On subsequent vacations, my dad would check the tourist books to see if an area had a less ominous drive-through animal park, always hoping to find something akin to a Barnyard Country Safari, where we could watch ducks and chickens, safely behind our rolled-up car windows.

We were comfortable only when we were certain that animals were separated from us by a retaining wall, steel bars, and/or moat.

"Go to a petting zoo," my mother warned, "and you are just asking for trouble."

My mother, indeed, feared any living creature that was not a member of her own species. She was convinced that all animals were our natural enemies and any one of them would attack if given the opportunity. Most, she elaborated, would go out of their way willingly to harass us. Furthermore, she believed that animals were filthy and disgusting and that her world would be a much cleaner and safer place if all of them were moved to, say, Europe. My father's favorite animal was steak.

My mother knew that the downside of having animals nearby far outweighed any possible benefit. So, I did not grow up in an animal-tolerant family. We never had any animal companions, and the only other living organisms permitted inside the house were in the form of friends, family, and workmen—and in yogurt. Vermin were eradicated immediately, squished if possible and professionally removed if necessary.

My brother and I were not permitted to have pets, since by definition "pet" implied "animal." And why would we even want one, since we learned over and over at our mother's knee that all but a few animals were venomous, evil, and that their fur was covered with deadly toxins? Just brushing up against one would cause us certain and agonizing death—that is, if the animal did not maul us to shreds first.

The closest we got to a real pet was a tiny, listless turtle my father bought in the local five-and-dime. This type of domesticated turtle was known in knowledgeable pet circles as a painted turtle, though from a spectral standpoint, the animal was a drab and fairly monotonous gray green. The typical painted turtle born and weaned at a Woolworth's was the size of a half dollar and a nearly inert organic mound, with little appendages jutting out evenly around its circumference—a head, four tiny clawed feet, and a tiny pointed tail, all of which looked identical from more than a few inches away, making it difficult to tell if the turtle was moving away from, or ominously, toward us.

The turtle lived with us for about a week before mysteriously disappearing. During its tenancy, we referred to it generically as "the turtle" because it was long dead before my brother and I could agree on a name. Besides, names are wasted on animals that refuse to respond to them. You could stand less than foot away from a turtle screaming its name through a megaphone, and you still couldn't get it to respond.

Unless children are permanently bedridden, turtles are generally not active enough to hold their attention for too long. In captivity, the creature exhibits only two observable behaviors: it is either moving or it is not. The cardboard box containing turtle food, which costs slightly less than the turtle itself, is often as entertaining to watch.

Still, this was the first animal that my brother and I were allowed to bring indoors. My father convinced my mother that living among wildlife would "toughen us up," and that of all possible choices of fauna, a turtle would be the least intrusive because it required so little ongoing maintenance. Once a day, and only if we happened to remember, we would give it some food, tapping out flecks of a special turtle entrée, nutritionally balanced for the sedentary lifestyle of an animal confined to a ten-inch living space. The food would float for a while on the surface of the water, totally ignored by the turtle, and only after wading around and bumping into it for a few hours would the turtle again remember that (1) this was food, and (2) it was for him. After the revelation, he would suck up a few flecks from the surface and, after this strenuous activity, would rest.

Feeding and occasionally adding some more water was the only husbandry necessary to sustain turtle life. Removing it from the bowl while it was alive for any reason was optional. Though it is generally prudent to take other pets outside regularly to deposit their waste in the yard, this is an unnecessary gesture when it comes to a reptile. A turtle's excreta pose no hygienic or aesthetic threat, and unless you are specifically looking for it, turtle ordure will be nearly invisible in the brackish water that the turtle collectively calls its home, its drinking supply, and its septic system. A turtle could excrete solid waste nonstop in its own bowl of slurry without anyone, including the turtle itself, ever caring.

Since servicing the pet would not require my brother or me to exhibit any behaviors that would be considered "responsible," my father concluded the turtle had a much better chance of surviving under our care than did a dog or a cat.

"It doesn't take much to make a turtle happy," my father would remind us.

So we didn't do much, thinking this is what the turtle preferred.

In truth, my father selected a turtle for us because it was cheap. If it died, which he assumed it would presently, he would be out less than a dollar. The only way my father could have acquired a less expensive pet would have been to go to a stream for a few minutes and reach in for something.

Beyond convenience and the fiscal benefits, a turtle would be an ideal pet because, as a reptile, it does not invite lasting emotional attachments, as do those animals classified by zoologists as "the fuzzy ones." When such a pet dies, it is seldom buried, mourned, or for that matter, even missed. In the event of its passing, a turtle is usually flushed without much fanfare, and the only additional attention its interment ever gets is in the rare case when a plunger has to be used if its corpse gets stuck.

It is difficult to tell when a turtle has died, and it is not uncommon for families to continue sprinkling in food without any inkling that the animal has been in rigor for days. The only evidence of death is that its "not moving" lasts more than forty-eight hours, or if it begins to smell even worse than it did when it was alive.

Our turtle spent most of its short life corralled in a round plastic bowl, a living space made of brittle semitransparent plastic, which provided the turtle very little privacy but did give it a panoramic glimpse of our bedroom. The see-through enclosure offered us a window into every aspect, albeit mundane, of turtle life. The focal point of the bowl was the signature spiral ramp leading out up to a plastic palm tree in the center, apparently designed to simulate the turtle's natural habitat, a small see-through island off the coast of South America.

One afternoon, our pet, apparently as bored as we were, hopped over the side wall to seek a life outside our loving home.

Confirming my mother's fear that we would not take the turtle's inevitable passing well, my brother and I, then six and ten respectively, were grief stricken when the animal disappeared. We felt hurt and rejected. For children entrusted for the first time with an animal that was not really just a toy *shaped* like an animal, we took its sudden departure personally. My brother was even more distraught, having forged a special kinship with the turtle because at one point, my brother still claims, it actually looked up at him.

It was difficult for us as children to understand why a turtle would even think about running away. In our home, it got everything that a turtle could ever want, which we presumed was simply "enough water."

But sadly, the turtle thought so little of our custodial skills that it was willing to take its chances beyond the safety of its plastic home. Beyond sadness, we welled up with guilt, assuming it was probably our fault, neither recognizing any of the traditional early-warning signs of reptile depression nor paying close enough attention to even notice its departure. Imagine then how much more ashamed we were to learn that it can take a turtle an hour to crawl four or five feet, and it still escaped unnoticed.

In fairness to my brother and me, it was not always easy to see the turtle. If you are vigilant about cleaning the bowl, which we were not, turtle water will be murky at best. Ours lived in a more lagoon-like habitat, maintained by a somewhat more relaxed cleaning regimen. When submerged, the turtle might not be seen for days, living in water that was nearly opaque, incidentally dark enough through which to safely view a solar eclipse.

Thinking they could console my grieving brother and me, and hoping to proactively fend off any lifelong emotional scarring that might only be annulled through long-term therapy and mild antidepressants when we reached adulthood, my parents sat us down at the dining room table and told us about how much the turtle pined for its home in South America. Though it knew we would be saddened by its departure, they confided, our pet left to look for its biological parents. My folks reminded us that we should think about the turtle's happiness and not just our own.

My mother placed her hands on top of ours and urged us not to be sad, because the turtle was OK and had been recently spotted by the Argentinean coast guard, lounging under a big palm tree on a tiny ramped island outside of La Plata. It would be weeks until my bother and I discovered that the story, though touching and initially convincing, hid the truth that the turtle had become disoriented after accidentally falling out of its bowl, rolled under the sofa, and died of dehydration, and that Bessie, the woman who came in once a week to clean, unceremoniously sucked up its dried remains using a vacuum cleaner.

Further, we should have been at least a little suspicious, remembering that my parents had used the same La Plata story a year earlier, shortly after my Uncle Rudy died.

No One Will Ever Call Me "Lieutenant"

CERTAIN PEOPLE ARE FEARLESS. NOTHING RATTLES THEM. They face dangerous tasks methodically, with the same calm you and I do clicking a remote control or unpacking groceries.

Courageous and unselfish, they accept a proxy for society's most dangerous jobs, becoming our police officers and firefighters, knowing that we are counting on them, confident that they have the guts and determination to do things other people cannot. Many of us remain safe today because these valiant strangers have selflessly put their own lives up as ante.

Driven by honor, commitment to others, and a more-lenient adrenaline-pumping system than most, they willingly volunteer to be our test pilots, Navy SEALs, and roofers. Unafraid to assume civilization's more hazardous duties, they take on jobs such as lumberjacks, happily packing chain saws, scaling mighty trees, and dodging falling branches and tumbling oaks. They willingly work in our slaughterhouses, wielding giant knives just so we can eat brisket, or hire out as body guards who, spurred by instinct alone, fling themselves between a client and a body-piercing bullet, no questions asked. In their ranks are millions of our miners, perennially filth-covered men and women, who agree to spend their working lives thousands of feet underneath us, in a dark, toxic, and claustrophobic tunnel where the air is stained with lung-coating coal dust and where a cave-in could squash them like bugs. In short, these unappreciated heroes embrace the jobs they know the rest of us cannot perform. They know that if they don't volunteer, the rest of us are doomed.

It is not that these people are never frightened, just that their sense of dedication smothers the fear that would paralyze the rest of us.

This is why a steeplejack can climb a 1,200-foot tower to change a lightbulb or rescue personnel will not hesitate running onto a collapsing bridge to save a Cocker spaniel. In research facilities, scientists seeking cures for deadly diseases routinely handle dangerous bacteria and viruses, a life-threatening job made even more so because if they catch anything, there isn't a cure, precisely the reason they are handling the viruses and bacteria in the first place. These are our professional risk takers, who routinely waltz with danger but don't want you to make a big fuss over it.

Without undaunted people such as these, our ranks of police would be filled with fearful officers gutlessly hiding behind their cruisers. Buildings and bridges would be constructed slowly by sweaty little guys who wrap their arms and legs around the girders and nervously wriggle a few inches at a time on their stomachs to move from place to place. Nothing big or with sharp edges would ever get built.

Alaskan crab fishers of the Bering Sea are thought to have the world's most dangerous job, one where accident is likely and a fatality is no big thing. Their workplace is the frozen godforsaken wash of ice water off the coast of Alaska. Here men and women voluntarily risk their lives just so you can enjoy an appetizer platter of crab Rangoon or a boiled entrée.

They work eighteen hour shifts, in a region that is dark most of the day, bouncing violently in a small crab boat. Thirty-foot swells tousle the vessel in choppy, super-chilled water. A slippery deck routinely pitches forty-five degrees. A layer of ice coats everything. They trawl night and day in the short, limited season when crabs are most likely to be carelessly duped into traps. Rugged men and women fight weariness in a work environment where one lapse of concentration can kill them or the person standing alongside. Without warning, a gust of wind can knock burly men into the sea. You could be standing next to three other people one minute and two the next. Even a minor injury can be fatal when you are thousands of miles from medical assistance.

In the perpetual night of winter in the Bering, the crabbers catapult heavy metal traps they call pots, which weigh several hundred pounds each, over the side. Whipping behind the quickly sinking traps are hundreds of feet of uncoiling line and floating buoys. A foot tangled in these cables will drag a careless fisherman to crab-depth in seconds. Hypothermia is a physiological prospect and can set in within minutes, not just to those falling into the icy waters, but also to anyone pecked for long periods by the cold sea spray air.

Even the crabs themselves, which prefer their quiet lives in the icy Alaskan waters to capture, will fight the boatmen to remain free. Equipped with pincers, crustaceans will not hesitate to use them. More than one fisherman has lost a finger to a crab that is making its preference for liberty known. Fortunately for the crabber, crustacean-induced amputation is painless, since all the fingers are numb from the cold most of the time.

Dropping off their catch, the handful of surviving fishermen will immediately return to freeze in the subzero winds, to be pelted ruthlessly by the sea once more in their gamble to get another hold full of shellfish before the season ends, while at that very moment, the crabs they caught a few days earlier are relaxing, enviably toasty, cozy, and in a great deal more comfort in a dish of warm butter.

Yet, when it comes to assuming risk, even the average citizen can rise to uncharacteristic heroism in the face of an extraordinary challenge. The most milk-livered among us have been known to rush into collapsing buildings to drag out someone heard moaning from inside, or heroically dive in front of a moving train to push an elderly couple from its path. Likewise, we hear stories of mothers who gain superhuman strength and are able to lift a fully loaded SUV after accidentally backing over one of the children.

The military is a good example where normal and easily frightened men and women gulp back fear, when a sense of honor and the security of others are far more important than the soldiers' own petty lives. Those who enlist in the armed forces, those who understand that freedom comes with a human price tag, are examples of common people to are willing to put the safety of the many in front of their own, and pleased to trade the remaining time they have on this planet for an ideal. I have often hoped I would be among that number.

But some people, and perhaps I am one of them, are not cut out for dangerous military life. My participation might actually be a deterrent to peace and freedom and jeopardize the effectiveness of the rest of our Defense Department. In short, it would be my patriotic duty not to enlist. If you would like me to give my life for my country, I will take a bullet gladly. I just ask that you save your time and mine and instead of sending me off to basic training and a war where others will have to count on me, you just take me behind the barracks and hack me to death with a bayonet on the day I arrive. I assure you that this will be more efficient, humane, and ultimately, much appreciated by my fellow soldiers.

It is a safe bet that no one will ever call me "Lieutenant." No one will hoist a rigid hand to his brow in a respectful salute and deferentially address me as "Sir," or will follow me blindly into a hail of bullets and exploding mortar shells. I freely admit that there are people better equipped to defend our nation, and America should be grateful that they are willing to do so. I have never been in the military or even in a marching band, and the only time I ever wore anything remotely resembling a uniform was during college when I had a summer job as a gas company meter reader. In the natural gas service, we were not issued guns and were empowered to kill no one, our stately blue uniforms notwithstanding.

The only basic training provided by the public utility to our platoon of new gas recruits was how to copy numbers in the right order from a basement gas meter into a meter reader's logbook, a skill whose sole prerequisite was the ability to recognize nine numerals by their shape. We learned that meter readers occupied the front line of gas service, and that the entire income of our multibillion-dollar public utility rested on our competence in reproducing numbers neatly by hand. Our superiors briefed us in only the most rudimentary of survival skills, limited to such things as what gas smells like just before we are asphyxiated by it and the warning signs that a vicious dog is about to maul us.

Though fraught with peril, defending ourselves against an aggressive bullmastiff so that our fellow citizens have the freedom to heat their homes with clean-burning natural gas is still vastly different from fending off enemy ground troops armed with automatic weaponry. So, meter reading remained a safe refuge for those of us in college who wanted to give service to our country, even if it was only reliable natural gas service.

Certain people are better cut out for military life: rugged outdoorsmen with a keenly honed sense of direction, men and women who are quick and nimble, those able to forage a rain forest or desert for enough insects to keep them alive, the kind of resourceful and courageous, self-sufficient men and women who neither shrink in the face of danger nor need to fall asleep using anything broadly defined as a "night-light."

I would never compare myself to the hale breed of individual who does not flinch at taking a life or minds wading neck deep through a leech-infested lagoon. Unlike them, I am not driven to defend to my death total strangers just because they coincidentally happen to live on the same continent as I do. In short, I am ill-equipped to protect others or myself. When it comes to serving my country, some of us would do a better job working a distance from the front line, concentrating on less demanding, less critical maneuvers such as stapling or keeping the country tidy when others were away. Regrettably, I am a member of the group that does not make useful soldiers, and I am not the type of warrior that others would turn to in time of crises. There are leaders and there are followers. Then there are those who can do neither.

It is easy to predict who will make the best and worst warrior. If you had trouble in gym class, it is likely that you will not be a very good soldier. Those who could not vault gracefully over a pommel horse or were unable to execute a simple lay-up shot without the unnecessarily clumsy flailing of limbs will most likely be written off early as the kind of soldier the enemy can pick off first. In gym class,

as team captains were choosing up players from a decreasingly qualified line of available participants, Howie Ives and I were always
among the last chosen, barely squeaking ahead of the Guttman twins,
Jake and David, who in coed softball games were generally counted
as girls. Lacking the level of athletic ability and competitiveness of
my more coordinated classmates, I could go an entire basketball game
without ever coming in contact with the ball, an objective shared by
both my opponents and teammates.

I never got better than a C– in phys ed, the lowest grade they
could give and not fit me for a mandatory leg brace. A barely passing
grade is bad enough in geometry or social studies. Getting a C or D
indicates that of all the organs in your body, one—specifically your
brain—is underpowered or out-and-out defective. But a C or worse
in gym is even more disparaging, publicly acknowledging that you
contain hundreds of thousands of faulty tendons, muscles, and skeletal parts, and the vast majority of them do not work well together. If
you were an animal in the wild, you would have been eaten at birth
by your mother.

I was first available for military service when there was a draft lottery. To ensure that both competent and inept young men had an
equal opportunity to operate artillery, draftees were called up randomly and according to their birthdays. Each year, the Selective Service Board painted dates on Ping-Pong balls and, in a nationally
broadcast sweepstakes that most draft-age eligibles hoped they would
not win, drew them out of a fishbowl one by one.

If your birthday was called within the first 120 drawn, it was certain the government would soon ask you to drop everything, leave
your friends, quit school, and postpone a sex life that was just starting
to gather momentum, in order that you join their army for a bit of
combat. You would be free to leave after three years of military servi-
tude or when you were critically wounded, whichever came first.

If you fell in the middle-third of the draft numbers, your chance
of receiving a notice to report for active duty dropped to 50–50, although the farther down the list your birthday fell, the less likely you
were to be called. Whether you had to serve or not was based almost
entirely on how well the draftees before you performed. If they

could keep themselves alive, the military would not need to replace them with you.

If your birthday fell within the last third, it was unlikely that you would be called at all, and if things were ever that desperate, you would find yourself in the same battalion as your grandparents.

My draft number was 362, which meant it would be just as likely for me to be drafted by the Norwegian navy. Lucky for me, my spinelessness and propensity for slip-and-fall injuries were now no longer even relevant.

I cannot stress more emphatically that not serving in the military was unquestionably in the nation's best interests. I am not necessarily very careful. My mind wanders. I get bored easily. I am often frustrated by complex technology. I can well envision the damage I could unintentionally inflict on both morale and military hardware. Certainly the armed service could try to help me, "be all that I can be." However, knowing the minimum military standards they like to meet, I still don't think that will be nearly enough.

Neither would training me for war make fiscal sense. It costs the government tens of thousands of dollars to take a raw recruit, build his body and spirit, fine-tune his senses, teach him to follow orders without hesitation, and unleash the aggression lying dormant in his nether hormones. Investing in my military training would be a waste of taxpayer money, since I would certainly be killed long before the military could recoup its investment and possibly even before I left basic training in South Carolina. It would be a highly visible loss, too, since I might inadvertently take a platoon of men and some pieces of expensive defense technology with me.

Furthermore, the love of guns and joy of soldiering are concepts foreign to me. I have never hunted or carried a firearm. The closest I ever came to handling a weapon was at a carnival, where I could win a stuffed panda if I could shoot enough water with a squirting rifle into a plastic clown's face to make his hat fly off. Regrettably, the skill required for this task is not transferable to any other activity involving a gun, and specifically not military service, unless of course the United States declares war against the Ringling Brothers and we have to get through a line of clowns first.

I gleaned what spotty information I have about military culture from an army ROTC recruiter who visited my college to convince my classmates and me that we should not waste our time studying electrical engineering, literature, and medicine, and instead ought to learn how to fire armor-piercing mortars. The Reserve Officer Training Corps, they claimed, would teach us how to be men in a way that no pansy-assed university ever could.

Through weekly ROTC drills and military strategy classes, the army trained college-educated young men to be "reservists." While I was partying on weekends and trying to convince women I wanted to date that it seemed unnecessarily harsh to wait until I was "the last man on earth," ROTC enrollees spent their free weekends in open fields crawling under barbed wire, slogging about in mud, firing pretend guns, and learning how to hunt down members of their own species.

For those students willing to sign up for four years of army or air force ROTC, the government agreed to pay a big chunk of their tuition and college living expenses, which must have seemed very seductive at the time. The scope of the future commitment didn't become apparent until these men and women graduated and only then remembered that they promised several years of their lives in active duty, during which time their substandard classmates, who barely squeaked through college with C averages, got the really good jobs they would have gotten themselves if they didn't have to go into the army for the next several years. To add to the indignity, once these officers left the military and were looking for corporate jobs, they found the midlevel executive interviewing them for an entry-level position was the same guy who used to sell bongs in the dorm.

ROTC alumni entered the military as second lieutenants, the very first rung on the officer ladder and a rank that would authorize these twenty-year-old military hatchlings to "boss around" enlisted men the age of their parents, who had been in the army for fifteen or more years and did not react well to being outranked by a kid who had just spent the last four years studying eighteenth-century poetry and attending mixers.

About twenty percent of our freshman class chose the paramilitary option. Those of us who did not enroll in ROTC—so we could preserve freedom and democracy, and could protect those taxpayers who were paying our scholarships and funding our student loans— would be allowed to opt out of our ethical and patriotic responsibility by taking two semesters of gym instead.

I was born into a generation far different from my father's. My dad graduated high school in 1941. Recognizing the importance of his upcoming commencement, the Japanese celebrated it by bombing the stuffing out of Pearl Harbor. Back in the 1940s, our country did not own Pearl Harbor outright, but instead, chose to "rent." To show our appreciation to the more-than-hospitable Hawaiians, we offered to take care of the greater Honolulu area in exchange for allowing us to keep our boats parked there. Even with the active volcanoes and an inedible foodstuff known as poi, Hawaii was still both a convenient and pleasant place for us to store military equipment. Since the Hawaiians permitted us to decorate our base with flags and other quaint examples of Americana, we pretended it was American soil, so an assault on our ships in Pearl Harbor was tantamount to bombing them if they were docked in Omaha.

The sneak attack on Pearl Harbor would stir the patriotism of millions of young graduates like my dad, who would answer the call to duty and enlist. For men of my father's generation, the December 7, 1941, unprovoked attack by the Japanese would be a date that would "live in infamy," though I must admit, not enough infamy to keep my dad and his contemporaries from buying Honda Accords some years later.

War brings out the best in some men. In Europe and the Pacific, the future of the free world hung on the courage and sacrifice of my father's generation, then mere boys of nineteen or twenty. When my friends and I were in college, we were considerably more irresponsible, people even our parents couldn't consistently rely on, and keep in mind, these were folks we knew and loved. So what chance would a nation comprised of a lot of people I never met have, wagering their freedom and way of life on the dependability of my college buddies and me?

I wonder how I would have performed as a part of the predawn launch of the invasion at Normandy. I know from experience that I cannot be expected to do well if I don't get a decent night's rest. So, if an officer announced that I would be storming a mine-infested beach while dodging the bullets of an enemy perched above me the next morning, and if he also mentioned in passing that there was a reasonably good chance that most of us would be killed the instant we stepped off the transport, it is unlikely that I would be getting much quality sleep the evening beforehand. Furthermore, I am always a little groggy when I first wake up, and don't trust myself before 10:30 or 11:00 a.m. with any important task requiring me to do reasonably good work. Both making the planet safe for democracy and selfishly trying to keep myself alive would technically fall into the category of "important tasks" where I would probably want to be doing "reasonably good work." So, a predawn attack, though strategically advantageous, might work better if they had some special arrangements for someone like me, who considers himself more of "an evening person." If I didn't miss the invasion outright because I slept in, I can only imagine my thoughts in the early hours before embarking.

There on the dark morning in June of 1944, I stand anxiously in a deployment area with a hundred thousand other men, waiting my turn to cram into a troop carrier. The sky is dark, and the air is cold and clammy, heavy with an early morning fog. General Eisenhower has issued his orders to proceed, and we know at the water's end twenty or so miles from here, there awaits death, destruction, and the future of the free world. I drift in and out of memories about childhood, family, and an uncertain future. The icy channel air slaps at my face. Though I am surrounded by tens of thousands of troops, I am alone in my thoughts, wondering whether I will see another sunrise and whether it is chilly in France and if I would be more comfortable if I maybe brought along an extra sweater.

If you are a soldier in battle, you are subjected to constant danger. Bombs are exploding everywhere, and your adversary is desperately trying to kill you. You are tired, scared, and hungry. You sleep, if you can at all, on the cold hard ground. Unwashed and unshaved, you wear the same socks and underpants for weeks at a time. With your feet already festooned with blisters, you march for days through mud and snow. You pray you will avoid ambush and the deadly bead of a sniper's rifle. War keeps your body in continuous, heart-pounding terror, and you are never free from the unrelenting fear that this is not safe.

Yet, in war, the most difficult task for me would be following orders unflinchingly, especially when doing so could mean certain death. I admit, at times I am a little self-centered.

On the battlefield, life is expendable, and you and thousands like you may be sacrificed, just to win a tiny skirmish or capture a few feet of foreign real estate, which might be nonchalantly abandoned the following day when it is determined to have no strategic value after all. Nothing personal, but those in charge do not necessarily think your life is as important as you believe it is. Your sergeant, a man who is your superior just because they happened to draft him a few days before you, is permitted to make you do nearly anything he wants. It wouldn't be so bad bowing to his authority if he were just limited to demeaning yet not potentially fatal orders such as, "Soldier, get me some coffee. On the double." But you will learn the squad leader has the power of life and death over you, a sobering thought when you realize he might be the very same guy who did your family's yard work before the war.

It terrifies me to know that any officer could casually order me to undertake a suicidal mission to capture a hilltop or a bunker, and he could do it without giving the decision as much careful consideration as I believe one involving my life requires. It wouldn't matter that I am the person who has to go out and do the work and that I am not personally convinced that storming that particular stronghold is a very good idea. In the military, there are few opportunities to graciously decline.

We are expendable, so an officer might yell out, "Corporal Goldstone, because your life is so meaningless to us, we'd like you to run up toward those people over there shooting machine guns at us and make them stop. Throw yourself in front of one of their bullets if you have to." He would pause and then add, "And before you go, get me some coffee."

If I were ever assigned to do battle, I would simply ask that our generals do not squander me senselessly just to win some trees or a distant gully, and if I have to be sacrificed at all, please trade my life for something really worthwhile, for instance, capturing the entire North Korean navy, destroying doomsday weaponry set to vaporize all known life on this planet, or rescuing some babies, through I would not be comfortable giving my own life unless someone could assure me it would save a minimum of say, three or maybe four of them.

Though I would make a terrible soldier, I would be even more ineffective prisoner of war.

I have seen documentaries about men who were captured and locked away in POW camps. Few wartime experiences are as harrowing as imprisonment by the enemy in such a place of torture and degradation, where the treatment and service on the whole could be expected to be discourteous.

The most successful armies are those populated by soldiers who can bravely endure imprisonment. Though fenced in like animals behind barbed wire, starved and mistreated, these heroic men and women survive, fueled by an unbreakable spirit and inner strength. When I registered for the draft, I warned the government in advance that I would not make a very good prisoner of war, unless they were defining "good" from the perspective of the enemy. As much as I love my country, I want to point out that if tortured, I will likely become what the military classifies as a "little chatterbox." I do not fare well with pain, so I would gladly consent to divulging national secrets if my captors promise not to hit me. The Pentagon can't say I didn't warn them.

These reasons alone are probably enough to dismiss me from induction into the military. But a final compelling reason may be that I just wouldn't be too good for the military's image. No belligerent country will be intimidated by seeing me on a recruitment poster, fumbling with my rifle and struggling awkwardly to keep it pointed safely away from people on my own side. Further, in time of war, I don't think that the enemy will consider retreating if they can hear whining off in the distance.

I am not the best candidate to participate in war, especially if our goal is "to win." In addition, I no longer look very good in uniform, and won't until the army adopts the Levi Strauss concept of tailoring and offers battle fatigues in the style known as "relaxed fit." Each year my new eyeglasses become a little more telescopic, and objects in the distance appear to be even farther away. The only hope I would have for hitting the enemy with a bullet is to ask them if they wouldn't mind standing a little closer and not moving around much.

Don't get me wrong. It's not that I wouldn't want to defend my country. But given a choice, I would rather do so when I am in my eighties, when I am suffering from constant muscle aches and incontinence. Then, I would proudly take an enemy bullet in the name of our Republic. I have many friends who would also gladly volunteer for service thirty to forty years from now. We could create an entire platoon of aged, gnarled-up old men who, because we have nothing to lose, would not hesitate for an instant to storm a fortified bunker. We cannot promise the element of surprise because we will be storming very slowly. Orthopedic footware will be involved, and you will just have to factor in us stopping quite often to pee.

So America, I apologize for not being tough enough, spry enough, and brave enough to defend my family and neighbors from invasion by a foreign enemy and its arsenal of incendiary, nuclear, and chemical weaponry. I would, however, be more than happy to don my blue gas-company uniform once again and proudly serve if my local gas utility ever declares war against the electric company.

Realistically, it is likely that when nations pick up sides and muster up all their able-bodied men for service, I will be among the last chosen, called up sometime after Howie Ives but well before the Guttman twins.

A Smudge in the Record Books

UNLIKE THE JELLYFISH, BANDICOOT, AND CANADIAN SNOW goose—which do not take risks just for laughs or to impress their fellow jellyfish, bandicoots, or Canadian snow geese—we humans are the only species that dabbles in peril for sport. Smart as we believe ourselves to be, some of us engage in behavior that even the most witless of lower animals would not be so foolish as to undertake.

Professional daredevils are our most visible symbols of voluntary risk takers, joyful participants in the game where "surviving this particular time" is but one option, and "living out the remaining days of life in a vegetative state" or "dying as a crumpled smudge under horrific circumstances" are two others. They jump into fire, not to save a puppy or loved one, but because it is dangerous and someone else is willing to watch them do it. We ask them to lick life's frozen flagpoles, and they gleefully comply.

They are born thrill seekers, reveling in the surge of adrenaline. Most are capable of such parlous escapades because they, unlike us, lack the normal mechanisms that trigger terror or personal responsibility. Perhaps they possess a special gene that thrives on danger, one that is happily absent in the majority of onlookers. Physiologists think that maybe they have an extra thingee on their DNA or perhaps are missing some kind of safety rung on their double helix ladder of chromosomes. Daredevils are the best example of those who ignore all the warnings, no matter how apparent and how loud the alarms blare. They are content to perform the same wacky things over and over, until we get tired of watching them or they get killed.

It is the daredevil credo to shock and impress onlookers. They take particular delight in arousing the morbid curiosity of those who would never consider attempting stunts so dangerous or silly themselves but are curious what death by that means looks like. Daredevils serve as our surrogates and perhaps as our society's modern-day gladiators, bored by the mundane lives the majority of us lead and looking for ways to separate themselves from the rest of the pack through feats of recklessness. Wired differently than you and me, daredevils elect careers where there is more at stake and where a bad day is not one when a copier jams or the cafeteria is out of nondairy creamer. Emotionally numbed to terror, they are unfazed that a small sector of the curious public would actually find it kind of neat to watch them get hurt badly.

If you want to find the greatest concentration of daredevils per square foot, visit the circus, where generations of show families perform death-baiting acts, repeating their courtship with danger twice a day, approaching daring tasks as others might real-estate appraisals.

Circus rosters include performers who voluntarily consent to being blown out of the front end of a cannon, allowing an explosion to fire them from a Howitzer by their ass and, if all things go well, to deposit them face first in a net three hundred yards away. In the name of thrill, they are willing to expose themselves day after day to potential harm to the bottom of their feet and their genitalia, not content to be just "A Human Cannonball," but continually seeking the recognition of peers and public as they aspire to become "The Best Human Cannonball Ever!"

Sharing the bill with them are trapeze artists, who carry on the family name and tradition. Often, as their wheelchair-bound elders look on, one aerialist hangs upside down clutching a swing with the back of his or her knees, arcing back and forth. For some spectators, seeing an Upside-Down Human Pendulum might be thrilling enough. However, the act is embellished by another family member swinging from a second trapeze, who at precisely the right moment, lets go and flings through the air, flipping and spinning about for a

few rotations, grabbing the wrists of the inverted catcher, whose trapeze, if luck will have it, happens to be in the right place at the right
time. Timing is everything, and from an early age, fliers learn it is no
better to arrive too early than it is a little late.

At ground level, knife-throwing acts offer yet another daring circus spectacle. A woman is attached to a large disk that is spun like a
Las Vegas wheel of fortune. Her arms and legs are splayed, and she
looks a bit like the Leonardo da Vinci drawing of the guy inside a big
circle. She is blindfolded, for perhaps good reason, and rotating
clockwise at dizzying rpm as her partner, usually her blindfolded
husband, hurls big-handled sixteen-inch surgical steel knives toward
her. If all goes well, the cutlery penetrates the area of the spinning
disc not occupied by the loved one's torso.

In center ring, courageous men and women calling themselves
wild-animal tamers entertain the crowds by provoking lions, tigers,
leopards, and other carnivorous jungle cats, forcing them to jump
through fiery hoops, balance on rolling drums, and perform other
tasks not required in the jungle.

These trainers do not "tame" jungle cats in the traditional sense,
but rather humiliate them publicly into performing silly and demeaning tasks. Wild-animal tamers all used to dress like safari masters in khakis, entering the cage armed with only a flimsy whip in
one hand and rickety chair with spindly legs pointed toward the
animal in the other. Through the years, they felt that they were safe
from attack, mistakenly believing wild animals have some kind of a
natural aversion to lightweight wooden seating.

Trainers remain alive at the pleasure of the animal, and generally,
the animals let their trainers live. Carnivorous beasts have learned that
as long as they remain caged, they must rely on the human for food.

"Eat the lion tamer today," or so concludes a savvy animal, "and I
will be fed for the day. Put up with the bastard, and I eat for a lifetime."

Clyde Beatty, one of the most famous of all wild-animal tamers,
carried a sidearm as a level of protection he felt would be more effective than the leg of a café chair. If the animals went berserk,
Beatty could shoot his way to safety, killing off all his animals one by
one as he fired over his shoulder in retreat. I do not think he gave

much thought to the long-term disadvantage of killing off all the animals he had taken years to train, or how a future act without lions and tigers, where Beatty would enter a cage alone with a chair, could offer much entertainment, unless you consider watching a man "sit" entertaining. I also doubt that he considered the consequences of shooting wildly from inside an open metal cage surrounded on all sides by circus bleachers filled to capacity, and how he would be much more likely to wipe out an entire family than to hit one of his attacking animals.

No circus family through history is more revered than the Flying Wallendas, a high-wire act, which kept the name "Flying" in spite of its connotation for the worst kind of tightrope mishap.

Under the stern rule of patriarch taskmaster Karl, the legendary Wallenda clan dazzled generations of circus-goers from the 1920s onward, inventing and performing some of the most daring high-wire stunts in all circusdom. They were the first to perform the deadly Seven Person Pyramid.

Four of the strongest and most iron-willed Wallenda men formed the bottom tier, yoked together at the shoulders with a balance beam upon which yet another pair of Wallendas stood. The second beam provided a platform to support a woman standing on top of a teetering chair. All of them held in their taped hands fifteen-foot balance poles that extended out on each side like cat whiskers.

This precarious human contraption would be extremely dangerous even as a stationary human sculpture on the ground, but to make the stunt even more breathtaking, they built it four stories above the cement circus floor and walked it along as a single unit across the slender high wire.

In the Wallenda tradition, the feat was performed without a sheltering net or safety harnesses, so with any miscalculation, any false step, or if a single Wallenda sneezed or freaked out even a little, a multigenerational circus tradition could come to a crashing halt. The Seven was performed regularly from 1948 until tragedy struck in 1962 with the collapse of the pyramid in Detroit, killing two of the Wallendas and paralyzing one other.

For the Wallendas, death was a regrettable but not a totally unexpected by-product of their work. "Don't go around whining if someone gets killed," appeared to be their motto. This was the chilly confidence that coursed through the Wallenda family genes. In typical circus tradition, the survivors performed their act, minus the Seven, the following evening.

The aerialists earned the respect of circus enthusiasts and have subsequently inspired clans of big top entertainers, many of whom have similarly attached action adjectives to their last names in homage, calling themselves "The Leaping," "The Soaring," or "The Winged," yet fervently hoping that history will not remember them as "The Hapless," "The Wheelchair-Bound," or "The Late."

For decades, the Wallendas were the most visible of all daredevils, that is until the self-promoting Robert "Evel" Knievel entered the fray. Clad in his comic Elvis Presley–style white polyester jumpsuit, he invented his persona as the world's most daring motorcycle rider, doing so by combining polished showmanship with innate wacko madness, and by committing a professional life to the kind of potentially deadly stunts most of us would not do even in the deepest of suicidal depression. Astride his motorcycle, Knievel spent a career catapulting his bike and himself over rattlesnakes, pools of sharks, rings of fire, and lots full of parked vehicles, the latter of which were lined with old and sharp-edged junker cars, buses, and trailers in such dangerous condition themselves that it would take a daredevil just to drive them into position.

He modified his motorcycles with performance-enhancing turbochargers, special tires, and mechanical accessories to help him reach extremely high velocity within a short distance. Speed, as they say, is a double-edged sword: a plus if you are trying to clear a line of school buses but a minus if you have fallen and are now sliding toward a line of concrete Jersey barriers.

Knievel earned his way-way-bigger-than-life reputation as a man who audaciously tackled the kind of motion feats that Sir Isaac Newton, Father of the First Three Laws of Motion and a respected expert on the subject, would have warned against. With some stunts, such as his leap over fourteen parked Greyhound buses, Knievel landed successfully, smiling and waving victoriously to the crowds as if he were a Roman solider returning from conquest. On other occasions, he was carted off in a crumpled accordion-like heap by EMTs. One widely promoted but failed stunt was his 1968 leap across the 150-foot-wide fountain at Caesar's Palace Casino in Las Vegas. Thousands watched as he cleared the reflection pool only to crash on landing. The resulting month-long coma and shattered pelvis would have been enough to push lesser men into a different line of work, but not Knievel, who continued to throw himself and his bike over anything that would consent.

His most outrageous stunt was an attempt to jump the Snake River Canyon, a leap across a horizontal 3,000-foot chasm, for which he would earn both the Guinness-sanctioned record for "The Human Flung the Farthest Distance from the Point From Which He Started," as well as six million dollars for his troubles. From the get-go he understood that even the beefiest of motorcycles could not hurdle that distance in normal Earth gravity, and that in all probability, a bike would soar off the cliff at high speed, arcing over the gorge gracefully for a few seconds, and even with engine screaming and tractionless wheels spinning manically, would slowly change direction from forward to downward, increasing velocity as it tailspun to the canyon floor below, ending with a fireball of metal and mangled flesh that would spread over a half square mile of riverbed.

So Knievel designed a jet-powered vehicle he called the Skycycle, a rocket-shaped motorized hybrid that mated a motor tricycle and the kind of ramjet contraption that you would envision Wile E. Coyote constructing from mail order Acme parts. His strategy was to launch himself at hundreds of miles per hour off a ramp, with the hope that his inertia and carefully calculated trajectory would carry him to the other side, landing him upright, with wheels grabbing the ground and able to gently roll him to a controlled stop. A huge crowd paid to see the event that some billed as "Man and Machine versus the Canyon." At that time, rumors were also spreading that Knievel was an alleged foul-mouthed racist and virulent anti-Semite, so in the grandstands on the afternoon of the event was a contingent of minority and Jewish spectators who were quietly rooting for the canyon wall.

The 1974 leap was televised and promoted as the kind of historical event you would kick yourself for missing. So with millions looking on, Knievel revved up his Skycycle and accelerated up the ramp. In one of the most disappointing failures in all of performance history, the craft impotently lobbed out a few feet over the chasm, prematurely deployed its parachute, and daintily drifted like an autumn leaf to the canyon floor below. Humiliated in front of a worldwide audience, and knowing he was a miserable and overrated failure, Knievel was consoled only by the thought he was still earning more than six thousand dollars per vertical foot he was falling.

I have heard that over his daredevil career, Evel Knievel claims to have broken something like 170 percent of his bones, meaning he probably fractured every individual bone in his body at least once, including that tiny one in the inner ear, and splintered the more accessible ones multiple times. When you repeatedly shatter your skeleton, speckle your body with random blotches of hematoma, and replace normal skin with continually rehealing scar tissue, I would imagine you are eventually desensitized to pain in the conventional "this hurts really bad" sense. Daredevils such as Knievel wear their tattered and buffeted bodies proudly and boast that broken skeletal parts are badges of honor. I am not an expert in such things, but it seems to me that if you break this many bones so often, there is a convincing argument to be made that maybe you are not really such a good daredevil after all.

In addition to Knievel, other daredevils have built careers entertaining the curious. At public events and on TV specials, you will find people willing to race around inside of a twelve-foot metal mesh sphere on motorcycles, drive an automobile headlong into a flaming wall, or balance gleefully on a device called the Twenty-five-Foot Spinning Wheel of Death. Some voluntarily set their clothing ablaze, while other leap off towers into a tub of bathwater or crouch down in a wooden box full of dynamite that they detonate in an explosion that spews splinters, dust, and jumpsuit material across an open field. If you want, they will do it for you time and time again. All you have to do is ask.

In movies, stuntmen and -women jump under trains, leap off buildings, and drive cars off cliffs.

Even our athletes put their bodies in the line of fire just to entertain us a little. Football players crash into each other like bumper
cars. Pro wrestlers, theatrical but not competitive in the Marquess of
Queensberry, sporting, best-man-wins-the-match-squarely sense,
heave each other outside the ring, withstand the weighty intrusion
of a 350-pound adversary crashing down on their necks, or smash
each other in the face with Samsonite metal folding chairs, the mag-
nitude of the latter punishment not fully appreciated until you learn
the number of people who injure themselves annually just by sitting
down on one too hard.

Rodeo performers, too, are members of an expansive roster of
popular danger jockies. At weekend events held throughout the West,
cowboys ride wild horses, which they ridiculously insist are the ones
about to be "broken." They jump off moving animals to tackle baby
cows, which still weigh in excess of three hundred-pounds. In the
most dangerous event, they willingly clutch their thighs around the
waistline of three-thousand-pound bulls for as long as the bull will
allow. Bull riding is a contest of man versus an animal twenty times
his weight, a beast specially bred and single-mindedly committed to
getting the skinny hat-wearing cowboy off its dorsum in order to
maliciously stomp on him as many times as possible. Once the rider
is thrown, a near certainty and usually within the first eight seconds,
his life is often saved only through the antics of gaudily outfitted
rodeo clowns, paid to distract the bull with wild movements, taunts,
and bovine slurs. It is their underappreciated job to convince the angry bull that it would be more fun to trample a cowboy wearing a
baggy gingham dress, a woman's wig, and thick makeup instead.
Even more dangerous to the rodeo clown than jumping in the path
of a very pissed ton-and-a-half animal is drinking in a cowboy bar
after the rodeo if all his mascara has not been adequately removed.

What is even more curious in bull-riding events is that the cowboy will use heavy rope to tie his wrist to the animal, so he can hang
on as long as possible. The downside is, if the rider is dislodged, he
will sometimes be unable to extricate himself and will consequently
bounce uncontrollably in random directions like a rubber ball connected to one of those kid's wooden paddle novelties with the

stretchy bands. Though I have never actually attended a rodeo, I would think that being thrown clear of a stomping bull, even if it means being hoisted twenty or thirty feet in the air, is preferable to being dragged by your wrist alongside one through the dirt.

So why are spectators, otherwise normal people who would never undertake impetuous stunts themselves, so keen on watching daredevils? Maybe it's because we all crave a little excitement, but prefer to get others to do our dangerous bidding, happy to watch them succeed or fail without putting us in the line of fire or making us directly responsible for their spinal-cord injuries. Maybe we are morbidly curious. Those of us who would never think to gore a cowboy with a pike ourselves are willing to watch one get speared by a longhorn.

As thrill voyeurs, we encourage others with the double dare, paying our daredevils to be risk whores whom we will forget about tomorrow. We take advantage of their need for attention, goading them on for our selfish amusement. As bystanders, we are immune from the danger, but for the moment our adrenaline can flow freely. We are safe whether the daredevil lives or dies, unless of course we are the victims of a fluke accident during which one falls to his or her death, landing on top of us in the bleachers.

Most daredevils, especially circus acrobats, perform their acts without benefit of a safety net. They believe that we, the circus-paying public, want this. This could not be further from the truth. My personal message to daredevils such as aerialists is the following: Your death or quadriplegia benefits no one. Sure, those of us who have paid to see you perform secretly want you to screw up a little, but very few of us really want to watch you die. From my selfish personal ticket-buying perspective, if you explode on impact as you hit the circus floor a few rows from my family, you will detract from much of the fun of our circus experience.

I would like to suggest that those daredevils reading this book consider using a net forthwith. You can still be as humiliated as you would like should you fall, but bounding into some nuzzling mesh unharmed will prevent all the children in the audience from lifelong trauma and reoccurring nightmares, wherein they relive your gruesome fatality over and over, as you splatter on impact like some organic piñata. Additionally, should you survive, my family can happily come back to see you when the circus returns and enjoy watching you fall time and time again.

Cutting Life Short in Your Spare Time

FORTUNATELY, MOST OF US NEVER ASPIRE TO THE HARUM-scarum world of professional daredevilism. But there are some among us who rise to a little amateur risk taking, engaging in some of life's chancier offerings, which the more sissified among us would politely decline.

Most hobbyist-risk takers have regular jobs but are willing to plunge headlong into dicey pursuits in their free time, believing that coquetting with danger is just plain fun. They feel that once in a while you have to make the jump across the bottomless chasm to prove you are, or were, alive. They use zest-hardy activities to prove to themselves and to others how well their mettle does in a test. They relish dancing blindfolded a little closer to the edge than required. They are not afraid to lose, just so they have a chance to play.

The fear-rousing organs, which risks takers love to light up at will, are quite serious at doing their work. Being so focused, the autonomic nervous system, the most nervous of all your nervous systems, is quite gullible, and is often so caught up in fright or flight maneuvers, it is unable to distinguish whether there is an actual intruder threatening or whether it is you just screwing with it. In the latter case, you can easily trick your body into endorphin-gushing physiological frenzy and sit back as it anxiously presses all your glands into action. It is not that your amygdala is stupid, it is just so singleminded that other parts of the brain can fool it easily and therefore make it the butt of their little cranial practical jokes.

Thrill seekers delight in turning the fear spigot off and on. They love the rush of a body running at peak capacity. They tingle whenever their innards are bathed in exotic action juices. So they enthusiastically dabble in fright-inducing activities as the excuse to mix up a batch, and they rejoice in getting all their hormonal valves to open wide and flood the body with intoxicating chemicals that are kept safely capped most of the time

Afterward, a backwash of well-being and a post-peril exhilaration drenches every cell. Victors emerge smiling, high-fiving, breathlessly blurting testosterone-fired primal utterances such as "Whoa!" and "Oh, man!" They wallow in a sense of achievement, jubilantly. Still quaking and a bit out of breath, some equate a thrill adventure with an orgasm. Call me old-fashioned, but I will stick to the conventional kind.

So these amateur adventurers climb mountains, go on safari, ride the killer surf in Hawaii, skateboard down mountainsides, or fly twenty feet in the air on a motocross bike. Like the Wallendas, they gamble with life, shrugging off a safety net, spurred to possible doom by their unwavering confidence in themselves. They revel in their avocational bravery, talent, strength, stamina, and agility. These people triumphantly walk away from a successful encounter, still wading in the residual pools of the body's principal pleasure fluid, still dripping with endorphins. They know their limits, but look for ways to stretch the boundaries out like a thick rubber band.

Medical literature describes a risk-friendly gene, a blip somewhere in the spiraling ladder of the DNA that makes an otherwise intelligent person do wacky things. For these people, it is not enough to stand their ground bravely when danger appears unintentionally, but instead they go looking for it.

While you will find risk takers in every age group, the majority of amateurs are young, many under the age of twenty-three. Perhaps their actions result from rebelliousness, defiance of parental authority, or perhaps, boredom. Maybe they suffer from a misguided feeling of immortality or are unencumbered by the inhibitions that hold back their elders. Perhaps their tiny brains have not yet developed an im-

class climber doubles, and all these conditions take a toll on the body, cumulative over the course of a climb. Each additional day a climber takes to acclimate saps a little more strength and increases the chance of malnutrition, altitude sickness, and frostbite. If your body's rebellion at the conditions is not enough, remember that the mountain is not going to make your trip easy for you, and bona fide physical danger precedes your every step.

Snow is slippery, and the most obvious danger is sliding off the side of the mountain. Stable-looking footing can collapse unannounced underfoot. Pitons driven into the rock can work loose, or rocks can fracture after a million years of previous reliability. Climbers, weighed down with backpacks full of gear, must often balance as they walk across narrow-edged ridges that threaten a three-thousand-foot drop on both sides. Mile-deep crevasses hide beneath a blanket of snow. You may be confident, even smug, knowing you are extra careful and highly disciplined, and can still be a victim yourself if someone a little more lax falls on you from above.

In permanent winter, you face the daily dangers of avalanche burying you and your company of Sherpas in a crushing tarpaulin of snow, sometimes racing down the slope at one hundred miles per hour. Fast-moving glaciers like the Khumbu Icefall threaten climbers with a constantly moving downhill current of giant ice chunks, some the size of icebergs and weighing in at millions of pounds. The pieces creak and tumble, so unstable that they tip without warning and squash anything unfortunate enough to be in their toppling path. They open giant fissures in the glacier flow that can swallow up teams of climbers before anyone notices.

Ice bridges tempt trekkers with precarious shortcuts across bottomless ravines. But just because one supported your stout climbing partner a few steps in front of you is no guarantee it will not collapse the moment you set foot on it. Whiteout snowstorms appear suddenly, and like a heavy fog, obscure anything more than a foot ahead. The searing brightness of endless sunlit drifts burns the retinas and causes temporary blindness. A sudden blizzard can bury a campsite. Winds approach hurricane strength, wafting with enough gusto to blow a team of mountaineers over the side. Girder-size icicles above, each a one-ton spear, delicately hang from sheer frozen walls, ready to break loose in a heavy wind, plummet straight down, and effortlessly skewer a tandem of climbers.

Team members rope together when traveling on glaciers and snowfields. Should one partner stumble in a crevasse, the other, in theory, can break the fall and then pull the first out. While tandem climbing seems safe, the danger of injury or death actually increases. Climbing alone, you have only your own missteps to blame for a fatal plunge. But with two climbers attached to each other, either one is technically capable of screwing up, dragging the other partner along with him, and effectively doubling the chances of either being killed.

Tragedy has struck expeditions in the alleged safer conditions of the camp when a climber wanders out of the tent at night for urinary relief, only to slide off the mountain mid-pee into a deep ravine. This is perhaps the most feared of all mountaineering accidents, not only because the steep fall is almost always fatal, but also because of the posthumous humiliation to the climber who will be discovered months later by rescuers with his hand freeze-welded to his penis.

The frozen, perfectly preserved body of Everest pioneer George Leigh Mallory, lost and presumed dead in 1924, was found in 1999. Debate still rages whether he died before reaching the summit or whether, as some Mallory supporters enthusiastically claim, he died on his way back down after reaching the peak. Either way, it can be argued that the expedition was not the rousing success Mallory had hoped for, since returning and not being found naked and dead three-quarters of a century later are inextricably linked to success. The Mallory expedition began nearly eight decades earlier when the costs were much less, but it has still turned out to be the most expensive mountaineering venture to date because much of Mallory's gear was a rental, and continued to accrue charges from 1924.

At one time, Mount Everest alumni were members of a very exclusive club restricted to the most elite alpine mountaineers. All had considerable experience. Today, anyone with $70,000 to $100,000 and a few months free can join an expedition, where along with a professional climber or two, they join fellow first-timers, including those who are retirees or on leave from their jobs as accountants, florists, and secretaries. A number of tour companies run Everest treks, advertising the mountain in the same way they might for Cozumel. Vacationers are encouraged to embark on one of the most dangerous and strenuous endeavors on earth, tricked into doing so by deceptively attractive brochure pictures of the summit on a bright sunny day and by promotional family specials where "Kids Climb Free!"

Your tour operators may not tell you that most amateur climbers do not reach the summit, and in some years, more than 1 in 10 aspirants die in the process. So unless you are predisposed to failure, go to the Caribbean, where you will not have to admit, "We got within three hundred yards of the resort hotel before we were forced to turn back," or more tragically hear others say, "We found his lifeless body in front of the ice machine."

It is the popularity of the mountain that is making Everest increasingly unpopular. Serious climbers find the trails and camps crowded, face delays, and get snarled in traffic congestion as teams crunch up at narrow passes and as amateurs a few steps ahead struggle to figure out how a piton works. Slow goers make ascent dangerous and extremely frustrating for those who, in technical-mountaineering parlance, "know what the fuck they are doing." As irritated as an experienced climber may get, little can be done except to wait for the novice to either voluntarily move out of the way or graciously topple off the side of a glacier. Faster teams, sadly, cannot ask one clinging for life on the ledge above if they can play through. With slow and disrespectful climbers in great numbers, we are beginning to hear about an increasing number of incidents of "mountaineer's rage."

You would also think those with a calling to a mountain would have a greater-than-average respect for the environment, but climbers top the list of litterers, polluters, and environmental slobs, leaving soup cans, broken gear, gum wrappers, discarded bottles, and spent oxygen tanks all over the mountain. Tons of garbage pimple the once-immaculate passes, spoiling the view and turning Everest into the highest-altitude trash dump on the planet. With no bathrooms, it is getting to be a tricky place just to walk.

Heavy foot traffic alone is destroying the natural beauty. Climbers are tracking dirt and debris onto the once pure white glaciers. Piton holes pit rock walls everywhere, on the Western Cwm, the Great Couloir, and the Hillary Step. You can scarcely find a place that hasn't been chewed up by crampons.

Some say the novice tours have cheapened the experience. The glory of conquest is becoming less meaningful to a master climber when he or she is followed by a Cub Scout troop. Now that elderly and Special Olympic tours are being held on Everest, professionals are desperately looking for new ways to differentiate themselves from the dilettante, by finding previously virginal routes, ascending barefoot, climbing without a partner or with a partner who is dangerously clumsy, or being a member of the first team to drag along a piano.

Why do people climb? Not because of some death wish. There are ways to kill yourself that are less expensive, more rapid, and less uncomfortable. Nor are climbers looking for pirate booty or hidden treasure.

For most, it is the challenge to walk along real estate inaccessible to the majority of others, to attempt a feat that draws on skill and strength that exceed those of their neighbors. Some undertake the adventure to compensate for other personal inadequacies. If you were picked on in gym class, you will have the last laugh at your next reunion when you nonchalantly pull out the picture of you with your Sherpa.

For many, climbing is a test of personal drive, the most primal competition between us and nature: our intellect, strength, and determination against the mountain's brute force and any obstacles it can litter in our path. Climbers listen to the little daredevil inside that goads them on, willingly putting themselves on part of the earth where God neglected to program mercy.

Many tackle a climb just for the bragging rights.

The mountain beckons. It is a hypnotic call that mountaineers say

portant lobe. Maybe they have been granted freedom but not the wisdom to use it responsibility.

Aside from the youthful body's bouts with acne, it is arguably much better physiologically than one a few years older. Earlier in life, we are spry and more coordinated, with sharper instincts and much faster reaction time. Our vision is more acute. Young people nimbly move out of the way while those a generation older flinch a moment before getting hit in the face with something. Young bodies have more endurance. Watch an eighteen-year-old play basketball for an hour, and compare him with a forty-five-year-old man, who every five minutes will stop, lean over from the waist, breathing hard, hold his palm against his chest and the other hand above his head, and pant, "I'll be OK in a minute."

The younger among us are generally stronger. Muscles have logged fewer miles. The body as a whole is more resilient, supple, and can absorb considerably more shock without shattering. A collision that induces fracture or coma in the skeletally brittle older population produces no more than a moment of inconvenience.

Our youth are our pioneers of new sport, our recreational test pilots. Their willingness to splinter limbs and flay themselves on rough asphalt are the reason we have skateboarding, Rollerblading, and aerobatic bicycling today. Without their discovery of hot-dog skiing, there would be no Olympic free-style medalists. Adventuresome young men and women have been willing to brave new activities long before all the bugs have been worked out.

In the late 1980s, the definition of athletics was pried open a bit wider to accommodate "extreme sports," a new breed of risky, heart-beating-out-of-the-chest pastime, which combine physical difficulty and outrageous danger into one composite activity, for example jumping off high platforms, performing aerobatic stunts on a various wheeled conveyances, racing down a seventy-five-degree trail on a mountain bike, or any number of challenging rough and tumble activities that promote danger as its own reward.

These nontraditional sports often meld two otherwise wholesome gambols, for instance bicycling and acrobatics, each relatively non-

hostile on an individual basis, but dangerous only when combined. Other extreme sports introduce obstacles such as big ramps, concrete barriers, bone-shattering heights, or the threat of criminal prosecution. These activities call out to enthusiasts who see conventional "Old World" sports such as golf, rugby, or bullfighting as "like way too calm."

Many extreme sports are noncompetitive games of high-risk solitaire, where an individual pits balance, coordination, and cool against conventional wisdom, in a personal test of skill, artistry, and physical resolve.

Bungee jumpers, for example, hurl themselves off elevated platforms, bridges, and cranes, face-first, to experience the sensation of plunging hundreds of feet in free fall. They are tethered to life at the ankles by a resilient rope called a bungee cord, a thin stretchy umbilical that is the only thing between them and being smashed into paste on the rocks below. As a bungee jumper, you will learn what it must feel like to fly, to accidentally topple off a medium-size highrise apartment building, or to throw yourself over a cliff or bridge in uncontainable despair.

The bungee cord stretches out behind the jumper to absorb the energy of the fall, and when fully extended brings the falling human anchor to a gentle stop. Stretched to its maximum, it rests at low point momentarily and now crammed with all this kinetic energy, snaps the participant back skyward at great speed. At the top again, jumpers feel the effects of zero gravity, floating in space for just a moment and experiencing a phenomenon called "air time" before gravity pulls them downward once more.

As a jumper, you rebound and fall, yo-yoing merrily until all the pent-up energy stored in the stretched cord dissipates and you finally come to a flaccid and gently swaying stop. Once your bouncing subsides, your friends above you haul you back onto the bridge deck by your ankles as if you were some kind of tuna.

Of primary importance prior to bungee jumping is (1) securing the cord properly around the ankles, then (2) remembering to tie the other end to the bridge or other structure from which you jump. These two steps are very important, so you might want to

write them on your hand or have them tattooed on a forearm or thigh, so you do not forget these crucial tenets in the excitement of the moment.

But most important—and even as a non-jumper I can understand the value of this—find a cord that is the right length. Many tragedies occur to people who forget that one of the remarkable characteristics of a bungee cord is its ability to grow longer, so it is imperative that the unstretched cord should be considerably shorter than the drop itself and all factors considered, an undersized cord is, and let me use the vernacular of bungee jumpers, "way better" than one that stretches a wee bit too far. Much of bungee-jumping's charm vanishes when the jumper smashes into the ground and does not spring back even a little.

Squashing onto the pavement or bouncing into a lane of oncoming truck traffic is only part of your worries. Even if you decelerate into the nadir unharmed, gently coming to rest for a moment, you will soon be hurled upward at tremendous speed and if you have miscalculated or strayed off a perfectly vertical descent, you will likely crash into the underside of the concrete bridge deck, and continue to bounce into structural pylons until most of the springiness in the cord has been exhausted.

Finally, those who have not been properly trained and do not understand the subtleties of bungee jumping may, in their excitement to get out and try it, mistakenly grab some less stretchy material such as rope or metal chain, which experienced jumpers will tell you will make the jumping experience a quite unpleasant one.

BASE jumping is an even riskier sport and is performed from a much higher elevation. The jumper, who is not leashed to the platform, leaps from upwards of a thousand feet and free-falls to earth, slowed by deploying a parachute. BASE is an acronym. BASE jumpers earn a letter after successfully leaping off each of four types of structures: *B* for building, *A* for antenna, *S* for spans, and by this they mean bridges (since using another *B* would mean the sport would be called BABE jumping, thereby spelling out a sexist term that is apt to be misunderstood), and *E* for earth, meaning cliffs and waterfall. Once a leap from all four venues is successfully completed,

jumpers are initiated into a secret society and the word BASE can be officially added to their sports résumés.

Special parachutes are designed to open quickly. Aside from one deploying sometime *after* impact, the most common parachute-related deaths result from tangled lines or winds that veer a jumper into a rock face, antenna guy wires, into the torrents of falling water, or toward the huge propeller blades of power company windmill farms. In most states, BASE jumping is illegal, but carries the post-James Dean cache as the "outlaw" extreme sport. In California and the Southwest where BASE jumping is fashionable, you read all the time about memorial services for its newest converts, many of whom are remembered by friends as only BA jumpers.

A particularly popular extreme sport is street luge, overtaking the alpine luge as the "sport of the insane." In the alpine version, men and women lie on their backs and slide down a twisting icy incline track in a skintight luge superhero costume on a flimsy little brake-less and barely steerable sled. Transforming themselves into an aero-dynamic stiletto to cut resistantly through the air, riders can reach speeds up to seventy miles per hour. Street luging replaces billowy snow banks and smooth ice with abrasive pockmarked asphalt streets, Jersey barriers, and parked cars. Like those on the traditional ice luge, street lugers lie face up in a stiff, feet-first, lying-in-state configuration that promotes streamlined efficiency. The luge rides on wheels like those on a skateboard and, similar to its alpine coun-terpart, is devoid of such niceties as brakes and a steering mecha-nism. Lugers steer by shifting their weight and, using momentum as their means of acceleration, can travel upwards of seventy miles an hour, as well. Wearing only a helmet and supposedly abrasion-proof clothing is the only thing that prevents crashes from scraping lugers skinless. Because of the inaccessibility of permanent racecourses, street luge competitions are held on city streets, where automobile traffic and intersections add to the excitement. You will not often see a street luger over the age of nineteen, for reasons that are painfully obvious.

Even a sport as leisurely as bicycling can turn demonic in the ex-treme version, no longer a serenely relaxing jaunt through the flow-

ered countryside, where the greatest danger is being chased by a dog or sliding off the shoulder of the road into a culvert.

In extreme mountain biking, cyclists barrel down near vertical mountain sides on trails that twist and turn without warning, saddled on an all-terrain, nubby-tired, two-wheeler, bouncing down rock-strewn paths, bounding over boulders and tree stumps, shooting over gullies and down embankments, and veering close to a cliff's edge as their tires slip and slide on dust, sand, and cinders.

If you ever try mountain biking yourself, you will discover mid-trek that your bike remains on the very cusp of controllability, and that you may be just a tiny shift of body weight from a catastrophic accident. A mishap on a steep trail begins a gravity-assisted fall, dragging you downward through gravel and debris that will be driven ir-retrievably deep into your skin. You will generally stop only after the hill does.

Should you unexpectedly tumble from the saddle of a dirt bike, you will likely continue on your own down the sharp boulder-littered pass, following the route intended for your two-wheeler, where you will bounce uncontrollably, alternating between contu-sions and lacerations, careening off outcroppings of rock, through thorn-vested vegetation, rasped against the abrasive grit of the trail, until you roll to a complete stop in some briars below. This is the kind of injury where gravity and clumsiness propel you down a mountain's cheeks just as fast as the dirt bike ever could. Incidentally, as you are somersaulting a foot or so ahead of your heavily outfitted mountain bike, which is even heavier because it is equipped with specialized shock absorbers intended to keep you from falling in the first place, you will soon learn that the cartwheeling bike is probably following the same trajectory that you are and will eventually and in-escapability catch up, just a moment after you abruptly thud to a stop. Sadly the bike will not land in some unoccupied plot within the vast expanse of nature at the bottom of the slope, but because both you and the bike were aimed in the same direction before your fall, will instead choose to land precisely on the tiny spot where you now lay buckled and bleeding, adding just one more wound to the collection of accumulating injuries that you amassed on the way

down. You will be pleased to learn that your bike will probably sustain no irreparable damage, since you will have broken its fall when your soft body absorbed the majority of its impact.

Of course, if mountain biking is too raucous, you can opt for a more traditional, leisurely bike ride through the country, but I warn you, you might just as readily be sideswiped on a bucolic back road by a passing farmer on a John Deere tractor or mauled by a pack of farm animals.

Kayaking, a more mainstream sport, offers adventure on water. As a participant in the Inuit-inspired sport, you slither into a kazoo-shaped boat, your legs extended straight, as the boat forms a watertight cocoon around your waist. You buckle your kayak around you, wearing it like trousers, and now you and the boat are inextricably one. You will use a multipurpose, two-headed oar for propulsion, for turning, for braking, for defense from attack by sea lions or rowdy people in canoes, and for keeping yourself from being washed out to sea. Should you lose the oar, you are pretty much screwed. A kayak tips easily, so if you flip upside down, your body will temporarily serve as the keel, though if you are effectively trained, you can jerk upward to right yourself, as long as you can do this before suffocating in hypothermia-inducing waters, or getting chewed upon by seals. While marginally safe, its dangers increase in more extreme versions such as white water or ocean kayaking. Extreme sport fanciers have not, as of this writing, discovered "street kayaking."

Parasailing combines air and water activities by towing a participant like a box kite behind a moving boat. The parasailer, either standing upright in a harness or seated in a special reclining chair, is attached to a jellyfish-shaped parachute canopy. As the towboat accelerates, the chute fills up with air and ascends, reeled out farther and farther on a winch line, often reaching an altitude of a hundred feet or more. As the boat slows, the parachute drifts back on its own toward the water, and the motorboater reels the parasailer back in. Parasailing fuses hang gliding with water sports, thereby doubling the danger and providing an opportunity for those not killed on impact by crashing into the ocean to die by drowning. Experienced boatswains must never forget they are towing an airborne parasailer

behind them and must remind themselves to never, and let me state this for emphasis, *never* drive the tow boat under a bridge.

I have a couple of friends who love the sky, not as I love the sky by looking up at it from the ground, but in their twisted case, from the sky itself. One is a skydiver, who spends a few Sundays a month with some buddies, packing parachutes and a few sandwiches, hiring a plane, and jumping out of it at altitude. They free fall, belly down, arms and legs spread outward like flying squirrels, spine slightly concave from the air pushing back at their appendages at a hundred plus miles an hour. When the ground seems to be getting too close, they open their chutes and drift gently into an open field. Sometimes skydivers perform acrobatics on the trip down, joining hands in midair, performing short aerial ballets, sometimes mischievously spelling out the word *HELP*, but generally enjoying every second of their communal fall. They describe the experience as the ultimate freedom, their minds free of all earthbound thoughts except for how nasty it would be to get nipped by a propeller or shot by a hunter who believes them to be impressively large ducks.

I know people who are pharmacist-pilots, elementary school teacher-pilots, banker-pilots, and allergist-pilots, who want me to believe that they are as good being pilots—the one day a month they are in the air—as they are being pharmacists, elementary school teachers, bankers and allergists for the twenty-some other days when they are earthbound.

A couple who live around the corner from me acquired glider licenses. For them, drifting silently in a lightweight, engineless craft with slender wings, rising on thermals of warm air like a bird, using nature as propulsion, is their newfound passion. From the moment they took up soaring, three years ago, they have repeatedly asked me to join them on one of their Saturday flights. I do not want to offend them, but I would not feel comfortable riding with these people, even in their Subaru.

So each week, I politely decline, and while I have been convincing for the past 156 weekends—citing nieces' bat mitzvahs and organ donations—I am not sure how much longer I will be believed.

A more dangerous and, for me, less appealing form of soaring is

done without the benefit of a solid, closed cabin airship in the sport of hang gliding, whose devotees clip on wings and dive off cliffs into the air. Harnessed to a lightweight fabric wing, hang glider pilots reshape the crafts aerodynamic profile by pushing or pulling a control bar, allowing them to bank, swoop, dive, or do any one of a number of things that kites can do when they are airborne.

Like more mechanical and comfortable solid wing gliders, hang gliders stay aloft by enjoying the warm updrafts that chimney upward and carry the lightweight apparatus with them. Paradoxically, thermals are often found near cliff walls, which as far as I am concerned would be outcroppings I would most like to avoid in a hang glider.

I have also known people who fly motorized crafts called ultralights, the smallest of powered aerobodies and basically a motorized canvas awning under which you and a patio chair have been tentatively secured. Ultralights are muscled by lawn mower-sized engines. I know that I am constantly restarting my mower each time I use it, so I am frightened by the thought of having to yank a starter cord numerous times as I tailspin back toward the ground.

But of all aerial sports, none is as beautiful as hot air ballooning. Large inflatable bags the size of Victorian homes, yet light enough to float, balloons demand the eye's attention, hypnotizing those on the ground to chroma upward. Balloons move so imperceptively, they appear pasted against a field of blue.

They are graceful, drifting mutely, punctuating the skies with bubbles of color, emerging in the summer when the skies are bright and clear, when the air is warm, when visibility is high and the currents of air are invitingly serene. At festivals, dozens of balloons hover overhead, hanging like fresh fruit. They paint the sky with dots of pure sunlit chroma, against a backdrop of absolute silence, with the quiet stillness of a cloudless sky occasionally broken by only the distant, faint cry of "Get me down!"

Suspended scrotally beneath is an open-air passenger compartment, a floating balcony from which the balloon pilot enjoys a truly spectacular, unobstructed, 360-degree view of hillside and meadow.

Passengers barely feel movement at all as the balloon is gently carried in the open palms of air.

Ballooning is the purest of aerial sport, and it is this very simplicity that is the lure to the enthusiast. The balloon is a captive of the wind, compliantly rambling wherever the whims of air currents dictate, neither hindered nor redeemed by motor, steering, or brakes. Pilot and passenger are generally just along for the ride.

The only direction that you as a pilot can control is up or down, so with enough warning, you will generally be able to avoid plowing into barns, the Sears Tower, high-voltage power lines, straying into the glide path of international airports, or drifting helplessly out to sea.

Balloons float because warm air is lighter than the cooler air surrounding it. Pumping an envelope with a sufficient amount of hot gas gives it the might to lift considerable weight. (To avoid confusion, I should clarify that irrepressible buoyancy is not the case for all objects containing heated air, because technically your furnace is a metal belly filled with great quantities of extremely hot gas, and you don't have any problems with it floating around the ceiling of your basement.)

A hot air balloon consists of three components, (1) a very large presumably leak-proof bag, (2) a heater to keep replenishing the supply of toasty air in the balloon proper and, (3) a passenger compartment to port its passengers.

The largest and arguably most important feature of a hot air balloon is the large overhead sack for which it is named.

You must remember that a balloon is only "lighter than air" after it is inflated. An uninflated balloon is quite a bit heavier than air, and if you drop it in that state from any reasonable height, it will crash to ground without exhibiting any aerodynamic characteristics, unless you consider straight down aerodynamic. Properly inflating it by stuffing heated air up its nether opening is the primary duty of the hot air balloon pilot, just ahead of keeping it from crashing into sharp buildings and breaking open like a puff pastry.

Today you will find many balloons in traditional teardrop shapes

and dazzling high iridescent colors. At summer hot air festivals, you will also see inflatables in all sorts of wacky shapes, sometimes as large stuffed animals, basketballs, killer whales, big-wheeled trucks, snowmen, pagodas, hot dogs, and split-level homes. Corporate entries feature huge pumped-up replicas of their products—for instance, cameras, soft drink cans, steel-belted radial tires, and artificial heart valves. You probably do not want to die in anything but a regular balloon to prevent people from giggling uncomfortably at your funeral when the eulogy mentions something about "a life cut tragically short dangling underneath a very big wiener."

The second component, the passenger compartment, hangs from the balloon's undercarriage. Known by its Italian name, *gondola,* the flimsy perch is made of rattan and is frighteningly similar in shape and structural strength to a laundry hamper. The wicker material from which it is woven is chosen because it is lightweight, but it poses a threat to your safety because frankly, it is lightweight. If you've ever sat on a white wicker patio chair, you can attest to its flimsiness and know the anxiety you will experience as the legs twist underneath you, recognizing that at any moment any one of them could collapse you and the chair in a pile of flesh and rattan splinters. Wicker is dangerous enough on a patio, so hoisted above treetops, some consider it downright foolhardy.

Air cools on its own, so to keep the craft airworthy, you must either reheat the air or lessen the load the balloon carries, for instance by jettisoning anything weighty or heaving one of the more expendable passengers over the side. Early in ballooning, pilots carried sandbags, tied onto the outside wall of the gondola. When the balloon lost some of its vertical punch, one of the sand weights was dropped, making the balloon a little lighter. The practice of dropping sandbags was curtailed, not for the safety of the balloonists, who might be a victim of vertical whiplash as the balloon rapidly ascended, but obviously for innocent passersby on the earth below, who would be instantly flattened by a twenty-five pound parcel of sand dropped on them from 1,500 feet.

Today, you keep your balloon airworthy by reheating the air trapped inside, using a propane-fired burner located above the gon-

dola. When activated through a blast valve, an eight-foot plume of blue flame shoots upward from the fire cannon into the inflated core of the balloon.

As a pilot, you must aim carefully to keep the giant blue flare from engulfing the lightweight canvas envelope in flames. You are also constantly reminded while firing a gas jet from this twelve-million-BTU flamethrower that you are standing in rattan, a dry flammable material that would make wonderful kindling.

Filling the envelope with hot air keeps the balloon playfully buoyant. Releasing air allows it to descend. Still, a balloon will ultimately come down where it wants. If you are lucky, this will be in an open field accessible by your car, but because of the independent behavior of balloons, you are equally likely to light down in a leeching pond at a sludge treatment facility, in the high-speed lane of the interstate, on an NRA rifle range, or into a residential backyard tenaciously guarded by a chow.

During the 1930s, colossal lighter-than-air passenger sky-ships offered Europeans the promise of safe, luxurious transcontinental and transatlantic travel. With thoughts of the Titanic and Lusitania disasters still fresh in everyone's minds, the Graf Zeppelin was touted as a better way to get around, since they were faster than steamships and unfettered by icebergs.

Germany and England were rivals in the race to develop rigid airship technology, and each began building huge steel-girdered envelopes, some the size of two or more football fields. Filled with millions of cubic feet of featherweight gas, these air colossi would float quietly on a straight line route over continents, mountains, and oceans.

The gas of choice to keep the crafts fluffily aloft was helium. Both the Brits and Germans knew the inert element to be safe, non-combustible, and non-toxic. Dirigibles would be immune from explosion and their passengers shielded from asphyxiation. In fact, even if a rupture of one of the many gas compartments occurred and helium leaked into the passenger section, the worst that could happen was that everyone's voice would get high and squeaky and sound very silly for a little while.

Helium, though safe, was expensive, so airship designers turned to hydrogen: cheap, ubiquitous, and easily harvested. Similarly lighter-than-air, it was sadly also more-explosive-than-air-or-anything-else-for-that-matter.

Impressed by their own engineering, which they claimed was flawless, German designers arrogantly assured that explosion was impossible and the hydrogen-packed Zeppelin would be the safest means of travel ever devised, and its dominion of the skies would last for a thousand years.

The sky-illuminating explosion of the Zeppelin Hindenburg over Lakehurst, New Jersey, in May of 1937 finally convinced advocates of commercial air transport that carrying fewer than a hundred travelers across the ocean underneath an eight-hundred-foot long, flammable, fabric-covered, passenger-filled bomb did beg some rethinking. The accident hastened the end of lighter-than-air travel, prompting a critical review of what went wrong and an objective assessment of German engineering, in the landmark scientific retrospective entitled, *Was Haben Wir Uns Dabei Bloß Gedacht?* Also known by its more common English title, *What On Earth Were We Thinking?*

The *Hindenburg* was the largest airship ever to fly, about four times the length of a 747. Photographers and news reporters were on hand for the May 6 arrival when, without warning, the dirigible blew up, erupting in flames that engulfed the airship end to end in seconds. A half a minute later, the burned-out skeleton of the ship lay gnarled and smoking on the ground. With newsreel camera and radio announcers serendipitously on the scene, the disaster was caught on film.

Radio listeners heard the trembling words of newsman Herb Morrison, "It's crashing. It's crashing. Terrible! . . . It's bursting into flames, and it's falling on the mooring mast." He sobs, "Oh, the humanity!"

Although his emotional account claimed, "This is one of the worst catastrophes in the world!" some later criticized Herb "Prone-to-Hyperbole" Morrison's statement as "as little over the top."

Though spectacular from a combustion standpoint, the accident, comparably speaking, was not even as deadly as some minor Amtrak

accidents. Furthermore, it's hard to muster much sympathy over the destruction of a German airship with a giant Nazi swastika logo painted on the tail, so if you had to put together your own list called "Tragedies I Am Not Going to Lose Much Sleep Over," the exploding *Hindenburg* would likely be somewhere near the top.

But the most vivid image ballooning conjures up is in the Hollywood ending of *The Wizard of Oz,* when a geezerly, bumbling Wizard, exposed as a fraud and rapscallion, tries leaving the Emerald City in a getaway balloon he apparently kept at the ready. Since Kansas is on the way, the Wizard agrees to drop off his visitors. But inexperienced at piloting a balloon, the Wizard lifts off prematurely, and leaves Judy Garland and her stunned friends stranded there in Oz, where disheartened, she eventually sinks deep into depression, alcohol, and drugs.

Adventure Vacations

HEN I VACATION, I PREFER A SAFE AND SUNNY CALYPSO-
style Caribbean island or a visit to some museum-laden European
capital where native speakers fawn over me because I am an American tourist, even if we, as Americans, are universally hated for what
we believe and tolerated only because we bring traveler's checks. I
like to limit myself to destinations that not only have electricity, but
sport familiar wall outlets that will graciously accept my shaver and
travel iron. I enjoy traipsing about countries where I can easily cab to
a Zagat-rated restaurant, where the water is drinkable, where there is
little chance of a military coup while I am visiting, and where I cannot actually see their sewage. I never like to be far from an on-duty
concierge.

A nice holiday includes languishing poolside at a beachfront property with a piña colada in hand and sunblock 9 slathered over my
sun-glistening body, where the greatest danger is shopping, if I
gullibly pay for something with a hundred-dollar bill and get back
what I think is my change in the indigenous currency but is, in fact,
a handful of colorful wrappers from their pastries.

For the rugged and thrill-seeking, adventure vacations offer an
adrenaline-triggering alternative to single's cruises or resorts serving
coconut shrimp. Intrepid tourists are willing to sign up for strenuous, unpredictable, and out-and-out perilous junkets to jungles and
glaciers, forgoing safety, comfort, clean sheets, and everything the
Occupational Safety and Health Administration stands for. The In-

ternet promotes trips down Class V white water, deep-sea explo-
ration of rusty shipwrecks, dog-sledding along the trail of the Idi-
tarod, auto racing, heli-skiing, and vacations where hunters track you
down in the deep woods of the Ozarks, reenacting scenes from the
film *Deliverance*.

Vacationers intent on trekking down one of these less-traveled
paths will politely pass up a week sitting on a padded stool at a casino
in exchange for an eco-vacation where they will spend seven days
and thousands of dollars to travel the remote Amazonian backwater
in a dugout canoe or sweat alongside the locals in order to build a la-
trine in a war-torn Rwandan village. Others choose to commune
with endangered wild animals, full well knowing that if one turns on
them, no other ecologically astute fellow adventurer will come to the
rescue for fear of harming one of the last members of the vanishing
species the group has paid to visit.

On these outings, travelers relinquish room service to be without
toilets and rudimentary hygiene, where the closest they will come to
a shower is getting sprayed unexpectedly by a urinating water ox.
Meals are often limited to grubs and tree bark. No one can guarantee these tourists' safety, especially in far-flung locations that are so
dangerous that the locals seldom live beyond the age of twenty-five.
This is the kind of non-pampering retreat where there is a good
chance that your luggage could return without you.

Safaris to the African subcontinent give urban dwellers a look at
wild animals up close in their native surroundings. As a safari goer, you
can be strapped voluntarily atop a chartered elephant, bouncing as your
mammalian conveyance lumbers along, hanging on as if you were in a
whitewater raft, knowing a twelve-foot fall out the back of the elephant saddle could be dangerous, but not nearly so much as falling out
of the front and into the path of your nonchalantly meandering mammalian vehicle, which, like a diesel locomotive can take a considerable
number of feet before it is able to come to a complete stop.

Alternatively, you can sightsee the savannah in an open-topped
Land Rover, driving through fender-height brush. Your vehicle travels slowly on the open plains alongside migrating gazelle, but is
poised for a rapid shift into high gear to outrun a rhinoceros, an ani-

mal with poor vision and who will charge you because it believes your four-wheel-drive vehicle to be either something to eat or something with which it can joyfully mate. For your own protection, you hire the Land Rover that has passenger- and driver-side airbags that safely deploy if you are rammed from the side by fauna. Safari vehicles may also put you at risk from the bite from a deadly black mambo if one decides to drop itself through your open sunroof.

Jungle expeditions may also expose tourists to certain dangers if they happened upon wildlife poachers, who as it turns out, are even more life threatening to passersby than they are to the rhino or bull elephant they are chasing. Not wanting to be later apprehended, poachers will hunt you down if they think you can identify them. You should assume that someone who does not care about killing one of the last twelve members of nearly extinct species will not hesitate to kill you, a human, and a member of a species that is not especially endangered.

Still, other amateur peril-seekers will pay a scuba guide hundreds of dollars in order to spend an hour in a shark cage, floating among a circling school of curious and perpetually hungry hammerheads or great whites, separated from these Chondrichthyes only by a lightweight cell whose thin security bars couldn't keep a neighbor's child out of your basement. Though you pay for the experience, the sharks are the ones most appreciative of the interspecies encounter, swimming by causally, pretending not to notice you, but actually eyeing you as some kind of a treat in a see-through box. No one can predict the exact day this will happen, but sometime in the near evolutionary future, sharks will figure out how latches work.

Following natural disaster has also become a popular pastime, most notably in the form of tornado chasing. Thrill seekers intrigued by the unrestrained forces of wind will spend part of the late summer in the rural plains of Kansas, behind the wheel of rental vans, crisscrossing the countryside in pursuit of twisters, reversing directions on a whim if they hear a bigger one is five hundred miles the other way. With video camcorders at their sides, they aim viewfinders toward the dark gray haze, recording grainy images of foreboding storm clouds. Tornado chasers are on the lookout for spiraling funnels that

drop from the under regions of clouds and point downward like giant index fingers toward the prairie floor. A reasonably endowed tornado can suck up entire sections of Iowa, leveling communities and spreading a wood frame home across two counties, leaving pieces no larger than a child's fist. Twisters move at over one hundred miles an hour and can overtake a four-cylinder rental car with very little effort. Midwesterners, who know better than to stand anywhere near such a powerful vacuum, hightail a retreat, amused, as they watch tourists gleefully heading in the other direction.

Those more interested in fire than wind hike on the rim of volcanos, looking down the throat of fire-spewing mountains at the elemental forces that gave birth to our stony planet. Deep in the earth's core is a continually replenishing supply of liquid rock, kept hot over billions of years in an underground furnace, ready to squirt outward to form new land masses when a breach in the previously formed crust allows it to escape to the surface. From this gurgling material, our continents and ocean floors have hardened into a number of floating plates, which bob merrily on top of our planet's slurpy mantle, moving about over time, careening into each other like slowly moving bumper cars. Where they rub, open sores form, which allow even more bubbling rock to seep out. After spilling over a mountainside through a volcanic peak, the overflowing molten rock called lava hardens, and in these places our planet becomes just a little thicker.

Both professional and amateur volcanologists are willing to journey thousands of miles to visit these sites and view the most violent of planetary forces close up. They get a factory tour of Earth and see firsthand how continents were created.

Of all types, the safest to visit is an extinct volcano, once virile but now feeble after its last eruption, choked off from its lava supply, safely stoppered and docile. With the shaft leading to the center of the earth congested, you are pretty much assured that the vent will never reopen and splatter you with warm lava.

Almost as safe as a fully dead volcano is one classified as a dormant peak, one that has behaved quietly for a few million years. It could be eons before it stirs, if it ever does again. Now cut off from its magma supply and the pressures from the under-geology, the summit is quite

safe, so much so that you might be tempted to act belligerently in its presence, daring it to explode, taunting its bottled-up power with cocky catcalls and epithets, calling it "an impotent spout" as you dance disrespectfully upon its plug with carefree impunity, assured its awakening in your geologically brief lifetime is highly unlikely.

Thrill-seeking hikers, those not content to stroll about the inert rock encrusted craters of sleeping or dead volcanoes, search out adventure aboard active ones. Most of Earth's fully functioning vents are located around the Pacific's edges in the so-called Ring of Fire. Each volcano is a time bomb, bottled up angrily for now, but waiting to let loose an explosion of rock, ash, gas, and lava with little advance notice.

Explorers delight in walking about the dorsal opening of an actively practicing volcano while it smokes and simmers. Fearlessly, visitors balance along the rim of a caldera, peering down the open chute into the belly of the planet, toward a cauldron where million-year-old magma bubbles. Even without lava flowing, searing blasts of Hell-borne thermal currents travel upward along the conduit's outer walls, ready to incinerate anyone standing top side. Hikers risk a tumble into a bottomless abyss, down miles of darkness until they land and instantly vaporize in the glowing igneous reservoirs. Noxious sulfur compounds and toxic gases, the poisonous flatulence of Mother Earth, spew upward to choke hikers during the literally breathtaking trek. These are the pungent aromas of planetary creation, so you gather from the experience that for the first billion years or so, the earth didn't smell too good.

Most frightening for a wayfarer is a visit at the ill-fated moment the flimsy cork holding the planet back at great pressure ruptures, spewing boulders and gases fifty thousand feet skyward as the crater's kettle lid blows off. Seconds later, the mountain overflows. Bubbling and gurgling liquid earth spills over the lip of the volcano and splashes soupy rock onto any nearby tour guides, their followers, and surrounding countryside.

Even if you are miles away from the mountain's herniated opening at the moment of eruption, you could be buried by a dense cloud of scalding volcanic ash, rock, and gases called pyroclastic flow, an av-

alanche of superheated geologic ejecta sometimes thirty or more feet high, which crashes down the slopes in a tsunami-like wave. The wall engulfs and instantly gasifies everyone in its path. With temperatures approaching 1,500 degrees F., forests are charred and stomped down like wheat fields. Unlike slowly moving lava, which you can deftly sidestep, the debris flow moves at hundreds of miles per hour, so you will find it useless trying to outrun the sizzling dust cloud as it buries you, your car, thermos, and camera and makes everything it blankets part of the ever growing pyroclastic flow. Still molten when it comes to rest at the bottom of the slope, the pyroclastic cloud cools into rock with a glassy surface. Here it is finally reunited with the lava, which has taken a more leisurely and scenic trip down the outer wall of the mountain.

Some visitors like to hike about the newly formed land outcrops shortly after a volcano has erupted, knowing they are the first to walk on earth's most recently manufactured rock, which is still cooling, born in the brief planetary episode occurring in their lifetime, and destined to outlast them by several million years. Lava fields harden from the top down, starting with a thin basaltic skin overlaying a still moist simmering center with the consistency of taffy. More than one unlucky hiker has broken through, like a chubby ice skater on a not-completely-frozen lake.

The volcano-based islands of Hawaii continue to expand through the concentric expansion of outflowing hot rock, annually appending new real estate for homes, hotels, and shopping malls, a fortuitous geologic event coinciding with the state's growing popularity, accommodating the need for new land in a way that Nebraska and other nonvolcanic states cannot.

Volcanoes dramatically illustrate the awe-provoking determination of the planet to create. On the other end of geologic life cycle is nature's, simply put, destructive nature. Earthquakes are acute attacks of Mother Earth's anger that can level cities, open serpentine creases along fault lines, and grind anything unlucky enough to get caught into bits. Within seconds, our lives and the monuments we have created can be consumed in the massive tectonic jaws of Earth.

More leisurely and determined, erosion is a diabolically destruc-

tive force. The actions of a gently flowing brook or a cool breeze, so innocent and serene, quietly mask the forces that are intent on destroying the planet behind our backs.

The determined gurgling of a stream will wear away the earth a tiny bit at a time, rubbing up against a sandy bank, dislodging an easily ignored fleck of gravel that is washed a few inches at a time downstream, nudging along a little blot of mud, and sometimes loosening up some silt from the bottom. Erosion is systematic destruction on a microscale, thinly spread over hundreds of thousands of years. So very little is abraded over the course of a single human lifetime, erosion often goes undetected—acting quietly, never greedy, never arousing suspicion—like an embezzler who is smart enough to steal just a tiny bit at a time in order to get away with it unnoticed.

Demolition is part of the earth's life cycle. What nature creates in one epoch, it tears down sometime later, keeping our planet in geologic balance, so that Earth does not expand unchecked, growing out of control like a tumor and imposing on the orbits of neighboring Venus and Mars. Erosion is nature's most patient force, and given enough time, it will flatten mighty mountains, reshape continents, and continually re-hem our shorelines.

If you want to find one of the most dramatic examples of erosion's abrasive might, look no further than the American Southwest and its Grand Canyon. Here you will stand awestruck at a mile-deep divide zigzagging along the floor of Arizona, flanked by walls of red rock towering up both sides. It is a laceration carved into the desert by six million years of rubbing by the Colorado River and the Southwest desert winds.

As you stare at its sculpted walls, it is hard to believe that this giant crease was created by two otherwise peaceful forces, the first being the trickle of water, merrily splashing downstream on its seaward adventure, peeling off the earth a little at a time on its voyage southward. Over time, the gentle tinkling ate a huge gash and exposed the desert in cross section. Its action stripped away billions of tons of riverbed, pieces of the states of Colorado, Utah, and Arizona, and dumped whatever it was able to carry over the U.S. border into the Sonora and San Luis Rio Colorado regions to the south. Geologists

will agree that much of Mexico today is simply "secondhand United States."

Delicate breezes, too, have contributed to the wanton destruction of the area, pushing the walls back farther, cutting the chasm wider, and sanding the canyon rough. Air, that substance delicate enough for us to suck up through our nostrils, is mighty enough to scrub back hundreds of meters of sandstone and shale, yet ironically, we can continue to breathe it in without it wearing away the much softer inside of our noses.

In any case, you have to respect the geologic workmanship of both the river and the breeze. Of all the earth forces around you, erosion is still among the safest, unlike a volcano that can erupt with little warning or an earthquake that can nervously crack open the ground and swallow you whole before you have time to sidestep it. You would have to stand in the same place in the Grand Canyon for a very, very long time for erosion to be personally dangerous to you.

The canyon's natural beauty and remarkable size defy articulate description by either cowpoke or poet. Where you might be content with the phrase "purple mountain majesties" or "fruited plains" in other situations, there are no words to satisfactorily describe the Grand Canyon, its magnificent rock formations, towering buttes, painted mesas that change color with the slightest shift in the posture of clouds, and ribbons of earth-red color running in parallel toward a distant vanishing point. Your lower jaw will free-fall as you survey the canyon's size and realize that the river, way down below you, was once where you are now. All it takes is standing in the magnificence of the Grand Canyon to make even the most steadfast atheist reconsider, maybe now concerned that if there is a God and He is now looking down, what is to keep Him from flicking a disbeliever off the north rim with an invisible poke of an Almighty index finger?

Of all the canyons in this hemisphere and perhaps the world, this one surely is the Grandest.

Many tourists are satisfied to see only as much of the Grand Canyon as is visible from the scenic roadway rest stop. They anchor their feet firmly on bedrock and peer carefully over the edge for just

a moment to the canyon floor below. Of all the views, the one from the upper plateau is the most convenient and can be done if you want to ogle the canyon fast.

No American born in the twentieth century can stand on the edge of the north rim behind a feeble guardrail, looking straight down a vertical mile, and not involuntarily flash the image of the previously mentioned Wile E. Coyote, the cartoon antihero who so often underestimated the effectiveness of his giant slingshot or misjudged the edge of the mesa when the roadway abruptly turned but he could not.

I know no one who cannot picture Coyote fruitlessly fighting the straight-line force of inertia and frantically backpedaling with his feet without success until he stops eight or ten feet over the edge, now suspended, stationary, looking at us and looking down, gravity not kicking in until that moment of enlightenment when he finally becomes aware of his tragic miscalculation.

We watch him plummet, with his arms and legs spread outward as he grows smaller and smaller and finally becomes a dot that produces a tiny puff of dust cloud rising up from the canyon floor when he finally hits, occurring at the same moment as the whistling generated by his fall ends with a quiet thud.

But the most impressive vantage of the canyon is the view from ninety degrees, looking straight at it eyeball-to-stratum. The cutaway view of North American geology chronicles the earth's story in a dirt retrospective, disclosing the planet's climate and animal population in the exposed fossil and mineral record. Embossed in rock are the individual snapshots, negatives actually, of animals whose representatives lived at a certain time and certain elevation. Long before the river ate its way downward, nature piled up marine deposits, one atop the other like flapjacks, forming the limestone, sandstone, and shale that give the canyon its layered look.

Those visitors to the canyon willing to make a trip down the escarpment will enjoy a detailed tutorial on their descent to the canyon floor, where the river, as the cliché would suggest, has made its own bed. A climb down offers a breathtaking backward journey, each layer a chapter that tells a little more about what the earth was doing at any particular moment.

Descending on foot is the most difficult and tiring means of travel, designed for the hardiest of tourists, though a pedestrian amble to the canyon bottom delivers the greatest visual return on investment. You spiral downward at your own pace, stopping, leaning over, taking time to observe, to smell, to touch, getting as close to the stratified walls as you want. The most rewarding of all descents, yes, but when tromping down the narrow cliff side trails in your shorts, you are also more likely to scratch up against a needling cactus or confront a coiled snake or upward-pointing scorpion. If you are painfully nipped in any of these cases, all you can do is "walk it off."

A narrow rocky trail hugs the outside of the canyon wall, jutting out in some places only a few feet. On one side, a sheer rock wall shoots upward, on the other, a precipitous cliff drops vertically with uninterrupted access to the canyon below. Along the route, you navigate thirty-five-degree declines, switchbacks, and hairpin turns. No one cleans the path regularly, so it is littered with natural trip hazards including litter, rocks, mounds of sand, tufts of vegetation, and the skeletal remains of previously thirsty desert animals. If you do fall over the edge, the paths on the side walls below are too narrow to stop you even if you are lucky enough to land on one, so you will sadly continue to bounce from terrace to terrace as you tumble through geologic time.

You descend thousands of years with every step, moving through the Permian Period, the Mississippian Period and the Devonian Period. You may reach the Precambrian by noon, stop to have some water or make a cell phone call from a half billion years ago.

The meandering route is frightening at first, and you must put your trust in your own sense of balance. You want to enjoy the spectacular view, but you spend a lot of time staring down at your feet and continuing to check the integrity of the trail. You recall that you have never thanked the balancing mechanism in your inner ear properly for its reliable work through the years, so you take a moment to do so.

Should you have limited time and do not mind spending extra cash, you can get to the canyon floor posthaste by taking a helicopter

ride instead, a cut-to-the-chase plunge to the bottom of the gorge. While others are choking on trail dust, some of which the helicopters kick up, you travel in cushy leather seats with an air-conditioning duct blowing directly onto your face. The most strenuous activity of your day will be leaning forward slightly to reach for another piece of paté.

The third and by far most popular mode of vertical transit is a slow and determined trip on the back of a pack mule. Although every fiber of my being tells me otherwise, descent via mule is reputed to be the safest means of travel down the steep cliffside trails.

Most people think of a mule as a rather stupid-looking animal, somewhat gawky with protruding ears and a repertoire of only two expressions, those being either "angry" or "bumpkin." It has an odd rectangular shape, much squatter than a sleek and graceful horse, the kind of shape you would imagine moves forward a few feet awkwardly, then jerks spasmodically just before it buckles and falls over. The hee-hawing when it wants to complain about something doesn't do much to win it respect.

A mule, the unfertile offspring of a donkey and a horse, does not look like the kind of animal with whom you want to entrust your life. But you will be surprised to learn that they are legendary for their sure-footedness. They have an exquisite sense of balance and do not fear heights. Mules are poised and athletic and do not stumble over rocks, nor when the going gets tough, do they fluster easily. Like magnets, their hooves adhere to the rocky ledges, and though you may see one wearing a bandana or a dopey straw hat with the holes poked out for their ears, they take their jobs quite seriously.

You never hear stories of mules tripping over rocks and tumbling head over tail for four thousand feet, or about one unexpectedly started by a Gila monster or snake and involuntarily backing over a chasm. I have read nothing of innocent tourists killed by an ungainly equine that has toppled onto them from a higher ledge.

On most days, you will see a platoon of these animals, marching in an orderly file, head to ass's ass, carrying their valuable human payload on the few-hour trip a vertical mile down. Helicopters, equipped with sophisticated navigational equipment have ultimately

proven to be more dangerous than mules, occasionally yawing off course and slamming explosively into the canyon walls or crashing into each other, something that even the most dullard of mules will not do.

Still, it does take considerable faith in the animal kingdom for me to forgo the comfort of a half million dollars in aero technology and instead put my life in the so-called hands of a farm animal who is stubborn, not very intelligent, and tolerates me only because I have just given him a carrot. Any joy I am experiencing in the breathtaking beauty of the canyon might at any moment be overwritten by the confrontational behavior of a bored mule who may want to demonstrate that he is not very happy, because (1) I am sitting on top of him, and (2) he has not fully come to terms with his own infertility and is a little moody knowing he will never get to screw anything.

I just pray he does not head toward the edge of the canyon, nonchalantly curtsy ever so slightly to the side, and dump me over the ledge.

On mule top, you will spend a number of rump-numbing hours spiraling down the trails, bouncing up and down incessantly in your unpadded, sunbaked leather saddle. You are a victim of this repetitive action as your entire weight slams downward thirty times a minute on a portion of your body only ten inches square. A physician you may not be, but you know that this jostling cannot be good for your butt and rectal valve.

You finally arrive on the canyon floor. It is dry and parched and not any nicer up close than it appeared from a mile up. You think about the trip back and how much harder it will be going uphill. As you stand near at the bottom of the gorge, erosion is continuing, so technically the longer you dawdle there, the farther your trip back up will be.

I imagine the inhabitants of the tiny parched desert town on the canyon floor are people who intended to visit for the day, but subsequently decided to spend the rest of their years living there rather than to undergo the torturous ordeal of returning topside.

Spectacular views are not limited to natural high vistas such as the Grand Canyon, Yosemite's El Capitán, or Africa's Victoria Falls. If you are not one to amble in natural beauty and prefer staying a short

cab ride to hotels, restaurants, and a twenty-four-hour pharmacy, you might think about the breathtaking high-altitude walk across the picturesque Sydney Harbor Bridge, located in Australia, a country already well established as dangerous to slog about.

The televised 2000 Olympics introduced the rest of us to the Australian city of Sydney, its skyline, the fan-petaled architecture of its Opera House, and the view of a spectacular deep blue harbor.

At four-hundred-plus feet, the Sydney Harbor Bridge, one of the city's most impressive landmarks, is the world's highest steel arch crossing. Built in 1932, the bridge links the city center in the south and the residential north, where previously a ferry ride or a twelve-mile detour with five bridge crossings were the only other transit options.

Weighing in at over fifty-two thousand tons, the beefy cantilever with its massive steel supports and neatly spaced nubby rivets is no skimpy overpass. Nor is it some gratuitously graceful, wispy, anorexic suspension bridge reaching bank to bank in some frilly backward aching ballet pose. No, the Sydney Harbor Bridge is not subtle, but a brutish crisscross of muscular girders, the hulking kind of bridge you expect self-sufficient and rugged Australians to prefer. A 160-foot-wide road deck carries automobile and rail traffic 150 feet above the shipping lanes, high enough that even the largest vessels clear it unimpeded.

Since 1989, the Sydney Harbor Climb has seduced tens of thousands of visitors willing to snap themselves onto a safety line and climb the superstructure to enjoy an incomparable panorama of Sydney from the height of a forty-story building.

Anyone who has previously taken the tour will tell you it is not to be missed. After a safety orientation in what is strangely the basement of the bridge, you don a loose-fitting gray jumpsuit equipped with safety clips and the all-important harness that will keep you from tumbling off the walkways. You may carry nothing, preventing you from accidentally or purposely dropping objects onto harbor cruise boats or car windshields. Because you will not be encumbered by cameras, soft drink bottles, or snacks, you will also have both arms free for grabbing safety supports or for unrestrained flailing in the

event that you do fall. I personally believe that the gray jumpsuits are used because the color helps you stand out from water if they have to look for you there.

You snap your mountaineering-style carabiner onto a safety cable on the guardrail. It will remind you of a dog run. You follow an open grid catwalk through the bridge pylon, out over the water, up an un-invitingly steep ladder that pops you out at deck level, first face-to-face with traffic and then after many more steps, well over the roadway. You climb another seemingly endless ladder where you join the eastern arch and begin the final assault of the 1,650-foot main arch girder. You ascend slowly and in single file, collectively traveling at the speed of the slowest in your party. The more cautious in your group climb hand over hand on the guardrail during the hour-and-a-half climb.

You plant your feet firmly on a walkway that is less than four feet wide. The railing and your snap ring convince you that you are safe, and if you slip or even if you are racked with an irrational impulse to throw yourself off the bridge, you will just dangle from the span about three feet from where you are standing.

You reach the summit, and if you have kept your eyes pinched shut on the climb and have ascended by "touch," you will probably want to open them briefly because (1) you have spent a lot of money to get here, and (2) you want to make sure that while your eyes were closed, everyone else did not leave and you are now alone on the top of this very dangerous bridge.

You roost a considerable distance above Australia. Exhilaration re-places fear as you stand on the girdered perch surveying a breathtak-ing view from 440 feet.

Alongside your half dozen or so fellow climbers, you enjoy the unfettered view in all directions, looking down at the busy shipping lanes where vessels appear the size of paper clips and cars are tiny moving rectangles of color. You look out toward the airport, where airplanes on final approach are passing through your altitude while still a distance from the end of the runway. Most impressive, though, the Opera House below you blossoms like some big cement arti-choke. You gasp, because the unobstructed view is spectacular. You smile, as they take your picture so you can convince friends back

home you were here. Vomiting from this distance would be both disgusting and dangerous to those below. You are continually comforted by the sight of your snap ring and safety line. You know that
without them, a fall to the water would be like hitting concrete, and
a fall to the roadway deck, a comforting 150 feet closer, would be just
as fatal because it actually is made of concrete. Even if you survived a
plummet from that height onto the roadway, you would not last long
sprawled out in the busy Sydney commuter traffic.

You are now one with the bridge and relatively safe, and the only
possible danger now is if the bridge collapses, since you will not have
time to unclip yourself from it before the massive span spirals to the
bottom of Sydney Harbor.

You can make the trip during the day, at dusk to see the Australian
sunset, or at night, wearing a miner's headlight on your cap. Each
tour offers the same vantage point but vastly different scenes, like a
series of Monet paintings. Even for the fearful, the altitude will offer
some consolation. Sure, you are more than four hundred feet above
the ground, but you should remember, you are also in a country populated with a disproportionate number of sharks and poisonous reptiles, and at least for the moment, you are as far from them as you can
get and still be in Sydney.

Not a fan of heights, I would be afraid of making it about a third
of the way up, and then realizing where I was, would panic, wrapping
my arms in an unreleasable bear hug around a girder, telling everyone else in my group that I did not plan to go any farther and please
just walk around me. For the next few days, other tour guides would
have to explain my presence and apologize for any inconvenience to
those in their groups, that is until the Australian coast guard finally
dispatched one of its medical evacuation helicopters to pry me off
the bridge and airlift me to safety.

Because I do not trust my own sure-footedness, I am still uncertain whether I will be making the trip to the top of the Sydney Harbor Bridge if I visit Australia, though I might consider the perilous
ascent if I could go up on some kind of a donkey.

The Revenge of Mountains

SOME RISKY ACTIVITIES PIT US AS HUMANS AGAINST THE obstacles that nature itself heaves before us, a pretty unfair match since nature has had at least a thirteen-billion-year running start.

Our mountains are Earth's most grandiose monuments, solidly planted and immovable. Embedded like molars deep into the Earth's gums, they tower above continents and rise up from the floor of oceans. Imposing free-form sculptures, rippling outcroppings of rock that have erupted from the core of our planet, they intimidate all those in their shadows. Patient and unflappable, they flinch at nothing short of powerful explosives.

In the presence of mountains, we are tiny and insignificant, a speck of untethered organic matter. We are soft and frail, not mighty and impenetrable. We are easily crushed by a casually discarded boulder a land mass brazenly flicks from its surface, to us huge and deadly as it rumbles by, but a barely noticeable cinder to a mighty igneous range. Should we slip off a mountain, we splatter at its feet.

Mountains are primitive and dangerous, with steep sides and sharp edges. They hide danger at every elevation and deal out the full spectrum of world climate within the span of five vertical miles, including searing equatorial heat in the jungle lowlands and subzero frigid cold and hurricane-strength wind at its ice-crowned summit. Some ranges live secretly submerged under thousands of feet of seawater, and others puncture the stratosphere. Our puny eighty-plus-year lifespan is an inconspicuous blip against the hundred-million-year

existence of this venerable geology. Our mountains, without brain or life, still humble us.

Climbing a mountain is a symbol of facing the most challenging of tasks. Triumphing over nature's most formidable obstacles demands extraordinary strength, bravery, endurance, and ingenuity that only the most daring among us will ever enjoy. In battling a mountain, the stakes don't get much higher. It is us against the earth itself. Climbers crawl up a mountain's skin while the mountain does its best to thwart their intrusions.

Among the purest forms of assault are the daring pursuits of the free climbers, who scale vertical cliff walls, not to reach a snow-capped peak, but just for the experience of ascending the rock face, alone and vulnerable, without benefit of ropes, hammers, pins, or any other climbing apparatus, which they see as unnecessary crutches. Free climbers confront the steepest mountainside one-on-one, armed only with, quite simply, their arms.

They powder their muscular hands and grab on to barely visible little nubs on the sheer granite cliff face, hoisting their entire body mass skyward by the strength of their fingertips.

Some climbers seek out surfaces that most of us would believe defy climbing, ascending surfaces whose complexions appear mirror-smooth and cut a climber no breaks. But this is the challenge that free climbers seek. Daring adventurers may claw upward two thousand feet or more. Others are content to climb extremely challenging faces a mere twenty feet off the ground, still knowing that a drop from that elevation can be just as fatal, and the only advantage is not having to scream in terror for quite as long before impact.

Like insects, free climbers adhere to ninety-degree surfaces as if by suction. They are equal parts acrobat and chess player, always thinking two or three moves ahead as they twist and contort to find a flake of surface to pinch or cleavage into which to wedge a toe or heel. Midclimb up a half-mile vertical granite wall, there is no place to rest and no easy way to turn back.

Climbers shove an elbow deep into a crevice and take advantage of any imperfection the mountain unwillingly exposes. Using the most expedient appendage available, they reach a leg upward and

grab a toehold on a shelf of rock well above their heads or reach an arm out as far as it will span to grab at a nose-size bulge on the cliff. While hanging in an uncomfortable position that does not offer much leverage, they summon up a momentary spurt of energy in order to lift their bodies to the next impossible position.

With every move, they face uncertainty, not knowing whether a piece of shale will support their entire weight or crumble in their fingers. And of course, climbers fear reaching blindly into a deep crack, pulling themselves upward, and finding to their disappointment that the crevice now at eye level had been previously claimed as home by a territorial mother snake.

Free climbers wear lightweight clothing and snugly fitting shoes, bottoms clad with sticky rubber soles. The chalk used to keep fingers dry enough to prevent the climber from sliding off the mountain is carried in a bag worn about the waist. This mountaineering purse is just big enough to hold a driver's license or laminated social security card as well, to make the subsequent identification of a fallen climber much easier than through a DNA match.

The majority of cliffs submit to conquest in an afternoon, so that amateur climbers can return to their desk jobs the next morning. The brevity of a four-hour climb does not diminish its danger or its difficulty, but even so, these intrepid climbers are considered mere hikers by alpine mountaineers, who are willing to invest months of their lives and endure the planet's harshest conditions to say they reached the summit of the world's tallest mountains.

Elite alpine climbers are the romantic heroes of mountaineering. They are portrayed in photographs, their beards covered with frozen ice and snow, skin reddened by the wind and unfiltered ultraviolet rays, and gloved hands wrapped around ominously lethal-looking ice axes. They cling to cliffs, tied to each other and to the mountain by ropes—driving pins into solid masonry, kicking saber-toed boots into ice walls, chipping away loose rock with a hammer, and inching up terrain that is fighting their every move. The exhilaration is counterbalanced by the realization that one misstep would be all it takes to fatally plummet back to the place they were camping a week earlier.

These men and women, able to withstand conditions that would make most of us run for warmth, do battle with nature's most terrifying obstructions. They look up at our mighty mountains, shake their fists in defiance, and vow to stand taller than their towering granite adversaries.

A climb is not a leisurely outing or even a hearty stroll, not a day trip or even a deep jungle hike, but a torturous expedition that demands months of careful planning and physical conditioning. Climbers are forced to endure hardships and extreme situations that are universally deemed "no picnic." They inch their way slowly, breaking through the cloud canopy, upwards of 10,000, 20,000, nearly 30,000 feet, past the snow line, past the tundra, to ice-capped peaks where it is always winter, beyond a line in the permanently frozen ground where the conditions are so hostile that even our trees, among the most resilient and forgiving of organisms, refuse to grow. Mountain climbers adventure toward the unknown, where weather can turn from unpleasant to lethal in a few minutes. Here a tiny mistake that would produce a polite "oops" at sea level can cost a climber and partner their lives.

Each inhabited continent has a slope or two lofty enough to summon climbers to their peaks. In northern Tanzania, Kilimanjaro, at 19,341 feet, is the tallest mountain on the African continent, and while 10,000 feet shorter than dozens of the Asian mountain giants, it is still no mountain for sissies. In South America, teams are eager to scale Antisana in the Andes and the peaks of Patagonia. In Europe, some ski the Alps while the more adventuresome prefer crawling up their rocky, icy rinds. You can attack the jagged limestone and dolomite peaks of the Alps from Switzerland, Italy, Austria, Germany, or France, continually finding new routes to explore. In Turkey, Mount Ararat is open to climbers who can climb to heights where Noah's ark is alleged to be buried.

Even the United States claims title to some of the more demanding peaks, including Mount Rainer in the Cascade Range of west central Washington State. Nearby Mount St. Helens vaults high above the state and remains a backbreaking assault, notwithstanding the recent volcanic incident where its summit was blown to

smithereens. That it has a lesser top now does not make it that much easier to climb.

The most popular alpine climbing in the United States is in the Rocky Mountains, a high stone wall that starts well above the boundary of Canada and zigzags its way south to New Mexico. In Alaska, Mount McKinley, at over twenty thousand feet, pointed and hard-edged and very difficult to navigate, promotes itself as the highest perch in North America.

The most legendary mountains, however, are found in Central Asia, and specifically in the Himalayas of Central Asia, which contain nine of the world's ten highest peaks. The penultimate summit, K2, rises 28,280 feet within the misty Karakoram Range in Jammu and Kashmir, missing by a mere 748 feet the laurel of tallest mountain. In its shadows, shorter, stout, yet equally toilsome mountains such as Kanchejunga, Manga Parbat, and Makalu stretch across the top fringe of the Indian continent. Annapurna in Nepal, poking the clouds at 26,545 feet, does not carry the panache of some of the mightier peaks, but climbers will tell you how they would not relish falling from it. A climber could spend a lifetime and never repeat the same mountain route twice.

Though many mountains have their own personalities and aggressive attitudes toward visitors, no matter where you decide to mount, you will face similar difficulties. You can count on the mountain remaining steadfast in its mission to prevent you from succeeding, parrying your assaults with cumbersome paths and nasty tricks. At the top, weather is the cruelest on all of Earth, more dangerous than the Arctic and Antarctic, dealing out climate so brutal, it will surely snuff out your unprotected life within hours. When it comes down to you versus the elements, the smart money is on the elements.

No mountain commands the respect of Mount Everest, topping off at over twenty-nine thousand feet, and at an altitude where pressurized jetliners fly. Like the rest of the Himalayan range, Everest was formed by the upward thrust of the Indian and Eurasian tectonic plates, which, acting like an underwire bra, forced the seams upward to form perky mountain peaks.

Located on the border between Tibet and Nepal, Mount Everest

juts up from the Karakoram Range of the Himalayas, a word by the way pronounced as "Himmel-LAY-yuz" by most, but occasionally with the more pretentious pronunciation, "Him-MAUL-yuz", though you should ignore this affected utterance because it is usually made by the same overbearing people who insist on pronouncing the words "EYE-ther" and "to-MAW-toe."

For centuries, Nepal and Tibet closed the mountain to visitors. Westerners, peering at it from more hospitable India, knew it only as an unapproachable distant land hump with the unromantic name of Peak XV. Its summit intrigued Sir George Everest, who was across the border in 1852 conducting the Great Trigonemetrical Survey, a project to measure the earth accurately, so it no longer needed to be casually referred to as "really big," but could be described scientifically as just "how big." Staring at the mountain from his comfy chair 160 miles away, Everest surprisingly calculated Peak XV to be 29,002 feet, a mere twenty-six feet shorter than its actual height.

Some years later, his English successors named the mountain after Everest, thinking that the people living in its shadows had perhaps never even noticed it and certainly never got around to giving it a suitable name. But in fact, this giant backdrop that covered a huge section of their sky was revered by the local Sherpa, who called it Chomolungma, which translates to "Goddess Mother of the World," a kind of name people would not waste on any ordinary mountain.

In 1920, the government of Tibet granted permission to Britain to survey the mountain from its north face. George Leigh Mallory, a schoolteacher and expert climber in his mid-thirties, was chosen to lead the three expeditions. Experienced, fit, and exuberant, Mallory was the ideal leader to carry the banner of the king. He assembled a team of gutsy climbers eager to map the mountain's uncharted regions, valleys, glaciers, cols, steep rock faces, passes, and cul-de-sacs. His climbers would venture into air thinner than anyone had ever wheezed, and perhaps in the process, the Mallory team would enjoy the distinction of being the first to reach its summit.

No matter how hard climbing Everest has been since 1920, no expedition was more difficult and potentially dangerous than this first one. No trail had been tramped down by earlier climbers; no treach-

erous obstacles had been courteously marked. Narrow passes were not yet littered with the retreating frozen bodies of previous climbers, an obvious clue to adventurers who can "read nature" that the trail ahead was a dead end.

Mallory's first expedition explored without benefit of maps, since going over there to create the first ones was rather the whole point of the exercise. So without much information in advance, they had no idea in just how many places they could get really hurt. With each tenuous stride, they ventured another foot into the unknown, where their moment-by-moment choices would either push them forward or be their last. The next snow bridge might offer a path leading straight to the summit or, equally likely, might drop them into a bottomless chasm.

Alpine climbing was a primitive exercise in the 1920s. Comfortable, lightweight, waterproof clothing was unavailable. Mallory made the trip through the death zone of Everest dressed in a tweed jacket and high knickers, carrying a walking stick and wearing a sweater his wife had knitted for him. He was an English gentleman and carried himself up the mountain with the British stiff-upper-lip attitude, which would be subject to additional stiffening in the increasingly frigid air. A veteran gunner of World War I, Mallory was unruffled by setbacks the mountain threw in his way, and was the man who casually stated that he climbed Mount Everest "because it was there."

I envision him staring upward, squinting as the sunlight reflected on the snowy peaks, continuing forward on a still nameless route. He stands, looking at the next obstacle as he tamps down tobacco with his index finger and puffs contemplatively on his pipe.

"I say, old boy," Mallory says, turning to his climbing companion, Andrew Irvine, "shall we jump the crevasse?"

"Jolly," Irvine nods, hopping over the bottomless chasm while grasping a walking sick in one hand and a meerschaum in the other.

Mallory's team made two climbs between 1920 and the end of 1921, both successful in gathering information, but neither taking him and his team to the still-unattainable summit.

George Mallory hesitated before committing to his final expedition in 1922, reluctant, telling his wife of his premonition that he might not be returning from this third junket.

"Don't be silly, Georgie," his wife encouraged. "And besides, I went to the trouble of making you another one of those sweaters you like."

During this third attempt, and a few days short of his thirty-eighth birthday, Mallory, along with colleague Irvine, disappeared. After an exhaustive and unsuccessful search, both were presumed dead, victims of what would become a mountain with a insatiable appetite for Europeans.

It would not be until thirty years later, after a dozen failed attempts, that a British expedition would finally succeed, reaching the elusive summit and coming back down alive, the latter achievement distinguishing a successful expedition from any other kind. The man to reach the summit was New Zealander Edmund Hillary, who was part of a fourteen-member team.

The expedition enlisted the help of the aboriginal people, the Sherpa, who lived at high elevation and were used to the cold. Hired as guides and porters, they would transport the tons of heavy gear, food, and other life-sustaining provisions up the mountain.

On May 29, 1953, Edmund Hillary, along with Sherpa guide Tenzing Norgay, reached the summit of Everest. Other members of the climbing team made it close before retreating, as weather conditions abruptly turned hostile. But only Hillary, who set out on a clear spring morning, was able to slog the few hundred feet more and make it to the peak. History would remember Hillary but forget the names of the other thirteen team members who put up with the conditions for just as long. You have to wonder if the others were chummy to Hillary's face in the years to come, but were also a wee bit miffed that he got all the credit.

Only a climber can sense the elation that Hillary felt standing on the top of the world, looking down through a carpet of clouds. No one knows for sure if these Westerners were really the first to reach the top or whether local Sherpas in the past had made the trip regularly or picnicked there with family but never bothered to mention it to anyone. The only thing for certain is that in May of 1953, one-time beekeeper and avid climber Edmund Hillary was the first person to come down and brag about it.

In recognition of this achievement, Queen Elizabeth knighted Hillary. By his side during the entire climbing adventure was his Sherpa porter, who sadly failed to get a fraction of the accolade, strange because Norgay Tenzing not only did everything that Hillary did, but did so while carrying all the heavy stuff.

For every would-be climber, months of preparation and physical conditioning precede many weeks of difficulty and hardship on the mountain. Mountaineers must be experienced technically, confident in the use of their gear, and competent in scaling walls and ice. Climbers must be strong. They are pulling their body weight and supplies by their own brawn up the mountain, when the conditions would plunge a weaker man into muscle failure. They must be able to ignore pain, freezing cold, and general discomfort, able to fight exhaustion and keep moving ahead in spite of very little sleep, food, or oxygen. A climber must summon up stores of energy and will when all oomph is depleted. An above-average sense of balance is also a plus.

Climbing gear is very specialized and not for those on a tight budget. Should you decide to scale Everest, you will need a supply of reliable pitons and carabiners, pins, and spikes, which you will wedge into cracks and fissures to support the weight of your two-person team. For some of the climb, you will rely on your physical strength to pull your heavily outfitted selves upwards. At other times, you will hoist yourselves with a rope and pulley like some drayage.

Movement is slow going, tedious, and not for the impatient. Two days' progress may advance you only a few hundred meters. Some nights, you will not return to camp to sleep but must bivouac on a mountain ledge, pounding slings into the vertical walls and sleeping in hanging cocoons annexed to a cliff by a nylon rope. Knowing you are suspended by a thin metal piton 20,000 feet up, you may not get much rest.

You pee off the side of the mountain, always maintaining proper cliffside etiquette and vigilantly looking down to ensure that no top

ropers in the middle of a tricky belaying maneuver are directly underneath you.

After weeks of climbing, you reach a top camp at about twenty-six thousand feet, leaving you one daylong climb to the summit. The final ascent starts at night, giving you sufficient time to reach the peak by noon of the following day. Your last challenges include the assault of a vertical wall of ice and snow, called the Hillary Step, rising up for forty feet, then an aerialist walk across a knife-edge ridge leading to the crown. At the top of a small rise, when you can go no farther, you will be standing on the uppermost shelf on our planet, from which there is no direction other than down.

You are in the death zone, a place where the human body can survive only a matter of hours, no matter how well conditioned. The weather here is so inhospitable and unpredictable that there isn't time to savor your victory, much less to dilly-dally. All that work to get to the top buys maybe a few minutes before you must head back down to the safety of a lower camp. So you take a few pictures or you make a cell-phone call, if you are not concerned about the roaming charges. The weather changes quickly, and thunderstorms, lightning, and hail can appear out of nowhere, so unless you turn around promptly, you may end up a "tragic discovery" that will take away a lot of the joy for tomorrow's successful climbers.

Even after you reach the peak, your troubles are far from over. Remember, you have completed only half the round trip and now have to get down safely, a process that has killed just as many climbers, whose deaths are not as much appreciated and often just hushed up in embarrassment.

"He was killed above Base Camp Five on his final assault of the summit," sounds so much hardier than, "He stumbled into a ravine while heading back down to the van."

For those thinking about a climb to the top of Everest, I remind you of the almost endless list of reasons to talk yourself out of it.

First, it is cold, even at Base Camp where a balmy day is one when your water does not freeze. At higher elevations, mercury can dip to a face numbing −40 degrees F. Add a brisk fifty-mile-an-hour breeze and its accompanying wind chill factor, and you will experience cold

that insulated parkas are powerless to block. You don't want to know how cold it gets at the summit. If you are whiny about typical New England winters and the ninety seconds of shivering discomfort you spend getting from a heated car to your front door, you will not be pleased to learn that as a mountaineer, you will spend six to eight uninterrupted weeks outdoors in subzero windy conditions, and the only warmth you will enjoy is when you crawl into a tent with nylon walls $\frac{1}{64}$ inch thick.

Additionally, climbing is exhausting work. Your muscles fail and your body aches. Your appetite wanes, so at a time when you should be carbing up for additional strength, you can eat very little.

You surrender to poor personal hygiene. Your fingernails are tinged with an unattractive rim of filth. Shaving is inconvenient. Little chunks of ice harden in the weave of your beard. Women will find their otherwise-buoyant hair limp and devoid of luster. Exertion still causes sweating underneath your Gore-Tex parka, but a good hot shower during the expedition is out of the question. The only reason that your own smell does not offend you is because the inside walls of your nostrils are frozen solid.

Discomfort and inconvenience may be enough to dissuade you, but real danger awaits you on the mountain.

The human body was not built for life much above twenty thousand feet. One deterrent is frostbite. In frigid temperatures, the cells of the body can freeze solid, causing something akin to, but vastly more serious than, the freezer burn you find on forgotten steak or chicken. Paradoxically, as the destructive process turns the fleshy tops of the nose, ears, fingers, and toes a necrotic blue, frostbite may not even be felt, masked by the anesthetic effect of the gnawing cold.

Many climbers return to find that the resulting gangrene will cost them parts of their bodies, bad enough when you are talking about your toes and fingers, but very, very bad when talking about your nose. Once you get frostbite, there is little you can do. It is one of the few muscular conditions where doctors cannot say, "Just go home and put some ice on it."

Hypothermia occurs when the body becomes too chilled to generate sufficient warmth for the heart, lungs, and other vital organs.

Strangely, as the body chills, the sensory effect is warmth, and some people on the threshold of death begin to strip off clothing because they are feeling uncomfortably hot. In the miraculous evolution of the human species, this is regrettably one of the mistakes that snuck by.

As altitude increases, not only does the temperature drop, but so, too, does the amount of oxygen in the air. At eighteen thousand feet, breathing is strained and the oxygen content in the air falls to 50 percent and at twenty-nine thousand feet, to an even more lung-deflating 30 percent.

Full-out altitude sickness results from rapid ascent into oxygen-stingy air. Without bottled air, you are likely to suffer pulmonary or cerebral edema, too medically complex to explain here, but let it suffice to say you do not want to get either of them. Mountain sickness causes dizziness, light-headedness, nausea, and disorientation, mimicking drunkenness: a problem because you will become faint and know you have to throw up, but might get confused and lost trying to find a place to do it. Oxygen deprivation will cause throbbing headaches. The brain is no longer sharp, you strain to keep concentration focused, and overall judgment is impaired at a time when sound decisions are especially valuable. Climbers hallucinate, some mention hearing orchestras or getting instructions from the Almighty. The thought that you can fly will prove to be troublesome, as well.

Slowing the ascent lessens the effects of altitude sickness, giving the body a period of time to adapt to the starving atmosphere. Climbers commute up and back a few thousand feet a number of times, using the trips to cart supplies to higher camp, spending a few hours there before returning to lower camp to sleep. They stay longer at higher elevation each trip until their lungs have accepted the fact that they are not going to get any more oxygen no matter how much they protest. In a day or two, the climber's body reluctantly adapts to the thinner air, and within forty-eight hours is ready to ascend to an even more oxygen-deprived elevation, making the one that is so uncomfortable at this moment seem like Cancún.

In this punishing environment, the resting heart rate of a world-

they cannot resist. Homer describes a similar overpowering call in the *Odyssey,* in the body of beautiful sirens playing their flutes and luring sailors to a certain death among the rocks. Mountain climbers know the loudest call comes from the rocks themselves.

Most of us would love to visit the rooftop of the planet, but know we will not be strapping oxygen on our dorsum, donning a suit made of Gore-Tex, and, as we wheeze for air, slugging up vertical cliffs of ice against gravity to reach the freezing heights where airplanes fly. Most of us would prefer a mountain appointed with paved roads, frequent rest stops, and shopping. Perhaps one of these days the Nepalese will put in a heated tram that promises to get us back down to our cars before dark.

To be honest, if the bragging is that important to you, it might be a lot easier to just lie and say you were there. Alpine mountaineers are so bundled up when they climb Everest, you could show friends pictures all day claiming they were of you, and no one would have any way to prove otherwise. You could save a lot of time, avoid cerebral edema, breathe oxygen-rich air day and night from the comfort of your climate-controlled home, and not have to go weeks without a hot shower. You would forgo dangling like a chandelier from a ledge at 29,000 feet. The money you saved could be spent on a luxury vacation in Belize, and you would know that if you were dizzy, woozy, and nauseated in a drunkenlike state there, it will be because you had actually been drinking.

Your lie will hurt no one and will not detract from the accomplishment of the honest people who attained what you only wish you could. Personally, I do not feel that your falsehood will cheapen the trips made by others and certainly will not in any way diminish my own triumph when I, Chuck Goldstone, reached the summit without bottled oxygen in the summer of 1991, accompanied by my Sherpa, Tsing Nootwig, a nearly blind man in his mid-eighties, whom I was forced to carry on my shoulders for the last nine hundred meters.

Flights of Fancy

MAMMALS OUR SIZE ARE NOT AERODYNAMIC BY NATURE. Drop us from any height, and we will plunge straight downward. Flap all we want, yet we remain steadfastly earthbound. Fling us high in an skyward arc, and we will follow a predictable trajectory and stay airborne for only a short time before we fall to earth gracelessly, no matter how desperately and spasmodically we flail.

Still, all but the delusional among us, who believe they already can fly, wish we could.

We envy the birds, though simpleminded and worm-eating, who taunt us with their freedom to penetrate the vast ethereal half-dome of blue above us. Ah, who among us doesn't wish we could trade some other evolutionary advancement, say, opposable thumbs, for the ability to fly, so we, too, could soar silently over mountains and lakes, flying straight and true over ground impediments we would otherwise have to walk around?

Determined to overcome our physical deficiencies, we have dreamed of mechanical contraptions that would allow us to break the suction that keeps us and other heavy objects stuck to terra firma.

Early attempts with clip-on wings, vehicles with oscillating fins, flapping ornithopers, and contrivances inspired by drawings of Leonardo da Vinci all proved disastrously unsuccessful. Many initial concepts were quickly abandoned, including those airships covered in feathers or made out of masonry, aesthetics notwithstanding.

Many would-be inventors of flying machines retired while other sacrificial visionaries crashed in violent smudging deaths into pavement and hillsides.

The era of powered human flight would be born of the vision and determination of brothers Orville and Wilbur Wright, two bike mechanics from Dayton, Ohio. Apparently unconvinced that bicycles were dangerous enough, the brothers were obsessed with the idea of a powered, heavier-than-air vehicle they could point and steer, one that would take them wherever they wanted to go, not only where a gust of wind unilaterally decided.

In spite of discouragement and ridicule, they worked tirelessly in their solvent-fumed garage, devoting their lives and fortunes to a belief that would violate every known law of physics and the entire body of collective mammal wisdom before 1903.

On the brisk morning of December 17, 1903, the Wright Brothers prepared their plane, optimistically dubbed *The Flyer,* for its test flight on a sandy beach at Kitty Hawk, North Carolina, an area thought to be softer than Dayton. Pushed forward on a small railed track by its propeller, the wood-and-cloth plane accelerated, and as an astonished crowd looked on, a gap of air opened between the craft and the ground. The plane lifted off, flying above the earth, not so high that Orville would have sustained more than a few brush burns if he had fallen out, but nonetheless detaching itself from North Carolina proper.

For a few seconds, the plane soared on its own power in controlled flight. From takeoff to landing, it traveled an astonishing 120 feet, barely the distance from the first-class section to the coach galley on a 747, but perhaps the greatest single accomplishment in the history of transportation to date. Orville Wright had completed the first successful flight of a piloted, heavier-than-air, self-propelled craft, skimming just above the surface of the beach. It was then the brothers realized they had invented more than just "The Giant Very Wide Hopping Bicycle." Observers, the first to witness the fulfillment of this archetypal human dream, could feel the surface of the earth shrinking beneath them.

It might be said that the twentieth century was born that day in

1903, thanks to the vision, invention, and pioneering spirit of the Wright Brothers, who believed in a principle and in themselves, who were willing to face overwhelming discouragement and sneering, risking their fortunes, their reputations, and their very lives.

The brothers would soon envision the carriage of letters and parcels from one end of the country to another, not in weeks but in days. They foresaw a technology that could lift us over mountains and oceans and would change the way we waged war. The Wrights predicted commercial air travel, where families would no longer be homebound and spend their entire lives within a circle twenty miles in diameter. They imagined a time when people would journey routinely from the Atlantic to the Pacific by taking off and landing at airports spaced 120 feet apart.

It is hard to believe that a little more than a century ago, we were traveling behind horse-drawn carts. Not long ago, a trip to Europe would take longer than it would to get to the moon today.

We now take air travel for granted. We sit inside a pressurized jet, flinging ourselves through thin air at bullet speed. It is hard to look up toward the clouds as a plane passes overhead, spewing white contrails in its wake, and not fantasize for at least a moment about the thrill of piloting an aircraft.

I know I do, but also being aware of my defective sense of direction and scant mechanical aptitude, I know it will never be.

Still, the sight of a plane creasing the sky makes me think about a poem called "High Flight," which begins:

> Oh, I have slipped the surly bonds of earth
> And danced the skies on laughter-silvered wings;
> Sunward I've climbed, and joined the tumbling mirth
> Of sun-split clouds . . .

"High Flight" speaks to anyone who has ever pushed a throttle wide open and aimed the pointy end of an airplane skyward, to pierce the ether in gravity-defying flight, surrounded on all sides by endless space, while the delicate gossamer of clouds turn to mist as they race past the cockpit and patches of blue and columns of light break through the billows like theatrical spotlights.

"High Flight" was composed by John Gillespie Magee Jr., a nineteen-year-old American volunteer serving in the Royal Canadian Air Force in World War II. Graduating as a pilot in 1940, he was sent to England the following year. There, he prepared for combat, electing the sky as his battleground and the airplane as his weapon, committed to freeing Europe from tyranny, but from above. Like other pilots, Magee knew mortality was high and his own future was uncertain, but a sense of duty veiled his fear of death.

Aviation changed warfare. After tens of thousands of years of human conflict at ground level, Magee's century was the first to allow its soldiers to soar above the battleground, swooping down like birds of prey. At no previous time had combatants ever seen the skirmish from this aerial perspective, flying above comrades and enemies. The only exceptions were the few unfortunate Roman prisoners who were loaded onto catapults and flung against distant castle walls.

The poem continues:

> Up, up the long, delirious burning blue,
> I've topped the windswept heights with easy grace
> Where never lark, or even eagle flew.

Magee's psalm rejoiced the solitude of flight. He sent the finished poem home to his parents. "Isn't this cute," I imagine his mom saying, beaming over breakfast, "would you look what Johnny wrote. And what pretty pensmanship!"

His poem ends with the words

> And, while with silent, lifting mind I've trod
> The high untrespassed sanctity of space,
> Put out my hand, and touched the face of God.

And touched the face of God! You do not have to be priest, rabbi, or imam to know that this is heady stuff. If any words could cause the most hardened, leather-skinned pilot to break down sobbing like a little girl, this poem comes closest.

We do not think of stalwart pilots, traditionally men, as a sensitive breed and comfortable expressing their deepest emotions openly. On the contrary, we expect our pilots to be technical, focused, detail-oriented, scientific, with little time or interest in reading unnecessarily sissified language, much less in composing poetry, and perhaps the closest they will get to literature is memorizing a ribald limerick that ends with some reference to vaginas.

Beauty for them resides in the right oil pressure and the glow of indicator lamps that come on when they should. Pilots waste few words and are not burdened by frilly speech or flowery descriptions. These are men who do not well up looking at art or listening to opera. Sit them down in the fanciest five-star French restaurant with a tureen of the finest bouillabaisse and the most emotive response you will hear is, "Hey, this is pretty frickin' good soup."

It is this lack of right-brain, weepy artsiness that we need in our pilots. We want hardened men and women, uncomfortable playing the violin and not overly distracted by a sunset. If a pilot and copilot are wrestling with a listing airliner as it side-slips toward the Sierra Nevada range, I would prefer they not pause awestruck during a thruster-controlled emergency landing when the hydraulics go out and flames are shooting out of the hind end of engine three, interrupting their Mayday to sigh, "Glory! Don't those billowing clouds look exceptionally sun-split?"

Yet Magee was uniquely gifted, able to straddle both worlds, as pilot and poet, at home at the controls of aircraft and equally comfortable finding the affect to describe them.

Several months after he finished his poem, in an unfortunate literary coincidence, Magee was killed over England when his Spitfire collided with another British plane, whose pilot might also have been paying more attention to "footless halls of air and the long, delirious burning blue" than to his altimeter.

Such prophetic poems, those that stun us with terminal irony and eerily portend the death of the author are quite common in literature. My classmates and I learned one of these in the seventh grade, in Mrs. Hill's English class. It is surprising that we remembered anything from her class, because the brain does not always convert short-term thoughts into long-term memory effectively under duress, and in Mrs. Hill's English class, we were in a state of constant trouser-soiling fear.

The elderly Mrs. Hill was arguably the meanest and most loathsome teacher to ever work in any Western Pennsylvania school. She seemed to enjoy the time-honored pedagogy of degradation and punishment, reflected in an educational philosophy that leaned more in the direction of Lizzie Borden than Maria Montessori, each day goading us into mistakes so she could unleash torrents of discipline and emotional toxins, crushing our fragile and still developing self-confidence in the name of poetry and prose. We envied the illiterate.

Mrs. Hill was a very tiny woman, perhaps no taller than four foot ten inches, but her cruelty per vertical inch made her all the more frightening. When she made eye contact, we could feel our retinas burn as if industrial lasers were aimed at them and cranked up to an "Etch Metal" setting. At the same moment, we could feel our youthful joy of living being remotely sucked from our beings.

Neither Heaven nor temporal assistance could save us if we answered a question incorrectly, if we relaxed for a moment from the artificially stiff posture she demanded, or if we squirmed in any way. No academic or physiological indiscretion went unnoticed, and after she gazed silently at any of us with her Death Stare, she would make a irrevocable notation in a grade book. Get three of these academic pustules in a grading period, and we could be certain that she would exercise her unquestioned authority to ruin our lives. Even God could not help us in Mrs. Hill's classroom, because He already had two.

There was not a day that my fellow junior high students and I did not wish Mrs. Hill dead, not a peaceful death passing away in her

sleep, no, but a violent, wretched, torturous death that involved mauling, parasitic infestation, or ritual evisceration.

Aside from being the cruelest, Mrs. Hill was also the oldest ed-
ucator in the district, starting her career teaching literature well
before William Faulkner, Tennessee Williams, and Ernest Hem-
ingway even considered writing. She was many years past the
mandatory retirement age of sixty-five, but had no intention of
stopping, knowing her life's work was not yet complete, and there
were still generations of 12-year-olds, yet unborn, to debase. Not
a single member of the school board, all of whom had been her
students over the years, dared to tell her it was time to leave the
classroom. Each still feared Mrs. Hill's grade book and no one,
not even those now grown up and successful in politics and community life, felt immune from the third pustule if she chose to
dispense it.

It was in her class that we memorized another tragically prophetic
poem, this one called "I Have a Rendezvous with Death," a sullen
verse about the life-stopping realities of combat, written by a poet
named Alan Seeger, who died in 1916 during the Great War. Mrs.
Hill loved that poem, as much as she could apparently love anything.
Though she claimed she was drawn to its descriptive language that
contrasted beauty with the ugly toll of war, we were certain she
made the sonnet part of the curriculum because it terrified the living
crap out of little children. Still, others were convinced that she was
drawn to it because sometime between 1912 and 1914, she had dated
Alan Seeger.

The poet would fight in World War I, but as the title suggested, he
had a funny feeling that he would not be there long enough to know
how it finally turned out.

Seeger wrote:

> I have a rendezvous with Death
> At some disputed barricade
> When Spring comes round with rustling shade
> And apple blossoms fill the air.

I have a rendezvous with Death
When Spring brings back blue days and fair.

It may be he shall take my hand
And lead me into his dark land
And close my eyes and quench my breath;
It may be I shall pass him still.
I have a rendezvous with Death

Closing with:

But I've a rendezvous with Death
At midnight in some flaming town,
When Spring trips north again this year,
And I to my pledged word am true,
I shall not fail that rendezvous.

America had not entered the war in Central Europe, so an adventuring Seeger joined the French Foreign Legion in 1914. As he strangely foretold, he was killed shortly thereafter at Belloy-en-Santerre on July 4, 1916. He was twenty-eight.

While not a particularly uplifting poem for a fragile seventh grader, "I Have a Rendezvous with Death" did teach us that if you want something badly enough—you can make it happen. In retrospect, I still believe it would have been much better for Seeger if he had composed a poem called, "I'm Hoping to be Back Home in a Couple of Weeks and Plan to Open a Dry Goods Store."

Like Seeger, pilot John Gillespie Magee would never live to see his poem earn critical recognition. But, as the posthumous spokesperson for flight, he penned words that would inspire generations of pilots and those of us who wish we were. He made all of us envious of his life as a pilot, except perhaps for the part where he was killed on impact as his plane nosed into the terrain.

Today, I recall Magee's poem when I look upward at a plane scribing a moist vapor trail across the sky, or when I tunnel through a Jetway into a commercial jet, realizing that this winged metal contraption, which is bigger than a fishing lodge, is capable not only of moving on its own, but of lifting itself off the ground, carrying me, a lot of fat people, their clothing, cosmetics, and a cargo hold full of luggage that these fellow passengers have again overpacked. I must admit I still get a little tearful whenever I return my seatback and tray table to an upright position.

While I would love to pilot a plane—and I am not choosy about what kind, whether it is a passenger jet or a fighter-bomber or even a dinky single-engine Cessna—I know enough about myself and am so at peace with my limitations that any fantasies are quashed by the grown-up recognition that this will never happen, in the same way that I have accepted that the majority of beautiful young women of Hollywood will not be bedding me any time soon.

My own safety is my primary, and admittedly selfish concern. I do not want to die at my own inept hands. But neither do I want the Goldstone name forever shamed by the memory of an out-of-control airplane crashing into a children's hospital.

Knowing my limitations and loving life as I do, I have settled for the purchase of a flight-simulator program for my computer, through which I can enjoy the sensation of piloting without endangering myself, passengers, or communities I overfly.

With this inexpensive, highly graphic software program, I can turn my laptop into a Boeing 777 wide-body jet or any one of a dozen or so commercial aircraft, planes that I can fly in absolute safety and privacy and conceivably ruin as often as I would like. My monitor is my windshield, and the keyboard my throttle and yoke. I control the rudder and air brake with the same kind of keystrokes I used earlier in the day to underline text. From my desktop cockpit, I look out over O'Hare, LAX, Heathrow, or anywhere else that my aerial wanderlust takes me.

Comfortable in my study, I captain a powerful air machine, watching the horizon rise, fall, or bank in response to the commands issued from my fingertips. Commercial pilots tell me that these programs behave with incredible realism and convincing graphic authenticity. You sweat as if you are a real pilot under real-life conditions.

The simulator prompts me through a preflight checklist to assure that my craft is airworthy. I can set the flaps and adjust the altitude as I would in a full-size version. The displays confirm the number of pounds of jet fuel on board, and I can even pump it from one wing tank to another to keep the plane properly balanced. An autopilot will fly the plane on its own, and for a moment, that seems like a nifty idea, until I remember that manually flying a jetliner myself was rather the reason I spent eighty-nine dollars on this thing in the first place.

My digital airplane is as receptive to poor judgment as a real one. However, I can fly confidently, knowing that a goofy mistake will not be newsworthy, and the worst injury I could sustain would result from leaning too far back in my swivel chair and tipping over backward, an embarrassment, yes, but nothing that will require identifying me only through my dental records. (I have always been a little fearful that if should I die in a real crash, total strangers will have access to my X-rays, and noting the number of fillings, will know I have not always taken the best care of my teeth.)

Flight simulators offer amusement, but also some valuable lessons. First, you will learn how complex a jet airliner is and how much we owe our faceless pilots who consent to drive us between cities.

The most revealing insight offered by the software is the profile of those who make good aviators. You have to crash a multimillion-dollar airplane only a few times to realize that you make a better passenger.

You learn that should you wish to become a real pilot, a good sense of direction is a must, not just distinguishing up from down and left from right, but reading navigational maps, understanding topography, determining the influence of crosswinds, and following the directions of air traffic controllers without making them repeat themselves over and over when you ask, "Is a right turn *toward* the river?"

You learn that above-average hand–eye coordination will come in handy. A good pilot should not get flustered easily when technology does not operate as expected nor should one resort to profanity and physical violence against the controls, believing that they are misbehaving on purpose.

Good pilots have faith in their instruments, trusting them over the body's more gullible senses, which falter when deprived of a stable ground reference. The body plays tricks in fog and turbulent weather.

Inexperienced pilots will often override the instruments, trusting their now confused inner ear instead, which may say the plane is on a level course when in reality it is nosing straight down like a pile driver. You must entrust your life to technology and cannot assume that you, a novice pilot, know more than a navigational beacon that does this for a living full-time. When the horizon indicator says you are flying horizontal and right-side-up, just assume it is right. When the altimeter suggests by its decreasingly whirring numbers that your craft is rapidly snouting downward, trust it to be true. On only a rare occasion will the instruments actually be broken. However, in the event this does happen, then you are probably screwed.

You learn that the most important characteristic of a good pilot is grace under duress. Those who make the best pilots are able to treat any emergency as if it were only a nuisance. If a uniform catches on fire, an unruffled captain, without much expression, might look down at the torso-engulfing inferno and chuckle, "Gosh, not again," while calmly smacking out the flames with his or her pilot hat.

A real pilot must remain composed and focused when trying to determine the cause and subsequent remedy of a problem. If you are in the cockpit of a real airplane, you cannot hit a couple of keys to stop the plane in midair as you think the disaster through for five or six minutes or check an online tutorial. Problem-solving time is short at twenty-seven thousand feet. While crises occur infrequently, you must always be prepared and must focus on the problems and not selfishly on your own looming death. Your response must be orderly and disciplined, running down a checklist methodically, rather than randomly flicking switches and twisting dials, hoping the out-of-control airliner will go back to acting normal again.

Even with flames shooting out of the nose of the plane, a good pilot must never alarm the passengers, instead making leisurely announcements that inspire calm in the cabin, convincing people it is OK to go back to reading their books and ignore all the smoke. With a friendly, folksy interruption, a well-intentioned captain will explain the plane's erratic behavior by using euphemisms designed not to arouse suspicion, for instance, claiming the bumpy ride is resulting from "airflow misconduct," "hydraulic fluid drought," or "engine nullification," all indicating catastrophic results but couched in more soothing terms.

Personally, knowing disaster is imminent and that it is up to me alone to save the lives of a cabin full of adults, the elderly, and babies, and more important still, me, I do not believe I could make a cool-headed, announcement such as, "This is Captain Goldstone. We are experiencing difficulty keeping this plane in the sky proper, and while we thought we would be able to make it to an airport, it now looks like we will just miss, but if it is of any consolation, not by very much. By the way, if you are wondering about the smell, it is molten aluminum, but it will become less noticeable once the cabin is depleted of oxygen."

Nor could I remain calm when I continue, "In the unlikely event that we can land without exploding into fewer than 320,000 fist-size pieces, please feel free to exit in an orderly fashion from the closest available gaping hole in the fuselage."

I know my voice would show fear when I end the announcement with the standard "We know you have many choices when you fly," but rather than thanking them for selecting us, I might finally loosen up and nervously joke, "Aren't you just kicking yourself for not taking an earlier flight?"

Booting up my own flight simulator, I pretend I am a dashing pilot, flying an Airbus 340, which I have configured for international travel with three classes of service. I believe I look particularly dashing in a pilot's cap.

Today I decide to fly from Paris to my old home town of Pittsburgh, eager to show a planeful of French where I grew up.

"There," I would get to say to my passengers as I fly over the downtown area, "that's the Monongahela River. When the steel mills were operating full tilt, the river was stained an opaque umber. As you can see, after years of environmental stewardship, the water is now just a little beige. Out of the left windows you can see the ballpark where the Pirates play."

I would then repeat as much of my speech as I could in my limited French, just to impress my judgmental Parisian passengers, *"Voici la Rive de Monongahela. Il est beige. Ah, la place ou des Pirates joué, bon frapper du baseball, n'est-ce pas?"*

I am on a linguistic roll, so I continue my pilot banter, trying to cram in all the other phrases I remember from my college Introductory French class.

"Jean et Marie vont a la bibliotheque," I ramble on proudly. *"Je demande une crème brûleé, maintenant. Ou est mon pantalon? Mon Dieu, Edith Piaf est morte!"*

I sit in my study, ready for takeoff. I follow the same preflight protocol as do actual pilots, but being in a hurry, complete only those I decide are really important.

I announce, "Flight attendants. Prepare the cabin for takeoff." I know this is common preflight parlance, but I have to wonder what equipment so critical to takeoff is located back there with the passengers. Mimicking other pilots, I request a "cross check," which I believe is offered as a courtesy to my devout Catholic passengers.

I browse the controls across the bottom of my screen. I am amazed at the number of digital displays: engine rpm, oil pressure, navigational coordinates, an artificial horizon if I somehow question the existence of the real horizon, and cabin oxygen levels. Warning lights inform me if my landing gear or brakes are not functioning, little cause for despair when I am parked at the gate, but a much bigger to-do if I am on final approach. I will ignore any readouts I do not understand.

Charles de Gaulle Airport wraps around me in 3-D. In the real world I would have a copilot, but in the simulator world, I can handle the seven-hour transatlantic flight myself. My pretend airline has graciously passed the savings onto my passengers with cheaper tickets and better quality headsets.

I taxi to the end of the runway and stop. My plane's undercarriage bellies over the thick lines painted on the far end. With the 340's brakes locked, I rev the engines, which begin to store up energy like a taut rubber band. Flanking me on both sides are runway lights. I could instantly make it night by toggling something on my keyboard, but I don't want to confuse my passengers, or make them believe we have been sitting on the tarmac for more than twelve hours. Two miles of pavement are all that separate me from the sky.

I release the brake and gently advance the throttle. The Airbus begins to roll, gaining speed faster than anything I have ever driven. More than three hundred tons of airplane accelerates as the pitch of the revving jets increases and the thud of the tires passing over the seams on the concrete comes more and more quickly. The painted middle line is slurped under the plane like strands of spaghetti. The ground speed indicator displays 160 knots, and I am committed to flight: my speed is sufficient for lift but I no longer have enough runway left to stop. So I pull the yoke toward my chest, rotating the nose upward. The horizon suddenly drops out of the bottom of my windshield, and the sky opens. The thumping of the tires instantly quiets and is replaced by the whirring sound of gear curling up into the plane's abdomen. A wedge of air now separates me from the airport. Following noise abatement rules, I cut back a little on the throttle so I do not piss off the Parisians living underneath me any more than they already are.

The checklist makes takeoff sound easy, but it is tricky to get a big plane off the ground and keep it from stalling at 1200 feet. It took me more than a dozen attempts before I was finally able to leave earth non-fatally, avoiding the kind of aircraft-ground incursion posthumously known as "pilot error," some resulting from me folding up the landing gear before the plane left the runway, others caused by my inability to judge where the runway would be ending, a few based on my unfamiliarity with unnecessarily complicated cockpit controls, and one occurring when I got a phone call in the middle of my rollout and, not wanting to miss it, chose to sacrifice my passengers instead.

In my Paris-to-Pittsburgh simulation, I reach my cruising altitude of 37,000 feet. Now all I have to do is (1) not corkscrew into the ocean, (2) avoid shutting off all the engines by accident, and (3) not fly into any plane heading from Pittsburgh back to Paris.

Once the plane is in the air, much of the fun of flying a simulator quickly vanishes, because you actually fly in real time and a seven-hour flight can take seven hours if you let it. In theory, I could sit in front of my computer into the small hours of the morning, just watching digital clouds stream by. So to amuse myself, I play with some of the dials, check my hydraulic-fluid level, and program new coordinates into the navigational system. Ten minutes over the Atlantic, I am bored silly and put the plane on autopilot, get up to make a sandwich, think about taking a nap, or imagine sex with any one of the female flight attendants who finds me attractive in a uniform and is willing to put her refreshment beverage cart on auto-deliver.

With this computer toy, I can also amuse myself by simulating all manner of airborne crises, including thunderstorms, a veil of fog, egg-scrambling turbulence, jammed landing gear, engine failure, incursion of other jets into my airspace, inaccurate instrument readings, and literally hundreds of other aeronautical hoops through which a real pilot might fly. I admit that not one of these emergencies results in a happy outcome for me or my passengers. If I thirst for even more excitement, I can even change the program options and try to land my passenger plane on an aircraft carrier or pretend I am warding off a squadron of Libyan fighters, swooping and banking with no offensive weapons on board aside from some tiny pillows and eighty pounds of roasted peanuts. But instead, I decide to truncate my tedious trip over the Atlantic, advancing on ahead to the Pittsburgh area, six hours and fifty minutes ahead of schedule.

Overflying Pittsburgh's Golden Triangle, I remind passengers about "*joué de Pirate baseball*" and head off toward runway 10R/28L at Greater Pittsburgh International Airport. With a length of 11,500 feet, this is the longest runway they have, so I request it just in case I do not remember how my brakes work.

Landing is the most difficult part of the flight. I line up with the straight ribbon of pavement and time my descent, planning to touch down as close as I can to the end of the runway. Should I misjudge, I prefer to err by landing farther down the runway and closer to the terminal, rather than somewhere short of the runway in nearby suburban Sewickley.

As I adjust the trim and go through the final approach checklist, I ask the passengers to return their seats and tray tables to the full upright position, a process they will perform numerous times as I repeat the landing sequence over and over until I can do it without causing the Airbus to explode in a molten heap of plane parts. For laughs,

I try the landing again at night, backing my plane up over the Squirrel Hill, turning the sky to dark, and aiming for a more challenging runway. Night landings can be confusing, and in my inexperience, I misread the lights on the ground, certain I am aiming my aircraft toward the runway beacons, but as I discover a little too late, I am actually about to touch down on the neon sign atop the Airport Radisson.

After a handful of catastrophes, at the conclusion of which I usually mutter, "Oh, the humanity!" I am finally able to bag a decent landing, roll to a stop, and taxi to the gate. I invite my passengers to visit the airport gift shop. They deplane, and at least for the moment, I can boast that I am the reason that 280 French will live another day.

In my handful of hours of simulator training, I have crashed an entire fleet of 777s repeatedly, some eighty-seven planes each time, with a street value somewhere about $800 billion U.S. Had these been real planes, I would have killed just slightly fewer people than Joseph Stalin.

Simulator packages have strangely added an additional level of safety to flying, training a segment of the passenger population to understand the aerodynamic behavior of the planes on which they travel, a backup that might come in handy should both your pilot and copilot suffer heart attacks simultaneously, succumb to faulty peach cobbler, or be inexplicably sucked out of the cockpit.

If you ever sit next to me on a flight, you can take some comfort in my four hours of experience piloting a desktop cyberjet. I am confident that I will be able to get you to the airport and possibly straight to your hotel room if you happen to be staying at the Airport Radisson.

Lacking mechanical self-assurance and a good sense of direction, I do not trust myself to pilot a real plane, so I will probably never experience the windswept leather-goggle-hat-and-scarf-traveling-behind-an-open-cockpit-exhilaration described by Magee in "High Flight." I doubt I have the courage to break the surly bonds of earth or to tread the high untrespassed sanctity of space.

Sadly, I am not confident enough in my own aeronautical skills to soar skyward, high enough to touch the face of God, but perhaps I could someday convince myself to fly just high enough to maybe touch His neck.

Your House Is Out To Get You

IF SOMEONE ASKED YOU WHERE YOU THINK YOU WOULD BE most likely to get killed, like most other people, you would probably guess incorrectly.

Topping the list of most popular death venues would not be under the wheels of a tractor trailer piloted by a drowsy long-distance trucker, not in a plane crash, not in a drought-stricken African savannah where underfed carnivores eye you from the brush, not in a foundry where hot smelted substances drip from weighty overhead cauldrons, not inside some crime-cultivating Pakistani brothel, or behind the steel containment doors of a Level 4 Infectious Disease laboratory where virulent Marburg virus sits out in open petri dishes.

The site of the most debilitating or fatal accidents is in the home, the cozy sampler-on-the-wall shelter where you go when you want to pretend to feel safe, the place where you huddle with your family to stay warm, the very enclosure where you walk confidently with bare feet over thick pile carpeting, and yes, ironically, the place you run to when you mistakenly think you are in greater danger somewhere else. It is here, under your own roof, that you are most likely to meet face-to-face with disfigurement or dismemberment. You are many times safer working in a meatpacking plant than you are standing on your patio.

If you were to kill yourself in a fall, it would be less likely off the slippery face of K2 than in your recently renovated bathroom. You may have used your stairs ten thousand times, but need to misjudge the edge of a tread only once for your neck to snap in two like some dry twig. Many owners of older automatic garage door openers, believing they can duck under one during a powered descent, have been severed by their carport's heavy metal doors. Climb under the crawl space of a house where hornets' nests spread like cancer, and you invite an attack from which a retreat unscathed is unlikely.

The electricity we invite into our homes is simultaneously friend and foe. It joyfully energizes the appliances that bring us comfort and convenience. It offers illumination so we do not have to perform other tasks in darkness. But fickle electricity will also kill you if given the tiniest opportunity. It travels invisibly in threads of wires just beneath the skin of our homes, packaged in fifteen- or more ampere circuits, with enough might to make lightbulbs and anything else it touches, including you, glow.

Like many Americans whose vision of success includes home ownership, I bought a house, not because I especially deserved one or because I demonstrated either an aptitude or sufficient responsibility to be issued a deed, but because I could come up with a down payment. Owning property does not demand prerequisite skills or test scores to prove worthiness. Unlike even fishing, which is a simple endeavor that is not tremendously life-threatening except perhaps to the fish, anyone can lay claim to a danger-stuffed house without a license and be allowed unsupervised access to heart-stopping electrical current, load-bearing walls, water gushing through pipes under great pressure, natural-gas lines, highly flammable creosote-coated fireplaces, gutters thirty or forty feet above the ground, and a salmagundi of other hazards that lie hidden and easily triggered, kinetically wound tight like the mainspring of a big clock, ready to uncoil in a slicing explosion, endangering the homeowner, his family, neighbors, and, when things go terribly wrong, an entire community.

I bought a house built in 1901, handcrafted by artisans who took to their graves the values of pride and workmanship, ideals that homeowners will agree are not generally practiced by contractors today. Underneath my home's weathered shingles is a house as structurally sound as it was when William McKinley was president. Back then, two-by-fours were what they claimed to be and not the anorexic 1½-by-3½-inch timbers you find now. Nails were hefty stilettos of steel that bit resolutely into lumber. Doors were solid, with each of theirs panels carefully inlaid. Wood was cut by hand, sanded, and joined painstakingly so that grains matched and seams evaporated. When people complain that things "aren't made like they used to," the time my house was built was the "used to" they are referring to.

Still, nothing lasts forever, no matter how meticulous the handiwork. You cannot expect most things built a century ago to be immune from wear and tear. Wood decays, iron rusts, old insulation crumbles. Electrical wiring and underpowered screw-type fuses strain and sooner or later fail as they try to keep up with the insatiable demands of today's frost-free refrigerators, air-conditioners, and microwave ovens. Horsehair plaster slathered onto walls when great-grandpa was a tot shows spider-vein cracks through a hundred years of chipping lead paint.

Even stalwart iron water pipes corrode a little and bathroom drains clog after thanklessly dispatching four generations of human waste. Windows rattle loose, and doorjambs warp. Outside, cedar shakes blemish after the repeated cycles of 400 seasons, and downspouts eventually leak. The best of houses must be renewed at regular internals.

Of course, my house is no exception. Every so often, it cries out for some mechanical intervention. Before do-it-yourselfing, the only sensible option for us as untrained homeowners was either to hire a contractor or ignore problems until they triggered others. Today, we are encouraged to try fixing things ourselves. So, many of us blindly plunge ahead, believing we are self-sufficient and can save a few dollars in the process.

I graciously admit that I am not handy. I know this from decades of retrospection, from the objective self-critique of my work, from the titters of other, and from a gallery of healed-over scars, small yes, but visible if you know where to look. I know where my talents stop and iffiness begins, and I am no longer ashamed to admit where I cannot be trusted.

I am smart enough to own up to my own limitations, when I am a danger to myself and others. I stay a safe distance from tools without finger-barricading blade guards or any implement that, with even the slightest provocation, can jeopardize my mission to remain intact. I undertake only projects that do not contain hidden dangers and repair only those hazards that can be proven statistically to be less dangerous to fix than to ignore. I proceed only when I am certain the projects will add to, not potentially detract from, the assessed value of my house.

I concede that I am careless. My mind wanders. I frequently disassociate from my immediate environment. I am easily distracted. I am absentminded, forever misplacing items I was just holding. If you are in the class of people who are always looking for your keys and it turns out they are still in your hand, you are probably not the kind of person who ought to operate a chop saw, though its name alone should be enough to give you pause. In all cases, I graciously extend the benefit of the doubt to the tool.

I lack good hand–eye coordination. Both my hands and my eyes operate quite effectively on their own, yet they do not appear to be on good speaking terms. I can be clumsy. I fumble with things and can get tangled easily in cords and string. It is not just in old movies that people continue to drop things while reaching down for something else that they dropped a moment earlier.

I lose my patience easily, and a task requiring precise microdexterity is often so frustrating that I stop being careful and gentle and resort to slamming things together out of anger just to get the task done. I settle for less than perfection, and I am perfectly happy knowing that an object that I gave up sanding from boredom when it was only half done is still 50 percent smoother than when I started.

I am not neat and meticulous. Because I am not consumed by craftsmanship, my signature woodworking pieces feature joints with permanent gaps that do not line up correctly, shabbily cut edges, and globs of cement prominently scarring over and dried as a translucent lesion on the skin of any two objects I wished to glue together.

Mismatched wood filler to mend a gash commonly overflows its banks. Painted walls and trim show vertical veining of hardened drips striping toward the floor like crusted stalactites.

Holes intended to line up do not follow any known pattern of symmetry. I still consider a right angle anything that falls within a window of 87–93 degrees, and likewise, two pieces I have cut do not have to be identical in all dimensions for me to consider them "the same size."

Though studs are theoretically sixteen inches apart center-to-center and my walls are dense with them, I cannot find a single one easily. I bore a hole where my twenty-nine-dollar electronic stud-and-joist finder assures me one awaits subcutaneously, but when the drill punches through a half-inch sheet of Sheetrock way too quickly, I know I have managed to miss it, and subsequently drill an uneven line of fifteen or twenty holes in ¼-inch intervals in my desperate attempt to hit a timber even by chance, eventually leaving me with the kind of bullet-ridden wall you might find after the St. Valentine's Day massacre.

Perhaps it is lack of patience or coordination, but for whatever reason, I am not very good at hands-on fix-it or build-it projects. If you examined my woodworking, you would be surprised to find it had been performed by anyone on my side of puberty. Even when it comes to verbally describing some problem requiring my attention, my native comfort with words evaporates. I blather on and cannot find the simplest sounds to communicate the most rudimentary concepts. In my helplessness, I describe the intricate workings of our universe using words like "thingee" and often have to rely on pantomime, for instance swinging my hand back and forth when I cannot remember the word for "hinge."

Because I am not genetically predisposed to home repair, I undertake projects cautiously if at all, acknowledging the dangers residing within most maintenance and upkeep, dormant for now but waiting for me to awaken them.

You don't need to look too hard to find the seeds of hardship in even seemingly harmless activities in your home, including installing a new faucet, changing a doorknob, replacing that copper floating sphere in the tank of your toilet, refinishing a chair, or assembling a simple storage unit to steckpile your unused doorknobs, floating copper toilet orbs, and the tools you need to deal with them.

I hold that it does not take a great craftsman to cut the lawn, rake leaves, and trim a few hedges, yet these are examples of modest activities that have the potential to heap damage on both property and person.

My lawn is just large enough that a manually shoved push mower is a nuisance, but not quite big enough to make using a power mower look anything but silly. Since I can live with silly, especially if it can save me time, I have relied on the motorized version through the years, independent of the size of my lawn.

I have owned four power mowers within the past decade. I know that many people are operating the same ones that they purchased in the early 1970s, but I do not seem to be able to keep a mower functioning for more than a few seasons.

My first lawn mower was a victim of a basement flood. Although the water receded within forty-eight hours, all the once-moving Briggs & Stratton pieces welded themselves into an oxidized solid, after which nothing, including the wheels, turned. The second unit was stolen from the yard when I went inside to find the manual to explain why it was smoking and making clanging noises. I am grateful that a thief saved me a trip to the dump. The third mower, an inexpensive plastico-metallico combo, refused to start after its third birthday, and the cost to fix the device was slightly more than I paid for it. Even at a new mower every two and a half years, I figure I am still saving considerable money over the cost of hiring a landscape guy.

Lawn mowers are examples of engineering simplicity, a two-stroke engine that spins a stubby shaft with sharp blades mounted on the end. This rotary scythe is housed underneath a protective cowling, and the entire blade assembly lies prostrate just above the ground, propeller perpendicular to the unkempt blades of grass. Four wheels give it mobility, and a long handle juts up at a bias and allows the entire noisy contraption to be pushed from behind, a much safer approach than holding a handleless fast-spinning sheering assembly by the edges like an hors d'oeuvre tray and moving it about the lawn on my hands and knees.

My father owned only two lawn mowers during his lifetime, both of which were better engineered than the devices available today.

The first was a hand mower whose blades whirred around fast enough to trim the lawn only if you could get its wheel moving by pushing it from behind.

The muscle-driven mower worked best on grass that had been cut recently. If the grass was short or brown-dead from underwatering, mowing was much easier for my dad. Getting me to mow it made it that much easier still.

We finally got a power mower after the rest of the neighbors did, thereby adding one more internal combustion engine to my family's woes. It was ruggedly built and started every spring in spite of the harsh winter living conditions in an unheated garage. The 1964-vintage cutter operated dependably year after year, and when my parents moved to Florida, a state where landscaping is often included, they traded it in toward a motorized Cushman golf cart.

I put off the purchase of my own new mower as long as I could, but soon the yard started to look wild and shabby, overgrown grass was blocking access to the mailbox, and my mailman refused to wade through hip-deep vegetation, fearing that deer-size predators could be hiding in ambush. Ignored sufficiently, even the most luxurious Kentucky bluegrass will eventually sprout tall pale-green stalks, and with a crown of seeds, it would sway gracefully in the breeze, patriotically reminiscent of the amber waves of a Kansas wheat field.

This time, I considered buying an electric lawnmower like my neighbor's. The fleet of conventional gasoline-fueled mowers I had owned previously required an adult aptitude for mechanics and attention greater than I was able to supply. Their engines demanded occasional maintenance, the insertion of oil every so often, and a stash of flammable fuel at the ready in the garage. They were difficult to start, requiring multiple yanks on the starter rope, most of the time climaxing in a stuttering tease from a pull not robust enough to turn the engine over. Each subsequent tug further increased my level of exasperation but not the likelihood of ignition. Internal combustion mowers were susceptible to fuel-line flooding, a kind of congestive heart failure for mechanical devices. Only after a ten-minute wait, valuable time when the grass continued growing taller and more resilient, could I try to start it again. Once the fuel ignited, the mower blasted out an oil-drenched cloud of choking smoke, sputtering as it revved to full power. I prayed the tank contained enough gas to finish the job, because I did not relish refilling a searing-hot engine by pouring gasoline into it.

But there was a clean-energy electrical alternative. Just as with a toaster, Norelco razor, or halogen lamp, you can count on an electric mower to obey when you plug it in and turn it on. Further, you can rely on it to keep working unfettered until you either (1) turn it off intentionally or (2) sever the power cord by running the blades over it. The benefit of such reliability is a compelling reason to invest in one over a petroleum-burning version, until you factor in the uncompromising attention demanded by an electrically assisted device.

With a conventional mower, you must certainly pay attention to the safety basics: not running over your own foot, your children or pets, or rolling over solid objects such as rocks, dog toys or sprinkler heads that quickly become rockets if accelerated by the whirring blades and fire out of the side chute.

With an electric mower, you add the danger of electrocution from shearing through the power cord, coursing with multiple amperes of invisible electrical current, while you are pushing along a highly conductive metal appliance with your bare moist hands. If the lawn is dew-covered, you are just asking for it.

Many electrically fired outdoor gardening apparatuses are susceptible to the problem of assisted self-mutilation, and millions of Americans every year carelessly bisect their Toro products, but do not send them for repair out of embarrassment. Walk down any street and look at the number of houses with only half their hedges neatly trimmed, and it won't take too long to figure out what happened.

It is not easy to learn about lawn mowers or even the best way to cut a lawn. You learn by trial and error. The first time you shoot a small rock into the yard two houses down from yours will be all the reminder you need henceforth to check the yard in advance for loose projectable items, children's marbles, and parts of the lawn-mower that vibrated free the last time you mowed. Likewise, the hour you spend after flipping the jammed lawn mower on its back to rip away the plastic bag, tiny piece by tiny piece, that wrapped itself tightly around the shaft after you ran over it will be a frustrating inconvenience you will not forget. If the mower startles you by revving back up to speed on its own while inverted, you will never go near its undercarriage again under any circumstance. No one ever touches the spark plug of a powered-up mower with a bare hand more than once.

Torn between the electrical versus another internal combustion mower, I decided to purchase a gasoline mower again, not that the apparatus was any better, but I figured with an electric mower, I risk both amputation and electrocution, and by getting a traditional petrol-fuel mower, I decrease the likelihood of serious injury by 50 percent.

I have often thought there might be a market for a computer software program called Lawn Mower Simulator, an instructionally entertaining product promising to teach grass cutting safely from a desktop PC, where you would be immune from danger, since there is no chance of hitting some virtual rock that will fly out of the side of your computer to knock over a table lamp or from losing a finger while reaching under the CD drive. On the screen, you would move a mouse-driven cyber-mower about a typical sod front and back yard, mowing around hedges and gardens with the same authentic realism heretofore available to only professional landscapers.

To make lawn maintenance more challenging, you could introduce such hazards as hills, coat hangers, house pets, garden gnomes, and toddlers or change the weather with an option for a flash flood, clobbering hail, or a fluke thunderstorm. The software would allow the user to practice in either novice or expert mode and to choose from (1) electric mowers with their dangling and vulnerable cords, (2) obstreperous pull-a-cord-to-start gas versions, (3) mighty John Deere riding tractors, or (4) for the traditionalists, the push mower. For a few extra dollars, you could upgrade the software with the purchase of a realistic winter snow-blower module, or outfit your mower with rockets and a grenade launcher.

Still, you don't have to consort with fast-revving razor-edged appliances to gamble away your life and the lives of your family. The most elementary home maintenance devices are brimming with adversity, even those absent moving parts and often before you get them fully out of the box.

I once bought steel shelving, an unadorned basement storage unit consisting of four steel vertical corner posts and a half-dozen flat horizontal pieces that screwed into them, an allegedly safe storage convenience that promised a lifetime of heavy-duty utility and pledged never to topple, no matter how much I loaded onto it, claiming to be the "Sturdiest Shelving Money Can Buy!"

The box assured me that as long as I could differentiate the "up and down" parts from the "side to side" parts, I had the requisite skills to properly assemble the unit. Yet, this seemingly simple home project would become the singular life undertaking that would bring me closest to bleeding to death.

Like many other items, steel shelving units come in pieces. This means the company that has stuffed the parts into the box is not technically the shelving manufacturer at all, and it has quietly shifted that responsibility to you. Such companies are quick to use this as an excuse if the item does not function as advertised, absolving themselves from any liability. They claim any problem is your fault and that you are lucky they are not suing you for taking their perfectly good product and sullying their name with your criminally shoddy workmanship.

When you buy shelving, you are not really buying storage space. Think about it: what you have purchased are metal dividers that subdivide the space you already have in your house. By compressing the unassembled pieces tightly in a box, the so-called manufacturer has extracted the storage part of the shelving prior to shipment, and you will have to "add your own space," as you put the unit together.

During assembly, I learned that machine-cut pieces do not always fit precisely and that whacking an out-of-plumb support with the palm of my hand to get the holes to line up is the time I am most likely to discover the jagged pieces of sharp metal protruding like daggers. It is no coincidence that they paint some of these metal shelves a deep crimson to camouflage stains resulting from your injuries. I should point out that the final step in the instructions told me to bolt the unit to the wall, which is apparently what makes it the "Sturdiest Shelving Money Can Buy!" One could argue that shelves made out of beef jerky would also be among the sturdiest money could buy if you secured plank-size pieces of dried meat to your basement foundation with carriage bolts.

Fortunately, no matter how sloppy and misshapen your wobbly product looks in the end, you will be safe from embarrassment and traumatic flashbacks because it will spend the rest of its bloodthirsty life hidden in your damp cellar.

Owning the same deteriorating house for twenty-plus years, I approach even the most innocent-looking activities timidly, not wanting to become another domestic statistic lost in a heap of coroner's reports, one more sad tale of an overly enthusiastic homeowner done in under, or in some cases by, his own roof.

I subscribe to a domestic Hippocratic oath that says simply, "Do no *additional* harm," and by "harm" I mean either to my house or to me. A successful repair is—how can I say this most plainly?—one where I do not make things worse.

I do not wish to suck any karma or market value from my house unnecessarily, so I am happy to delegate many of my projects to a professional. Certainly there is a good chance that I am being overcharged because the contractor knows I will pay anything to have anyone but me do it and he can tell by my previous work that I am not an expert in such things, and that I may not even know if he is doing it properly. But I am comforted in the knowledge that, by finding a professional willing to take a splinter on my behalf, I remain ambulatory and laceration-free. By accepting my shortfalls, I avoid the humiliation of hearing that the object in need for repair is no longer fixable, but would have been had I not tinkered with it.

I blame my father for my craft deficiencies. Unlike my mother, who was outright afraid of tools, my father simply was not good with them. He was not quick to fix things that broke, and instead preferred to wait until a sufficient number of house features failed, at which point he would convince my mother that it was time to buy a new home. The Goldstones left a trail of broken houses in their wake throughout Western Pennsylvania.

Many kids and their dads bonded by doing home projects together, by building a swing set or a tree house. My neighbor Andy and his dad worked every weekend for a month to build a Soap Box Derby racer, an aerodynamic, gravity-powered vehicle, sleek and wooden, stylish, and painted red with a golden lightning bolt running down the side. It was the only conveyance that a ten-year-old was allowed to drive. Whether the little coaster won or not was unimportant, subordinate to the experience of father and son working together. My father never helped me built a soap-box vehicle, offering the excuse that, "Our people do not competitively race."

The only father–son project I can remember from childhood was a birdhouse, which we learned later did not have enough room for an avian visitor to turn around. Once stuck inside, birds flapped futilely, died, and eventually decomposed, and since the birdhouse hung on a tree out of our reach, we were unable to use the backyard for weeks at a time.

During both childhood and now adulthood, I cannot think of more than a couple of projects my dad and I ever tackled together. My dad's basement had only a limited selection of tools so he would not consider addressing any problem that could not be solved by tightening it, pinching it with pliers, or thwacking it soundly with a mallet. We would talk about something we should fix or a project that would improve the house—assembling a laundry table for the basement, installing a small flagstone patio where my parents could put some plastic outdoor chairs, or hanging a ceiling fan. I am sure we both thought about how nice it would be to actually put something together communally that had a chance of working. But then we would look at each other and remember how pitiful the other of us was, and instead would decide to have something to eat or maybe take a nap.

My parents retired to southern Florida and purchased a nice house overlooking a golf course. They also bought a service contract that takes care of most of the major repairs, but when I visit, my father and I occasionally consider undertaking an intergenerational fix-it project, a process that starts with us opening up an old metal toolbox, pointing to either the hammer or screwdriver, and as we both stand over it for a while, trying to agree on which end we believe to be the handle.

Instruments of Our Personal Destruction

SINCE THE TIME OF DARWIN, WE HAVE KNOWN THAT *HOMO sapiens* ascended from the same bloodlines as monkeys and apes. Try as you might to distance yourself from lower primates, which zoologists rightly claim are downright stupid compared with the majority of us, you are probably aware that 98 percent of your human DNA, the genetic blueprint that accounts for everything you are, is identical to that of primitive simians and that it is only by a mere 2 percent fluke that you were not born a gibbon.

To promote self-esteem in their human subjects, anthropologists have looked for the single, most fundamental characteristic that separates us from the beasts. Recognition of some simple but distinctive talent would offer our species a psychologically comfortable cushion to distance the human race from more dispensable animals, and give us as *Homo sapiens* something for which we could be collectively proud.

Some years ago, social scientists settled on a rather curious definition: that humans were unique in all the animal world as its "sole toolmakers and tool users." Our prototypes learned to adapt simple objects from their surroundings to help them solve problems and perform tasks more efficiently and productively, and this is ultimately the reason why our species has been able to create cities, literature, automobiles, and elected government and why, say, the ibex has not.

This definition surprised a lot of people who felt we had a lot more going for us.

You would think that a species that was smart enough to figure out that it was different from other animals would settle on any one of a number of loftier, more dignified, and frankly, more obviously discriminating attributes such as, perhaps, "Humans can talk. They can think critically. They invented mathemetics. They write books. They came up with the idea for pesto, for God's sake. They are, well, just better."

In an attempt to keep it simple, social science insulted all of us who take our upright bipedalism seriously.

A few years later, someone noticed a tiny oversight in the theory, finding that other animals also employ rudimentary tools. Chimpanzees, for instance, use saliva-moistened twigs stripped of bark to scoop out little insects from the hollow of a tree, and use rocks as handheld mallets to smash their way inside nut casings, remarkable feats of problem solving and dexterity that were well-documented in the film *Jane Goodall and the Wild Chimps* and further confirmed in the lesser-known sequel *Jane Goodall and the Wild Chimps at La Scala*. Her observations forced anthropologists to rethink the theory of implement making and to backpedal delicately, all the while trying to save face by claiming, "Well, what we meant were *power* tools."

But to the credit of social scientists, they did notice that humans have become keenly aware of the benefits that tools offer.

In the last hundred thousand years, as we have widened the social and intellectual gap between other primates and us, our ever-swelling brains have devised implements to help us perform tasks we could not do with our hands alone, thereby extending our dominion over both the animate and inanimate. We discovered elementary laws of physics that had always been available, but that our progenitors were not yet ready to understand. Early versions of Man learned the practical application of smashing, twisting, hoisting, pinching, and squishing, and fashioned the simple lever, the taper, the hefty sledge, and the auger to help. All hand tools are inert without the fuel of human toil but offer a powerful mechanical advantage when married to a little muscle and determination.

Using our keenly honed flint axes, we could fell giant trees and cleave freshly quarried stones, collecting the materials from which we would build shelters to insulate us from the elements and savage predators. We developed weaponry, outfitting ourselves with pointy spears to increase the chances that, after a hunting expedition, we would be the animal that was doing the eating.

Even if tools did not make us unique, at least they nudged us a few rungs upward on the evolutionary stepladder. With them, we built communities, roadways, and civilization. It was through the use of these devices that our society has been built and repeatedly fixed.

I am an occasional tool user myself, but feel fortunate living in an age when I do not have to hone my own stone ax or venture out to find my own flint, since I do not hone well and haven't the foggiest idea where I would even begin to look for flint.

Thankfully, I can rely on retailers who have assembled a hundred millennia of tools and building materials, often preassembled, boxed, and stuffed with some kind of instructions that make using them easier for people like me.

I am grateful to emporia such as the Home Depot, which have gathered an impressive array of items on my behalf, some I know I will someday need, but the majority that will remain darkly mysterious, and their their purposes never adequately revealed. I am likely to buy them anyway.

I look at the Home Depot with the same jaw-dropping awe and wonderment as I do NASA's Air and Space Museum in Washington. Both are cathedrals to the mechanical achievements that have sprung from the uncorked human mind. Both pay tribute to mammalian ingenuity. Both make me swell with pride at the unbounded capacity of man-the-animal to master his surroundings. I stroll though the Home Depot, starry eyed and spellbound as I peer upward toward machinery that is as mystifying to me as a solid-fuel rocket booster.

The Home Depot do-it-yourself superstore was an idea concurrently brilliant and diabolical in its conception. Founded in Atlanta in 1978 and now the world's largest building materials supplier, the no-frills retailer single-handedly changed the way every American looks at pipe flanges and Spackle, and in doing so, unleashed an epidemic of amateur construction projects that the firm has convinced home owners are actually "improvements."

The store brags that it stocks more than 35,000 individual products, most of which the typical do-it-yourselfer does not need and about 10,000 items that the do-it-yourselfer should not be permitted anywhere near. Products tower above the rapt shoppers through open-faced shelving. Here, under a single roof, professionals and novices alike stroll amid acres of merchandise—everything a person could need to build a home from scratch or replace any one of its individual pieces, from its subterranean foundation to its shingled roof.

Inside the store, someone can point you to every type of domestic treatment, from quarry tile to Berber carpet, kitchen cabinets, hinges, stainless-steel appliances, sump-relocation pumps, bath spigots, and even specialty fixtures that put boiling, flesh-scalding hot water in little faucets next to the regular hot-water valve, just asking for a tragic family mishap. You'll find all manner of ecologically beneficial flush toilets that use half as much water as your old commode but are not quite powerful enough for you to flush only once. The store offers an arboretum of little trees and shrubs that appear healthy for the moment because they are in some kind of temporary remission from the botanical diseases that they carry, but you can be sure will return to the fringes of death not long after you plant them at home. You will also find mailboxes, millions of oddly shaped carriage bolts, and lighting fixtures that beg to be connected to potentially life-snuffing electricity by any well-intentioned novice with a screwdriver.

Outside, a parking area capaciously entertains thousands of cars, stretching the overall retail footprint over acres of land that you remember used to be a productive family-owned farm or protected wetlands.

The character of the building captures the gritty, uncoddled sensibilities of the "hands on" man and woman. Bare-bones simple and with no flashy trappings, the store's design values size over aesthetic splendor and function over customer comfort. The unadorned treatment reflects the belief that building America is a rugged job, not the place for dandies and the pampered. It is a place to get a little dirty. The Home Depot is proud that it is the kind of retail establishment where Paul Bunyan would have shopped for his axes or Mike Mulligan for spare parts to service his steam shovel, Mary Anne. It is no secret that the store's architects spent a fortune to make sure the place looks as crappy as it does.

Each store is a giant box, its outer boundaries defined by cinder block walls and a high open truss ceiling. Inside are row after row of evenly spaced aisles, each two hundred or three hundred feet long, where like items congregate with their own kind in banner-draped departments: garden, electrical, paint, plumbing, kitchen and bath, door and window, flooring, appliances, and hardware. Toward the end of the building, raw, untamed lumber is neatly arranged in its own wood-corral.

In each aisle, muscular metal shelves tower up four or five tiers, bolted together with girders as beefy as the skeleton of a new office building.

The floor is a neutral gray, poured from the effluvia of dozens of concrete trucks. Pathways are shared by pedestrian shoppers, their children, and always-busy hydraulic forklifts, which skitter from one end of the store to the other, purposefully toting hot-water heaters and pallets of cinder block, with their pointed dual prongs extended outward, ready to gore any customers hidden in the driver's blind spot. From far overhead, mercury vapor lamps spray acres of merchandise, customers, and sales people with a sickly purple-tinged light.

So vast a world inside, it beckons sparrows and robins, which make the store their avian home as they flutter above, landing momentarily atop the paint aisle before migrating south to electrical and plumbing.

Prior to the emergence of the Home Depot and its kind, our fathers and grandfathers relied on the local hardware store when they needed to build or fix anything.

The neighborhood store was the adhesive holding the community together, a shop you could count on to stock parts of things and the tools to connect the parts to the things themselves.

The store was not very large. A bell on the glass door tinkled as you entered. A dingy wooden floor, darkened by spilled liquids and years of grimy work boots, creaked. The ceiling was sheathed with the original tin. The place smelled of aged wood and paint thinner.

Behind the counter was the owner himself, a trusted guy often named Carl or Roy, who never seemed to take a day off. On those rare occasions when he wasn't there, you could count on his assistant—who had been there for as long as you can remember—to help you, but if he couldn't you need not worry, because Carl or Roy would be back in five minutes.

Here you bought tools, paints, nuts and bolts, plumbing supplies, and electrical apparatus. Experts in all things hardware, they cloned your front door keys, matched paint color perfectly by eye, and could tell you the steps to repair a squeaky hinge or how to stop a toilet from running long after the flush should be silent. The tiny store always had what you needed, whether it was a rubber washer, an oddly shaped spring for a mortise lock that hadn't been made since 1926, or an esoteric wood stain with a name like Smudgy Oak. If Carl or Roy did not have the actual part, he could find you something that he last remembered seeing in 1973 in a box downstairs and thought might work just as well.

"Bring it back if it doesn't fit," he would say. "Try to remember to pay me if it does." If it didn't, and you did not break the piece while trying to install it, Carl or Roy would return it to a bin in the basement, where it would hibernate until one of your neighbors might need it eight or nine years later.

The hardware store was also a repository of generations of collective repair wisdom. Here, no home maintenance question went unanswered, and few dream projects went unfulfilled.

"This is how to rewire the lamp," the owner would say as he began sketching a schematic on the back of a Benjamin Moore paint brochure. Then putting the pencil down, he might look up and shrug, "Just bring it in, and I'll do it for you."

The hardware store owner was a friend, a neighbor, a trusted resource, and an ombudsman, encouraging us to perform tasks we did not believe we could handle, but equally committed to dissuading us from projects beyond our abilities. His honesty was borne of his friendship with us, to be sure, but he was also a realist, knowing that a paralyzed neighbor would not be a good customer for the long term.

"Chuck," my helpful hardware store owner would chide, "I will not sell you this tool because you will likely put your eye out."

I would leave, remembering that he had lectured me about such things before, and though frustrated that I would be unable to complete my home project, I was thankful that his candor and willingness to remind me of my shortcomings would allow me to continue walking around my neighborhood without the aid of a specially trained dog.

With seductive merchandising, greater selection, and the promise of better prices, giant Home Depot–like stores have lured in people like me, and in doing so have all but wiped out the local hardware store. Dazzled by thousands of tools and flashy packaging, we have forgotten about loyalty, as well as about paying Carl or Roy before they went bankrupt for a pipe flange that ended up working just fine. Huge retailers replaced the familiar visage of my sage repair don with a fleet of faceless part-timers who understand SKUs much better than they do shower fixtures and R13 insulation.

Most nefarious of their tactics is the effort they put forth to stir unjustified confidence in the otherwise prudent. With encouragement that borders on the criminal, the Home Depot types goad us into buying sharp-edged implements we are not qualified to handle. They urge us to buy "assembly required" products, and make us believe we can end up with something that looks like the one displayed.

If we cannot figure out on our own what domestic projects cry for attention, the chain offers us lavishly illustrated "idea" books that show how simple repairs can be, relying on big color pictures to illustrate the steps for, say, installing a dimmer or a dormer. No project seems difficult, because none take up more than two facing pages. If you plan to upgrade to a hundred-amp electrical service yourself, you might see three drawings. The first shows a guy removing the front panel of an old circuit box above the caption, "Remove the cover." In the middle illustration, all you can see is the shoulder of the do-it-yourselfer obscuring the work he is doing, with text that says, "Remove all the old breakers, and carefully install the new ones according to code, making sure you do not do anything dangerously moronic." The final picture is of the proud homeowner looking up and smiling as the room brightens. Most of the book features illustrations of white men, although every few chapters, you find a project undertaken by a drawing of a black man, who is actually the exact same white man, just with his hands and face printed a little darker. Listed on the bottom of the page are the tools and materials we will need to buy, which coincidentally, they happen to sell.

They convince us we are vastly competent, with hidden talents that we have yet to recognize. Products beckon us, and television ads convincingly proclaim, "You can do it." While the ad tagline that follows says ". . . and we can help," you will soon find that "we can help" does not mean that the salesperson is actually willing to come over to your house and help.

They would have us all believe we share something in common with the skilled laborers and artisans who built our nation, those riveters of skyscrapers, the farmers whose plowshares laid perfectly straight furrows across Kansas, and the men and women who toiled in our factories and foundries. The Home Depot's encouragement would bring to mind black-and-white photographs of workers captured in the WPA images shot in the 1930s by Lewis Hines, images featuring shirtless men covered in a veneer of dark sweat, oil, and filth, muscles momentarily strained as they tightened a Frisbee-size lug nut with a five-foot wrench, welding fearlessly as they balanced on the narrow girder of a fetal Empire State Building eighty stories above the pavement, or straddling the cables of a still-floorless Golden Gate Bridge with air hammers in their hands. In each case, these are the men and women of photo mythology who fashioned the skyline of our country. "You can be just like those guys," the do-it-yourself stores suggest, making me forget, at least for the moment, that I do not look all that good shirtless and oiled down.

The Home Depot has become one of the most profitable companies in the country on the backs of gullible homeowners who are assured that there is no magic to operating a granite-shearing wet saw and that anyone who does not own a 4-horsepower lathe and a cement grinder is just plain sissified. They ruthlessly dispense dangerous apparatus and solvents raging with brain-dissolving fumes to the competent and the mechanically halt alike, never distracted from their quest to increase shareholder value at any cost. An unrepentant sales force offers anyone with cash or credit all manner of tools that spin and buzz, vibrate, or reciprocate. The store won't hesitate to sell a carpenter, a veterinarian, or a rabbi a pneumatic nail gun that can effortlessly blast a 16-penny nail with a single air-driven burst deep into a ceiling joist, into a gerbil, or completely through the Talmud, respectively.

Emergency rooms are overflowing with the hapless, convinced they were handier than they really were. Home-improvement stores have worked the cost–benefit numbers, knowing that there are a hundred million homeowners in the United States, and even if they killed off or maimed fifty million of us, there would still be a sufficient market left over for them to gross more than forty billion dollars a year and remain a Fortune 25 company.

"The strength of the overall retail economy," they might defend, "is far more important than the petty safety of any one individual."

Still, I shop at home improvement stores like the bulk of property-owning Americans. Why? Maybe it is because of the overwhelming selection. I have never seen so many things in one place. My house has many parts, and in the sprawling retail center, I can find at least one of each. I could build my house from scratch just by filling my cart a sufficient number of times.

Perhaps I spend thousands of dollars a year there because I am taken in by the attractive packaging. A beautifully photographed object on the box looks exactly the way I hope mine will look, installed in a professional workmanlike manner, absent dangling wires and mars from whacking it to fit where it is supposed to go. Looking at the picture, I mentally remove the generic house and family in the background, and in its place, I envision my own.

The artistically designed package conceals the inherent danger of novice installation, so you seldom if ever see a family like your own on the box with a child wearing a tourniquet, a nurse administering CPR to a man in order to restart a heart stilled by a 30 amp electrical discharge, and certainly not anyone face down in a pool of his own blood. The picture of a happy family in a beautiful home, with children looking up at a father they can respect because he has just built a swing set or added a game room is usually enough for me.

I find it easy to buy an item I do not need at present, but imagine I might someday. I have filled my house with these materials, for projects that I know I will tackle when I have the time. The purchases eventually get lost in the garage clutter and will be nowhere to be found when I really need them, so I will be forced to go back and buy a duplicate, only discovering the original some years later. I spend a hundred dollars a year on various plastic containers and shelves to house the extra one of everything I buy. I leave the store proudly, my cart overflowing with impulse purchases, sometimes getting home only to find I have neglected to buy the one item I drove out there to buy in the first place.

Perhaps I shop at the Home Depot, because I have been persuaded that goods are cheaper there. Point-of-purchase signage suggests that these are the lowest prices anywhere, and the gaudy four-inch-high bright orange price tags, big enough to be seen by people with cataracts, scream out for attention and assure me in a none-too-subtle way that this is "a bargain that only a complete ass would pass up." I have not done any comparison shopping, but the store looks like a warehouse, so I foolishly assume I am playing pennies over their cost. I am the just the shopper their market research people drool over.

I probably shop there because I am also convinced that even with the twenty-minute drive, my trip to a sprawling improvement center is quite convenient. I am willing to park my car in a space whose distance from the entrance is just a little farther than the walk from my house to my neighborhood hardware store.

I shop there because the professionals shop there. I am surrounded by men and women who build, paint, plumb, and roof for a living, and the Home Dept is giving me, Chuck Goldstone, access to the same items previously reserved for members of these guilds. The store is willing to sell me the same materials that a contractor would buy on my behalf and mark up by 200 to 300 percent before tacking on his labor charges. So if the professional journeyman shops here, I should, too, for the same reason that I am most comfortable eating in a Chinese restaurant frequented by lots of Asian families.

But the most compelling reason I am comfortable at Home Depot is because I am likely to be around "my own kind" there: the Sunday do-it yourselfer, the glassy-eyed suburbanite, the guy who wants to impress his neighbors, and the weekday executive bent on proving something to himself. We wander the aisles wide-eyed and vulnerable, our Levis neatly laundered, our complexions pasty from working during the week under cool white fluorescent tubes in air-conditioned offices, and our hands as smooth as a woman's. Highly prized among loyal customers like me is the attitude of the store's sales team. No matter how brainless our questions, they are trained not to laugh or roll their eyes, at least not to our faces. As I look around at my colleagues, I convince myself I am just as good as the rest of these amateurs: the junior high school student getting supplies for a science project, the newly married couple, the lesbian condo owners, the recently landed immigrant who during the past week here has gotten a job as a taxi driver, learned to drive, and found an apartment that will be habitable once he puts cheap wood paneling over the exposed chipped plaster and lath chewed open by vermin.

Looking around me, I know if I am about to destroy part of my home while performing a repair that I am not qualified to undertake, I will not be the only one in America doing so.

Patio Peril

ONSIDERING ALL POTENTIAL HAZARDS IN YOUR HOME, YOU may be surprised to learn that the innocent-looking patio grill is one of the dodgier items you will ever buy. Behind its simplicity and good intentions, a home grill offers up the danger of both personal injury and property damage, and unlike the chain saw, which can hurt you only when you use it, the barbecue bulges with hidden peril, starting with its purchase, continuing through transport and assembly, and climaxing with cooking and consumption of food prepared on it. Most people do not know this, but more Americans die each year from patio-grill accidents than from home-lumbering and septic-tank tragedies combined. When you buy and operate a barbecue, you are, as the old saying goes, playing with fire.

Still that does not stop us from enjoying one of summer's most pleasant pastimes, when we get to frolic with friends and family and share food prepared under an open sky in the most primal fashion. Perhaps the experience beckons us with thoughts of our primitive past and the call of the wild, to our species' nomadic days, when our hunter-gatherer ancestors seared fresh kill over an outdoor fire and shared it among a circle of squatting family and neighbors.

The smell of meat searing over an open-charcoal flame stirs up my childhood memories of summer grilling. Our neighbors, the Hertzmanns, were committed to the primordial ritual of barbecuing, and they served as a model for the rest of the community. So serious an enterprise was their Saturday and Sunday family picnics, the

Hertzmanns built a colossal brick-and-mortar barbecue pit in the center of their backyard. It was a large institutional barbecue, a dedicated free-standing edifice that was five feet wide, almost three feet deep, with a masonry chimney that rose up more than seven feet, disbursing meat emissions to higher elevations of the atmosphere. The Hertzmanns' spacious barbecue pit looked like a religious shrine and was made out of the same building material as their garage.

A ledge extended from both sides of the grilling surface, large enough to hold trays of uncooked and cooked meat. In the center was the pit itself, a hollow able to accommodate a bushel of charcoal. A metal grate straddled the pyre, blackened with a hardened past-meat residue, which looked and behaved like asphalt but was in fact a crusty compound comprised of burned carbon, smoke, and organic matter, chubbing up the eighth-inch chrome slats over time so they were now the diameter of an adult pinkie. But this coating only added to the mystique of grilling. A cast-iron front door swung open for the removal of ash. While these commodious in situ constructions were common to picnic pavilion areas in local Renziehausen Park, you would only occasionally see such a large and ornate one in the private sector. If it hadn't been filled with soot, the structure would have made a perfect playhouse.

Avid barbecuers, the Hertzmanns enjoyed nature and escaped each summer weekend to the backyard. They were a hearty Bavarian family, of Alp-loving, cuckoo-clock-wielding, not-too-ashamed-to-have-once-worn-lederhosen German stock. The Hertzmann kids—Jackie, a year older than me, and Billy, two years younger—lived with their parents, Frank and Ingrid, and with Grandfather Gustav, an ill-tempered old man in his mid-80s with white hair and tufts of alabaster stubble on parts of his hollowing cheeks where he missed shaving. Gustav Heinrich Hertzmann came to McKeesport as a young man in the 1920s, old enough to be blamed for fighting on the wrong side in World War I, but detached by a sufficient number of decades to fend off any association with the Nazis.

The Hertzmann family lived together in a meticulously well-maintained white frame house. Just beyond a small-but-weedless strip of grass was a spacious front porch, whose centerpiece was a porch glider—an outdoor mechanical furnishing that was a combination vinyl sofa and rocking chair. A glider is able to sway gently because of a complex assembly of unguarded metal gears, razor-edged braces, and pinching levers operating underneath, exposed and ready to chew up the fingers of anyone reaching under it for a lost Wiffle Ball or anything else that could lodge near its privy mechanics. Every summer evening, the Hertzmann family sat quietly under a yellow insect-repelling lightbulb, gently rocking back and forth on the glider until time for bed. Next to the Hertzmann house was a beautiful garden, healthy with tomatoes, corn, globes of lettuce, and a few intimidatingly statuesque sunflowers.

Once a year, the family would open their fence gate for a neighborhood barbecue. The Hertzmanns had very little to do with our family otherwise, and my father's limited contact with them was making an occasional phone call to Frank, requesting that Jackie beat up my brother and me a little less often. During the rest of the year, the Hertzmanns would not so much as look over to wave hello, and when our mail was delivered to their house in error, they would be more likely to drive it back to the post office so the mail carrier could redeliver it to our house than to walk across the street.

During this annual fete, however, they were friendly, charming, and actually pretended to like us. The social amnesty would always remind me of the Christmas Eve football game sometime during World War I, when opposing armies entrenched for months put down their guns and met in the battlefield between them for one night of camaraderie, when sportsmanship and humanity displaced hatred for a few hours, at least until the sunrise when they would return to blowing each other's brains out.

On this particular barbecue Sunday, our family would be one of a dozen on the guest list for the neighborhood potluck picnic. We showed up because we knew the Hertzmanns were not as likely to talk about us if we were there.

Each of the invitee families was required to bring along some kind of grillable meat, all of which would be deposited upon arrival into a communal meat trough, abundantly overflowing with commingling hamburger patties, hot dogs, barbecue-sauce-sopping chicken wings, Italian sausage, and Bavarian bratwurst.

You placed your food order with Mr. Hertzmann, who would reach down with his bare hand and choke off a fistful of ground beef from a ten-pound meat mound, using his two cupped hands to squeeze it into the requisite burger shape, a process that looked like making a snowball, just one that was a little flatter and, of course, made out of meat.

Frank Hertzmann, it was widely held, was to ground chuck what Henry Moore was to sculpture. As he laid the patty gently onto the grill, the burger let out a whoosh, almost sighing in pleasure as it began its journey from raw pink to tasty charred. Plump hot dogs or sausages would snuggle in the furrows between two parallel slats of metal grating, lined up head to foot, their undersides next to the coals blistering over and their tops rupturing in celebration of their doneness.

Mr. Hertzmann manned the grill alone, needing and wanting no help. His work demanded complete attention, and distraction was unwelcome—fine for him, because he was not one for small talk. Say what you will about his social skills, Frank Hertzmann was an artist and expertly skilled in grill management, knowing when to move partially cooked food from the hot spot on the grate to a slow-cook region, continually rearranging the position of items, choreographing a meat ballet to make the best use of space, and creating an assembly line so there was never more than a minute or two wait for anything on the menu.

He was armed with his long-handled fork and spatula, intuiting the moment to puncture and flip a grill-top item, standing back to watch the leaking fat fuel the fiery coals and ignite a momentary plume of flame upward, which engulfed the food. He poked and stabbed, and to this his burgers would respond with a sibilant hiss. Each burger bubbled on top, releasing disgusting globules of escapings lipids, which thankfully disappeared from the surface an instant before the burger was handed off to a patiently waiting consumer.

At the moment of perfection, that tiny window between the time a grill item is "not quite done" and "a little dry," Mr. Hertzmann gently unseated the patty or dog, lovingly sliding the metal spatula underneath and nestling it onto a bun. The unclaimed overflow was placed on a platter to the right of the grill. An hour or so later, a half-dozen disks of graying dried meat and elderly-looking wieners would grow cold on the neglected plate. They would become a resting spot for flying insects, but more important, a symbol of the generosity and artistry of Mr. Frank Hertzmann.

All the cold drinks were chilled in a large washtub filled with ice and water, now super-frigid and keeping the contents on the verge of freezing. The bottle we wanted always seemed to be on the bottom, darting away from us like frightened fish, so we needed to keep our hands submerged in the hypothermic water for ten or fifteen unbearable seconds in order to capture the specific Nehi we thirsted for. Our fingers numbed, and soon we were unable to move them. When retrieval was just too painful, we settled for whatever was close, usually a cream soda, drinking it reluctantly while the capillaries in our hands thawed.

Jackie and Billie Hertzmann's mom was the concierge of condiments and side dishes. She set out an array of auxilliary slaws and macaroni-based salads, fruit-embedded Jell-O moulds, a pot of yellow mustard, a selection of colorful relishes, diced onions, and sliced cheeses, all arranged buffet style on a picnic table temporarily upholstered with a floral-print plastic tablecloth. Since we lived in a town within driving distance of the Heinz bottling plant, ketchup was cheap and abundant, so no picnic would be without an ample supply. A new bottle sat on the table, though no one wanted to be the first to try to dislodge the plug of solid ketchup that coagulated around the spout. The standard method of initiation was spanking the bottle on the bottom and waiting for a larger than necessary glob to blurt out from the neck onto anything beneath it, while the more demure treatment to break up the tomato logjam was stabbing it gently with a knife until the condiment flowed freely.

Neighbors brought chips, pretzels, and pies. We ate few salads back

then, but we did have hothouse tomatoes from the Whitford's vegetable garden, prized because of their enormous size and squirting
ability.

Mrs. Hertzmann made a German variation of potato salad, which
took perfectly acceptable potato salad and contaminated it with a
beaker of vinegar. German potato salad is a shock to an American
palate, which does not expect a burst of sour to assault the tongue or
the smelling-salt effect of vinegar fumes to pierce the nostrils and
cause the eyes to tear uncontrollably. If you look at a bowl of it sitting on a picnic table, nothing about its posture warns you that German potato salad is an astringent and is tolerated only by peoples of
Germanic-Prussian-Austrian ancestry. This is a side dish that Germans have endured for centuries, and some historians speculate that
the advent of both World War I and II could be attributed to Germany looking throughout Europe for better potato salad.

We dined and chatted with the same neighbors we avoided the
rest of the year. Before the afternoon was over, someone would invariably hand my mother some kind of pork wurst. The Hertzmanns
were unaware of my mother's dietary restrictions, and, not being
Jewish themselves, did not know that she did not eat pork, and in
their limited familiarity with the Torah were under the impression
that "kosher" just meant meat "raised by Jew farmers." So when
handed a bratwurst, my mother would secretly feed it to the Hertzmann's schnauzer.

My family was not to be outdone by neighbors who already out-
landscaped us and drove newer cars. My dad was determined to
prove that we were as capable of searing meat outdoors as the next
family, so he convinced my mother that henceforth on Sundays in
summer, we would be grilling outside, too. I do not believe that until that time my mother had ever eaten outside, but she knew it was
important for my father, so she agreed he could buy an outdoor charcoal grill if he insisted.

Back then, the alterative to a permanent brick structure was a
portable charcoal grill, a thirty-inch-round by four-inch-deep pan
that appeared to be the prototype for today's broadcast satellite

dishes. The cook pan connected at waist height to a footing of spindly tripod legs. A round metal grate sat a few inches above the bed of coals.

It might be obvious once more that the Goldstones were not the rugged outdoorsy types. My brother and I had little experience with a world that was not carpeted, and the only sure thing we knew about the outdoors, which we learned from our mother, was that we should not track it indoors. Barbecuing would give our family a chance to learn about rustic dining and allow us to commune with nature, if only from the safety of our fenced-in yard. The character-building experience would remind us of the days when families survived by procuring their own fresh meat and would further confirm how lucky we were to be living in an age when we could eat in a newly renovated kitchen for the other six days a week. Such a primal Sunday meal would bond us as a family and we presumed from seeing others do it, would be fun. We would consider the outing a success if we didn't burn down the backyard or if neighbors did not discover the four of us the following Monday morning piled up near the stuck patio gate and charred beyond recognition.

On all days except Sunday, the new grill lived in the garage next to a bag of charcoal chunks and a leaky can of charcoal fluid, stored up against a wall next to our car, which through the years had dribbled its own blot of flammable oil and gasoline on the floor, contributing to a condition that was both combustible and slippery. In the event of fire in a petroleum-slick carport, we imaged slipping and falling prior to being engulfed in flames, in our gawkish attempt to escape.

Sunday afternoon, my dad wheeled out the barbecue, dragging a bag of briquettes and fuel with it. He dumped a heap of these marshmallow-shaped charcoal pieces into the grill, but in doing so, released a flammable cloud of very fine black carbon dust that silently hung over the backyard, momentarily turning a bright day overcast. On a windless afternoon, the patio was a powder keg, where a spark, even from static electricity, could ignite the air in an explosion akin to a grain elevator blowing up, sending a backflash of flame toward the house and simultaneously defrosting anything inside on the kitchen table.

Charcoal, because it is the compressed ashen remnant of a previous fire, will not combust easily on its own. Getting a briquette to light with only a match is not much different from trying to set fire to a cinder block. Hold the match under it for as long as you would like, but the briquette will not cooperatively ignite unless you saturate it first with some highly combustible petrochemical. The truth is, you could probably make firefighter uniforms out of charcoal briquettes, and they would be a successful fire barrier so long as you didn't douse them beforehand with an accelerant.

So arranged in a tightly packed pyramid, the briquettes were drenched with charcoal fluid, a solvent more explosive than jet fuel. The charcoal was thought to be sufficiently primed if was shiny and dripping with the highly flammable solution, no longer able to absorb moisture through its pores, swimming in a puddle of excess flame juices in the pan below. The air above the heap of briquettes would be wavy with the escaping volatile fumes.

Once the briquettes were sufficiently marinated, my dad ignited them in a ceremonial detonation, throwing a match into the grill as my brother and I looked on from a safe distance. A plume of flames shot up a dozen feet, then gently receded, smoldering for a few minutes, then pretending to be asleep as the coals began the leisurely process of turning from powdery black to flakey white. Across the street, a tall and stout cumulus of smoke billowed from the Hertzmann's yard, deep black smoke like they would get if they were burning logs or as members of the Hertzmann family who did not leave Germany in the 1930s would get when they were burning books. In our yard, no more than fifty feet away, a more slender thread of smoke nervously twitched above our little barbecue. Not quite strong enough to make it over the fence and not as impressive as the Hertzmanns', it was still our smoke, and we were proud of it.

It takes a good twenty minutes to a half hour to rev up the barbecue to cooking temperatures. In the transformation process, the coals lose their solid black sooty texture and turn a glowing "al blanco." Only after the majority of carcinogens have burned away and the petroleum fumes have dissipated are these little heat-radiating briquettes able to sear meat without imparting the subtle soupçon of diesel fuel.

The quiet state when the charcoal nuggets are still turning white can deceive an impatient chef, making it appear that the metamorphosing has stopped and the coals are no longer internally ablaze.

At that time, when the coals were externally dormant, my father, like thousands of others, believed that the preparatory fire had gone out and would not continue without his intervention, which meant impatiently spraying one more tinkle line of fluid from the squeeze metal can onto them. The flammable liquid would ignite instantly as it hit the still-burning charcoal, blasting another soaring wall of flame skyward. We prayed that the incendiary did not follow the spray of fuel back to the can my dad was holding. The fire ritual ended with my mother screaming something at my dad and reminding him what he looks like when he has no eyebrows. My father answered by grumbling to himself.

It was my mother's job to ready the raw meat for barbecuing. A burger can be prepared in one of two ways, either by taking the ground beef, rolling it into a flattened ball, and putting it directly on the grill or by mixing in some bold spices before the meat is shaped into patties. My mother used the more elaborate preparation method, convinced that my father liked his burgers better that way, but in reality he only said that to get her off the patio so he could squirt more charcoal fluid on the flames.

My father consented to wearing a cooking apron when he grilled. Men of my father's generation felt unashamed to wear one on only two occasions, the first while barbecuing and other when operating an arc welder. Outside these venues, my dad, like Frank Hertzmann, would be as uncomfortable in an apron as he would be in a prom gown.

We learned to be a bit more forgiving of the look and texture of barbecued food. Hot dogs blistered. Chicken was easily overcooked in a process that extracted most of the juices, making the wings and breast so dry that I could feel them trying to distill humidity from my mouth. A hamburger often arrived at the picnic table with a charred shell protecting a tiny pellet of still frozen raw meat at its nucleus. Fish was often a culinary failure because of its innate flakiness and tendency to disintegrate into tiny shards, falling irretrievably through the grate and onto the dirty hot coals. The only good news was the charcoal did impart a rather unique smoky trout flavor to subsequent burgers and hot dogs.

But still, it was outdoor eating, and my brother and I were so excited about it, we couldn't wait until the first wave of food was ready. My safety-conscious mother reminded us that running toward the grill eagerly with a plate in our hands was not a good idea, especially when my dad was holding a long pointy barbecue fork.

The family ate off paper plates, which are an invention that works much better, with no pun intended, on paper. Their scalloped edges collapsed easily under the weight of food and increased in flaccidity in the presence of anything moist. I am generally amused that so many people refuse to buy the better quality, stiffer paper plates which might cost a few pennies more, but will instead buy the value brand but double them up. Paper plates do not require washing, unless of course you are even more pathologically value oriented and want to continually reuse the same ones.

When the food was done, we would sit down at our backyard picnic table and eat until the bugs arrived, at which point my mother would grab the platters and herd us into the kitchen. Here, we finished the meal, now no different from the ones we ate on the previous six nights, only tonight, we were eating badly carbonized food from drooping platters that disintegrated as they slid around the kitchen table, and we were armed with nothing more than brittle plastic utensils that could cut nothing and would break trying unsuccessfully to spear even the most unassertive chunk of potato salad.

If I learned anything from college, it was that barbecues had an almost mystical power to impress women. And a good thing, because those of us who were not athletic or did not drive nice cars looked for any means to help us move up the social ladder from invisibility.

Barbecuing had little in common with more conventional modes of cooking. College age men do not know much about kitchen science. We were only a year or two detached from our too-often-unappreciated mothers who had previously prepared all our meals. Our dorm rooms were close to the university cafeteria, where the food was admittedly not very good, but was plentiful. At any moment of the day, we were never a few hundred yards from someplace that served life-sustaining hamburgers or pizza.

Prior to getting our own off-campus apartments, there was no legitimate reason for any of us to know how to operate a stove. Few of us were aware that a skillet could be used more than once, so long as the burnt food was scraped off before it permanently bonded to the fry surface.

Once on our own, we would live exclusively on fare that could be eaten directly from its container. Preference was given to meals we did not have to heat. We generally bought only food that would keep in a refrigerator for a semester or longer, and avoided anything that started out green, since it would be difficult for us to tell when it went bad.

While having an apartment was a boon to our social lives, we understood that no college male in his right mind would invite a coed over for a meal prepared in his kitchen, for fear that the evening would end with a drive to the infirmary.

Barbecuing, on the other hand, was an activity within our limited cullinary capabilities. Grilling required no special attitude. There were no fancy recipes. Preparation did not extend much beyond checking to see that all the plastic packaging had been removed. When a grilled item no longer looked raw, we felt confident to serve it. Even char-encrusted carbon, so unappetizing on our pots and saucepans, was perfectly acceptable on our grills.

My women friends, who grew up watching their mothers slave in the kitchen, knew traditional cooking to be challenging, requiring skill, patience, and sound judgment. They had no idea that one could barbecue without a clue about how food worked, and that grilling had more to do with luck than talent.

Barbecuing got me dates and impressed women who were both eager to escape cafeteria food for even one night, and willing to give me more credit than I deserved.

By preparing a hamburger, I was a heroic figure. Add a potato to the menu and I was sure to stir a woman's heart. A steak and dessert could get me laid.

In our frugal college days, we often sought out meat that was not too costly, gravitating to butchered items displayed by themselves under the "Manager's Clearance" banner, a separate section of the beef case promoting meat the store was desperate to sell because it was beginning to smell up the rest of the butcher department. The price per pound continued to drop as the meat grayed.

Our grill-by-default back then was the hibachi, a tiny steel cigar-box-size barbecue perched on squat wooden—and please note that wood is flammable—legs. These stumpy lower appendages were only about two inches high, giving the hibachi a dachshund-like appearance and placing it within sparking distance of our equally flammable wood porch. Because the entire enterprise sat at ground level, we would squat down on haunches with spatula in hand to conduct our cookery business on it.

Like many impoverished students at the time, I was grateful that the hibachi had been invented in my lifetime and could be purchased for less than four dollars, and, in some cases, was offered as a bonus if we bought three or more pounds of ground meat.

For me, the Japanese-style hibachi brought outdoor cuisine to the University of Pittsburgh, and Fused Western Pennsylvania and Eastern cooking. The name hibachi (pronounced *ha*-BOTCH-*chi*) revealed its ancient Asian grilling roots. Its name was derived, I assume, from the word "ha" meaning "to laugh," and "botch" meaning "to ruin."

I was confident that I was helmsman to the same device that had been used by fifty or more uninterrupted generations of Japanese and whose origins could be traced to the feudal days when the shogun threw the occasional warlord get-together. As it turned out, hibachis like mine had no association with the peoples of Asia at all and were manufactured a few miles outside of Englewood, New Jersey. Because the stoves were made so inexpensively, I understand they were exported for sale to Osaka. Still, the name hibachi brought more charm to the culinary experience, so I would not have to offer up the less romantic invitation, "Do you want to come over for a dinner I will cook for you on my very tiny outdoor stove?"

We kept the hibachi on our third floor back porch, which was just outside the kitchen door. Through the years, the house had shrunk around the door, gripping the jamb with the full shrugging force of a four-story building, making the door impossible to open and a fine security barricade, impervious to breaking-and-entering. This same characteristic similarly prevented us, the rightful occupants of the flat, from exiting onto the porch unless we climbed out the window next to it. Legally, the kitchen door was not considered a second means of egress in an emergency anyway, because once we got onto the porch, the only option for escape would be jumping off a forty-foot-high deck.

When you could get to it, the small roofed-in porch was the apartment's most charming attribute. It overlooked some parking and still had the extending clothesline, recalling a period when people aired fresh laundry in public, unabashedly displaying their underwear and towels like little Tibetan prayer flags across the back of the house.

The porches stacked on top of each other, all resting on wooden posts missing a real foundation, so over years of wood fatigue and settling, our porch listed slightly downward and away from the house proper. The business space on the deck was about eight feet by eight feet and made of aged, dry, splintery wood from which all moisture had been drained. We believe it had been last painted in 1946 with a flammable oil-based lead paint, now faded gray with no clue what the color might have originally been, and balding in spots down to bare wood. So brittle and thirsty for any moisture was the flooring that you could almost hear the wood asthmatically wheezing, hoping to suck any molecules of water vapor from the air around it.

Sharp erectile slivers pointed upward at various angles to snag a sock or piece of foot, and even with the thought of driving a wedge of termite-ridden wood into a bare heel, it was still less dangerous than walking across the decking in wool socks on a dry day, when the air, rife with static electricity, could spark a flash fire that would quickly ignite the back of the house before raging out of control.

The town fire marshal would have cited our back porch as a fire hazard had the building inspector not come over and cited it as a structural hazard first. We knew that setting up a hibachi there was risky, but even with the possibility of a flash ignition of the eight-unit apartment building, the grill on the porch seemed so much more convenient than on street level, three walk-down flights below us.

The hibachi's simultaneous advantage and disadvantage was its size, small enough to be snuck up past the landlord who did not permit any kind of grilling, but too small to hold more than about eight briquettes and cook more than a few square inches of meat at one time. The cooking surface accommodated two steaks only if placed head-to-foot in a yin-yang configuration. Otherwise I would have to prepare a steak that my date would eat alone while I would be on the deck preparing one that I would eat by myself a half-hour later. The hibachi could seat up to four burgers, or in another configuration, a maximum of twelve hot dogs, but in the latter case, a candlelight roof-deck dinner over a plate of six hot dogs each was not going to be all that romantic.

Further, do not expect the handful of charcoal embers to give off a lot of radiant heat. If you measured thermal output, the grill was at its hottest for the one to three seconds following the explosion of fluid vapors. Food cooked slowly. I often wondered whether a hamburger would be prepared just as quickly in an Easy-Bake Oven, broiling under a 25-watt lightbulb. But again, a miniature turquoise Easy-Bake range would not promote the rugged outdoorsy effect I wished to have on women.

House pets were particularly fond of hibachis since they put stealable food at their level. If you ever look into a dog's eyes, you know the gesture is not unappreciated. Sufficient time has passed so I can now confess to many women still living in Pittsburgh that the steak they so enjoyed decades earlier on my back porch had to be wrested from the jaws of my college roommate's Irish setter.

Our only concern was for the safety of an elderly woman who lived above us. She was not very mobile, and we feared she could be an unintended victim of smoke inhalation from the clouds of thick smoke that wafted from our porch directly into her bedroom, and we were always afraid we might hear that she died mysteriously, slumped over her walker on her way to closing the back window.

Still, we loved our hibachis. Had it not been for them, many of my friends and I would have remained virgins until after graduate school.

I have owned a number of grills in my postcollegiate days.

Winter in New England is the best time to buy a patio grill. While others are off buying skis, which I tend to look for in July, I find that deals in barbecue equipment are abundant when it is brutally cold, and even better during a blizzard just before roads have been plowed, when the thought of spending a moment on a snow-inundated patio deck, shivering inside a puffy down parka and trying to hold a spatula with a mitten just to flip a cooking steak over onto its back is the furthest thought from any sane New Englander's mind. Granted, the selection of grills in the snowy season is not plentiful as in midsummer, but the prices are usually very good, and the commissioned sales people, who are grateful to you for rescuing them from loneliness, are gushingly attentive.

Just before the New Year, a consumer bent on buying a barbecue might discover one or two cookers cowering in a clearance corner of the store, next to other slow-moving summer sundries, such as a lone badminton racket, some chaise lounges with their webbing missing, a round Lucite patio table with a hairline fracture running down the center—and a special buy because it has only three of four matching chairs still intact—and a few bug-dissuading citronella candles on Caribbean-style bamboo stands for those patio-goers who want to discourage intruding insects from visiting but are too humane and ecologically pious to use the more festive electric patio bug zappers.

The advantage of buying a remainder grill is that it is already assembled, a fair trade-off even if it had been a demo. Sure, there may be some scratches and few knobs broken off, it may be missing the lid, and might have a small pinhole in the tubing leading from the propane tank—and yes, that means it will leak propane, but just a little. Still, it will cost you a hundred dollars less, and not to repeat myself unnecessarily, it comes already assembled. If I haven't stressed this sufficiently, it comes already assembled.

Jealous of my Southern California friends, I am willing to bundle up and brave the patio in core of winter to enjoy grilling year-round. My barbecue is located on my back deck, so if I put on my mukluks and heavy flammable parka and grab my shovel, I need only to look for the biggest snow mound on the porch. The tarp is frozen and comes off in the same shape as the grill body. I clear the snow off the deck and chip the ice from the propane tank and regulator valve. My mittens can barely hold a barbecue fork, and they are totally in-effective at shaping a hamburger patty, but I relive summer in my head and on my palate. The grill must work harder in winter to cook the meat while the arctic air is competing to refreeze it, so a simple burger can often take a good chunk of the evening to cook. Friends have an outdoor hot tub and think nothing of bubbling during a snowy gale, so I figure that grilling in winter will be less of a physi-cal hardship, and besides, I do not need to be naked on my deck in twelve degrees.

From the moment you decide to buy a grill onward, every inter-action with it exposes you to potential bodily harm. Long before you open the valve of the propane canister or squirt charcoal lighter onto an open flame, you put yourself in the path of one of America's riskiest pastimes. Your first foray with danger is just buying the grill.

You have two choices today. One is the traditional charcoal grill, now updated in the popular kettle version, a sinister-looking black cooking orb that chars meat in a sealed sphere of unventilated dark-ness. The kettle splits equatorially at its midriff, with a lower bowl to hold a bed of charcoal, and a mirror-image upper lid that fits snugly to trap the food and force the heat and smoke inside to swirl about madly. Meat is seared and slow roasts, asphyxiated in a continually whirlpooling jet stream of carcinogens and fat-saturated fumes. Meat emerges from the kettle a dark umber, for no other reason than it is covered in a think layer of soot.

I personally find the principal advantage of a two-piece kettle is during the lighting phase, when I can hold the top dome like a Ro-man soldier's shield, as a guard protecting me against flash singeing from the inevitably explosive column of flame generated during charcoal ignition.

For sheer ease and convenience, nothing beats the now-popular propane-class grills, fired by a tank of gas and producing a blue flame identical in every way to those produced by the jets of your kitchen gas range. Modern grills are imposing appliances weighing up to 150 pounds, consisting of a cast-iron trough with a heavy hinged lid and appointed with shelves on at least one side. Big rubber wheels allow grill owners to quickly and easily move the hefty grill about, useful for shuttling it out of the way to extinquish a smoldering section of patio deck. A gas-fueled burner heats artificial stones, which are scattered across the bottom, and it is the radiant heat from these lava rocks that roasts the food arranged on the top grate. Do not expect a smoky charcoal taste from these faux briquettes. Because the grill is fired by propane, you will more likely get the infused fumes and subtle flavors of hydrogen sulfide and carbon monoxide.

When buying a grill, you will need to decide whether to purchase one preassembled or not. Pre-assembly will assure you that in the hours to come, you will not sustain unnecessary cuts, puncture wounds, or the indignity of a heavy part smashing down on your knuckles. Pre-assembly will save you time when you get home and permit you to eat in the same day you buy the grill, a benefit seldom enjoyed by those who buy grills unassembled.

As a traditionalist, you may want to assemble the grill yourself, thinking, "How hard can this be?" Besides, saving forty dollars is saving forty dollars, which will buy you a number of decent steaks.

Your first challenge will be getting the boxed, unassembled grill to your car, a difficult chore because the grill still weighs upwards of 150 pounds, including the weight of the wheels, which are at this time packed in a plastic bag inside the sealed carton and sadly doing you no good. Not until you lug the hefty container to your vehicle will you discover that the boxed grill is too big to fit in the trunk, and while the stockroom guy who helped you to the parking lot will make a halfhearted attempt to ram it into the backseat with his shoulder, your only hope of not having to abandon your expensive purchase right there is to remove it from the carton. Unencumbered by the grill's bulky cardboard and protective padding, you can finally squeeze the sharp-edged metal cooker piece by piece into the backseat, where it is free to bounce around and hurt itself or drive one of its pointy parts into your leather upholstery on the way home.

However, if you do transport the grill in winter, you will enjoy the last laugh. As other cars you pass are fishtailing all over the highway, yours will be clinging to slippery pavement on a sure path, the beneficiary of over a hundred-plus pounds of ballast in the back.

You erroneously believe it should not take more than an hour to put the device together, telling your spouse confidently to go marinate some meat. It will not be too long before you discover the Hell you have voluntarily entered. But unlike the more conventional Hell, flames will not be involved. The exercise of assembly, seemingly so straightforward, will trigger physical harm, psychological turmoil, self-doubts, a wave of personal worthlessness, and the alienation of family and friends. If you could relive the last few hours, you would gladly pay many times the forty dollars you thought you saved to have someone else do the assembly. Figuring there are thirty parts to a grill set, not counting the nuts and bolts, there are over nine hundred possible configurations, and only one of them will give you the gas grill depicted on the package.

Unless you have put together a grill before, you are likely to turn to the printed instructions. Some people do OK without them. Some people need them. Others are still helpless whether directions are provided or not.

Manufacturers consider directions a frill, putting their energy into making products with the least number of flaws so that organizations such as Consumer's Union will not deem the items "hideous death traps," or "worthless pieces of consumer pig-filth." Manufacturers politely ask you not to judge the quality of your purchase by the lucidity of the printed directions.

Remember, the instructions were translated into English at the same offshore factory that fabricated the many metal parts, a place where English may not be widespread, so, sentence structure and syntax will differ from conventional English markedly and you will

struggle to decipher the writer's intention. Verbs will appear in unusual parts of the sentence, and some phrases will not be understood
without numerous rereadings, for instance, "Placing the lid knob on
to, make twist." You will find words badly misspelled; others such as
"ape wrench," "screwing driver," "washee," and "gas relugator" will
be understood only in context; you will find some words that do not
appear to be English at all—"fligrin," "charanrd," "bip"; and there
will be terms you will not figure out no matter how you try, such as
"flexible meat part."

An explanation of how to attach the grill body to the legs and
lower shelf will be ambiguous, cryptic, and elliptical, with many hidden meanings and levels of understanding. Some instructions will
seem to contradict those described a page earlier. You will critically
analyze sections many times, wrestling with meanings, especially
stern warnings that seem like they should not be ignored, such as,
"Nut to leg wrench tight make with you. Don't!!!"

You assume the task of writing the instruction leaflet was an af-
terthought and given to any employee who appeared to have a passing knowledge of, or at least interest in, English, who convinced his
boss having best English be try him, yes?

You may also believe that instructions lavishly illustrated with
black-and-white line drawings will be helpful, but again, you will
learn you are a fool. Illustrations will depict objects that you will not
find inside the box, or were drawn using a non-Euclidian perspective
that will make recognition of them close to impossible. The last page
will include a disclaimer saying, "Your parts, at least the ones we have
included, may look different." You wish that the instructions were
done as 3-D stereograms, so the completed grill would pop out of
the page and you could visually walk around it.

You will need to find an open space to spread out your project,
first making sure that the doorway from the room where the grill
will be assembled to the outside is wide enough to allow passage of
the fully mobilized cooker; otherwise, you will end up with another
unvented indoor range or some kind of cast-iron hallway planter.

During construction, you will throw down parts in anger and will
have difficulty finding them later when you need them. You will curse

prolifically. You will be loath to figure the "secret way" two pieces should be conjoined. At times you will waver between self-flagellation, thinking it is your own fault for not being able to complete this simple task, and full-out anger at the Third World foreigners who are subjecting you to this trial, a feeling that will slowly grow to racism and a fantasy of U.S. military occupation of the factory. The snarl of assembly will trigger uncharacteristic wrath and the seeds of depression. In the middle of one of your tantrums, you will find yourself impulsively slamming your fist down in anger on the still-unassembled project, but will do that only once after you are reminded that it, like so many other metal items, contains many sharp protruding pieces.

Finally, and perhaps the most important warning—do not undertake the project with the help or even in the presence of loved ones. In preparation for the task, it is best to send the family shopping or on holiday to protect them from a side of you they have never before seen, and to prevent you from saying something that you will regret for the rest of your life. Assembly of a product intended to bring a family together is often the catalyst to rip it irreconcilably asunder.

Once your device is assembled, you are still not out of danger, exposing yourself to potential harm each and every time you stoke up the firebox. Remember, you are playing with propane, C_3H_8, a natural compound of the alkane series of hydrocarbons, easily angered and mighty in its retribution. Propane is highly flammable, and that, quite frankly, is the reason it works so well in a grill.

So it is prudent to check the integrity of connections. You can ignore a small pinhole or two in a garden hose, but not so in a propane feeding tube. A bag of charcoal cannot explode all at once, but a propane tank can, with the power to launch your patio deck into the next city block.

You are most at risk while lighting the grill. To energize a barbecue, you open a regulator valve to permit controlled leakage of gas into the burner ring. By striking an electronic igniter, a spark detonates the gas that streams out neatly from the tiny apertures along the metal burner's top. After releasing the gas, do not dawdle. If the propane does not ignite immediately, do not continue to punch the igniter over and over for the next thirty seconds, since a number of cubic feet of unlit gas will continue to accumulate in the grill body, along the top of the lid, and as a small invisible cloud around your face and hands. Should the spark finally execute correctly, you will flash-singe every follicle from your waist up.

Your food, the focus of the entire barbecue experience, harbors dangers, as well. Undercooked meat is a health threat, especially with ground beef or raw chicken, which is resident with an organism called *E. coli,* bacteria that will bring a level of sickness you previously considered beyond the talent of your body. If you are exceptionally unlucky, your burger or pinkish chicken can cause death.

E. coli makes its home in the excrement of animals and through sloppy slaughterhouse-keeping, can find its way into your food. If the bacteria alone do not make you consider a vegan life, the thought that your burger may contain a little bovine or poultry waste might. Overcooking meat will kill *E. coli* by sucking out all the moisture and facilitating the parching death of the deadly microorganism. Even so, it will still be hard to eat without thinking about the dung thing.

As picnickers, we accept wider latitude in sanitation rules. People who are quick to complain about a smudge on the water glass in a restaurant will quietly pick up a plastic fork that has fallen onto the driveway, wipe it off on the shirt they have been sweating in all afternoon, and resume using it to carry coleslaw to their mouth. The idea that you can gently brush off pathogens picked up from the sidewalk or pressure-treated deck is a fallacy.

People who wouldn't think of using a pot still caked with yesterday's now hardened meat sauce will stoke up a barbecue grill, placing burgers and steaks onto a grate that was too hot to clean immediately after its last use and was therefore not cleaned at all, and is now not only encased in solidified meat drippings, but in drippings that have been exposed to the elements and flies who find that congealed lipids make a wonderful place for them eat, sleep, and soil. Once on the grill, your aromatic meat will attract the attention of even more insects, whose tiny hairs and sticky feet carry terrible disease. Insects that have recently frolicked in the area where your golden retriever relieves himself may find your grill a fine stopover on the route to open jars of mustard and sweet relish. When you come down with terrible flu-like symptoms or suffer from gastritis sometime later, you may never think that it was because a fly with dirty feet landed for a moment on your bun.

Guests are regularly poisoned at barbecue outings. Food at room temperature hastens the propagation of bacteria, and in less than two hours, your meal could be teeming with battalions of illness-producing microorganisms. Meats will give you a clue visually that they are no longer approachable, not only by turning cold, but also by darkening and shriveling up, forming a tough outer dermis. More dangerous are side dishes or salads whipped up with a mayonnaise binder, which will turn toxic in sunlight, simmering at low temperature but giving little visual warning of their evil and ability to unleash gastrointestinal hardship.

Many cooks have also been injured in fluke accidents, stabbing themselves with unwieldy foot-long barbecue forks, slamming their hands underneath a 35 pound cast-iron lid, searing a palm on a sizzling grill top, or catching their aprons on fire. In this latter tragedy, victims are not usually done in by the blaze itself, but rather by overzealous family members eager to smack out the flames, who, in their adrenaline-charged frenzy of seeing a loved one combust, have successfully extinguished the fire but have sadly beaten the smoldering family member to death in the process.

And of course, the final danger in eating outside is that as you relax with a wonderful meal, sitting outdoors in nature, surrounded by your family and friends, as the evening stars are beginning to poke through an azure evening sky and the young crickets begin to grind out their tunes, as you lean back content that summer life does not get better, an intruder could be inside robbing you blind.

After all is said and done, you may find, just like the million-mile frequent flier who unexpectedly wakes up one morning pathologically fearful of airplanes, that you will someday inexplicably return the grill to the garage, afraid to ever use it again. You will henceforth cook all future meals indoors, seduced by a dangerously false sense of safety, forgetting about the thousands of people every year who lose a finger to an electric can opener or scald themselves with soup.

Life Is Risky: An Epilogue

THE WORLD WILL REMAIN A DANGEROUS PLACE. NO MATTER what you do, there is an accident lurking somewhere ahead, spring loaded and ready to discharge.

We need warnings. But perhaps we would be better served placing them on people and not on products, acknowledging once and for all that it is the person and not the item that is usually at the core of senseless tragedy. The warning tags will let retail stores, restaurants, manufacturers and bystanders know which folks must be protected from themselves. Maybe we need to rally around a phrase such as, "Chain saws do not cut people's arms off; people using their own chain saws do."

If corporations and individuals continue to be the targets of lawsuits, they should be allowed to take preemptive action and refuse to sell to those they know in their gut will injure themselves and their innocent children, proactively denying access to items for their customer's own good, no matter how much these consumers protest or threaten. Sellers will just have to learn to say, "No!"

People might carry ratings like extension cords to indicate the amount of risk they can safely handle before endangering themselves or others. The burden to prove trustworthiness will fall to the customer, and there will no longer be an Assumption of Competence, per se.

It is not as if we do not have legal precedent. The state issues a driver's license only after we can prove that we can start and stop a motor vehicle, move it backward without crashing into anything stationary or knocking over the elderly, park it into a space twice its size, and rotate the steering wheel so we can get it to point elsewhere. Our society discourages people from practicing medicine without attending a medical school. If you want to fire up a Rolls-Royce engine on a Boeing 777, expect to show someone your paperwork.

At amusement parks, you are not admitted onto certain rides unless you are a minimum height, and no matter how much money you flash in front to the ticket taker, absent the arbitrary stature they predetermined, you will not be welcome. Would-be riders parade past wooden cutouts of Howdy Doody, Smurfs, or Pokémon characters, and those who do not measure up are publicly culled from the line.

This stringent Customer Protection System is obviously not without problems. One that comes to mind is how an abnormally gangly ten-year-old would be OKed for a thrill ride while an exceptionally short athlete would be turned away. Certainly it would be a bit humiliating for a fit but diminutive company CEO or Supreme Court Justice to be denied admission to a roller coaster just because he is not quite as tall as Hello Kitty. Still, we may have to accept offending a stunted adult every so often if we want to protect our children.

Any number of possible scales could be used to rate purchaser competence, the simplest being a numerical designation from one to ten, with 1 indicating the most inept. If you are a 5, sales people will know you can safely operate an implement such as, but no more dangerous than, a power paint sprayer, rated at 5.0. Any tool with a 5 or under will be happily wrapped and charged to your credit card, while the store would know that a 6 in your hands will likely trigger a minor injury, and 9 or 10 makes disability a near certainty. Another ID scheme would be color coding, starting with blue, which would indicate experience and common sense, working up through the spectrum to eye-searing red, no coincidence that it suggests the color of carnage. Anything in the warm spectral range would tell salespeople it is best to completely ignore you.

Perhaps our designation would be worn about the wrist like a

MedicAlert bracelet, clipped on to our clothing like a ski-lift ticket, or perhaps displayed as a tasteful lapel pin. In the most extreme cases, a tattoo visible on the side of the neck would be easy to check. There will be some who say it is discrimination to refuse to sell certain groups of people items such as tools and hot beverages. Sure, "sales profiling" will invite a rash of lawsuits from overly zealous civil libertarians claiming an infringement on personal freedom, and it may invite the ACLU to selfishly test the legal principle on the backs of the weak and bungling, a shortsighted exercise that will literally not just figuratively cost America an arm and a leg.

In the end, we may hear a sales associate apologetically say, "Sir, I cannot in good conscience sell you this electric hedge clipper, and while I know that the money I make here helps me feed my children and buy them clothes so they do not have to play naked and filthy in the dirt behind our house, I could not sleep at night knowing that I have placed in your hands an implement of your ultimate demise, and because I love my children dearly, I want to protect them from the grisly television news footage of your mangled, dismembered, or disemboweled body discovered in your yard by the neighbor's dog, and the knowledge that this needless bloodshed and wanton carnage was born of their father's greed."

Indeed, the world is a risky place. We survive if we heed its well-posted warnings and know where dangers hunker in wait. We also need to willingly acknowledge deficits in our own talent inventory, and we must respect, no, we must *celebrate* our limitations, unashamedly and unapologetically, bowing out of those activities we know we cannot handle, even if the majority of others around us can. We don't have to live a sheltered life, pathologically fearful of everything that crosses our paths. We just need to avoid being unnecessarily stupid, by harnessing our brain as a tool for survival, and not letting its senseless wanderings and overconfidence make it the instrument of our destruction. I still hear my mother's warnings resonating. If you pass along your phone number, I know she would be happy to call and warn *you* about things too.

Today I am still a bit cautious. My own risk-taking is restricted to a little on-street bike riding and some not-very-hazardous fix-it jobs around the house, with most of these chores requiring nothing more life-threatening than spackle.

Lighting a propane grill is about as reckless as my life gets these days. I still sometimes struggle on my back deck with a finicky gas ignitor, and I usually win, but when laws of combustion and my grill conspire against me and I get an uneasy feeling that my life and the lives around me may be in jeopardy, I am content to move indoors, knowing that my kitchen range has a perfectly adequate broiler. I err on the side of caution. To paraphrase my mother, "No hamburger, no matter how succulent, is worth your life."

But I do occasionally think about an earlier, more carefree, perhaps naive time when my friends and I lived in the company of adventure. I remember my old buddy Jeff, the flatus-igniting college dorm neighbor, whose sense of theater and willingness to entertain overrode any concern for his personal safety. No one asked him to light his bowel gases; he unselfishly did it with joyful abandon to amuse his friends and to help him define the man he would eventually become.

Though I have not spoken to Jeff in a very long time, I am tempted to pick up the phone and call one of these days. He is a very successful corporate merger and acquisition attorney and now living with his wife and kids in New York. I have no interest in hiring him for any legal work, nor do I think we still have much in common after all these years. I'm just thinking how much easier my Sunday barbecues would be if I could find some way to hook him up to my patio grill.